SEX AND WORLD PEACE

SEX AND WORLD PEACE

Valerie M. Hudson
Bonnie Ballif-Spanvill
Mary Caprioli
Chad F. Emmett

COLUMBIA UNIVERSITY PRESS   NEW YORK

COLUMBIA UNIVERSITY PRESS
Publishers Since 1893
New York   Chichester, West Sussex
cup.columbia.edu

The authors and Columbia University Press gratefully acknowledge the support of the David M. Kennedy Center for International and Area Studies and the Women's Research Institute of Brigham Young University in the publication of this book.

Library of Congress Cataloging-in-Publication Data

Sex and world peace / Valerie M. Hudson . . . [et al.].
   p. cm.
   Includes bibliographical references and index.
   ISBN 978-0-231-13182-7 (cloth : alk. paper)—ISBN 978-0-231-52009-6 (ebook)
   1. International relations—Social aspects.   2. Sex discrimination against women.
3. Women and war.   4. Women and peace.   5. Peace—Social aspects.   6. War—Social aspects.   I. Hudson, Valerie M., 1958–
   JZ1253.2.S49 2012
   303.6′6—dc23

                                                                                    2011048554

Columbia University Press books are printed on permanent and durable acid-free paper.
This book is printed on paper with recycled content.

Printed in the United States of America
c 10 9 8 7 6 5 4 3 2 1
References to Internet Web sites (URLs) were accurate at the time of writing. Neither the authors nor Columbia University Press is responsible for URLs that may have expired or changed since the manuscript was prepared.

To Hope Rose and Eve Lily: May your lives be full of joy, confidence, meaning—and action!
To Zakia Zaki and Fawziya Ammodi: We are impoverished by your passage from our world. (D&C 123:13–15)

   —*VMH*

To my daughters, whose strength and wisdom astound me.

   —*BBS*

To my wife, Laura Chapin, for always believing in me.

   —*MC*

To my mother, Norda; my wife, Marie; and my daughter, Sarah. Their goodness inspires me.

   —*CFE*

CONTENTS

LIST OF MAPS, FIGURES, AND TABLES

Maps

Figure

Tables

Tables in Appendix B

PREFACE AND ACKNOWLEDGMENTS

THE TEAM OF AUTHORS for this book is multidisciplinary, and this is re-flected in the text. We have two political scientists who specialize in inter-national relations (Hudson and Caprioli), one geographer who specializes in the study of Islamic societies (Emmett), and one psychologist who specializes in the relationships between socialization, gender, and peace (Ballif-Spanvill). These interests manifest themselves in the literature and examples cited in the book. For example, some of our most detailed micro-analyses are of Islamic nations. This emphasis reflects the in-depth knowledge of the circumstances of these nations held by Emmett. Similarly, the socialization examples are drawn primarily from the psychological literature, and not from political sci-ence, reflecting the expertise of Ballif-Spanvill. We believe that this diversity of background and professional training enriches the manuscript.

This book would not exist without the goodwill and hard work of many individuals.

First, we would like to thank the WomanStats coders past and present, including first and foremost our director of operations, S. Matthew Stearmer, without whom the project could not have accomplished what it has thus far. We would also like to thank Jana Pope Badger, Brooke Greer, Thelma Young, Jo Cozzens, Rachel Ligairi, Amy Stevenson, Julie Johnson, Evis Farka, Meg Wilkinson, Becca Hall, Hope Buckman, Tania de Oliveira, Joanna Lon-don, Dan Phelps, Melissa Paredes, Leah Raynes, Mary Ann Tanner, Ashley Custer, Emily Pomeroy, Casey Fowles Cox, Nichola Taylor, Katie Phelps, Jason Anderson, V. Matt Krebs, Meghan Foster Raynes, Sarah Roessler, Col-leen Johnson, Julianne Parker, Amalia Smith, Margy Hannay Elliott, Doug-las Melvin Hansen, Carl Brinton, Laura Summers, Becca Nielsen, Patricia Campbell, Charla Finnigan, Autumn Smith Begay, Lindsey Hulet, Diane

Bailey, Melinda Hardy, Caitlin Carroll, Luke Warnock, Maren Reynolds, Tiffany Stanley, Erin Roundy, Lindsey Johnson Leon, Becky Perez, Analiesa Leonhardt, Rebekah Butterfield Wightman, Grady Deakin, Vanessa Nielsen Molina, Alixandra Lewis Adams, Michael Hall, Aimee Farnsworth, Kendra Arguello, Lauren Smith, Andrea Kelly, Rachel Fairclough Zirkle, Julie Ford, Jessica Hogstrom, Michele Trichler, Arielle Badger, Kinsi Suttner, Crys Kevan, Stephen Cranney, Morgan Wills, Nick Griffin, Eliza Houghton, Jeramy Ferguson, Victoria Fox, and Jillian Wheeler. It has been a complete joy to work with these young people.

We also wish to thank those who provided funding for our efforts. Among our supporters are the Women's Research Institute; the David M. Kennedy Center for International Studies; the Department of Political Science, the Department of Geography, the College of Family, Home, and Social Sciences, and the Office of Research and Creative Activities, all of Brigham Young University; Hunt Alternatives; the Office for the Vice President for Research, University of Minnesota, Duluth; the Sorenson Legacy Foundation; Ruth Silver; and several anonymous donors.

We would also like to thank Mark Jackson and his students at the BYU Library Geospatial Services Center for producing our maps, and Hwanhi Chung for handling the endnotes for two of the chapters.

We would like to thank several scholars whose work has inspired our own, including Rose McDermott, Alma Don Sorensen, David G. Winter, and J. Ann Tickner. Thank you for what you have written, and what you have taught us.

We thank *International Security*, *Foreign Policy*, and the *Journal of Peace Research* for permission to use portions of articles we have published in those journals.

We would like to thank Anne Routon for her confidence in us, as well as two anonymous reviewers who were most helpful in developing the vision of the book.

Finally, we would like to thank our families for giving us the courage and the time to write this book.

SEX AND WORLD PEACE

1

ROOTS OF NATIONAL AND INTERNATIONAL RELATIONS

When society requires to be rebuilt, there is no use in attempting to rebuild it on the old plan. No great improvements in the lot of mankind are possible until a great change takes place in the fundamental constitution of their modes of thought.

—JOHN STUART MILL

OUR ANALYTICAL MINDS rarely tend toward a holistic view of complex systems, such as national and international relations. For example, take a moment and picture a tree. What do you see? Perhaps you envision a tall tree with many leaves and a big straight trunk with long branches. Do you think about the root system that is sometimes larger than the part of the tree aboveground—the roots that keep the tree alive? What alternatives would you have to heal sick trees or to grow new trees if you never considered the roots? We rarely consider the whole picture, and Mill is right that our own modes of thought are the key to effective and positive change. In this book we ask that you consider the whole picture when examining the world of states and international society. Although often overlooked, sex and gender play a big role in world affairs. By overlooking sex and gender, we limit the policy alternatives that we see in the quest to find solutions to world problems.

In this chapter, which is oriented to undergraduates in international relations (IR) classes, we introduce some of the theories you have been taught about national and international relations and then show you the "roots" of them. We also examine some foundational definitions and concepts that may help us begin to see the roots more clearly. The point is to see the entire tree—not just the part aboveground and not just the roots.

You were taught that a sustainable population meant population control, but were you told that empowering women will naturally restore the population balance? Slowing population growth does not necessarily entail population control—the restriction of the number of children women are allowed to bear. The best approach is to support reproductive freedom for women. With reproductive freedom, women tend to have fewer children. Population control rests on a top-down approach that punishes rather than empowers. Reproductive freedom, on the other hand, gives women choice. If you weren't taking a gendered perspective, you might see population control as the only alternative. Yet when you take into consideration the empowerment of women, policies based on reproductive freedom become viable alternatives that are arguably more effective.

You were taught that the U.S. economic recession that began in 2008 may have altered the landscape of power in the international system, but were you told that this meltdown may have been aggravated by the exclusion of women from important decision-making roles in society? If women were to make up one-third of corporate boards, it is possible that the likelihood of a banking failure would be diminished because women tend to be more risk averse. Women and men working together as equals create a more balanced perspective. In addition, studies have shown that women tend to be less corrupt than men. Without taking a gendered perspective, you might think that the recession precipitated by the banking failure was inevitable, but once you look at gender you realize that the global economy is profoundly affected by the structural power of each gender in society.

You were taught that AIDS is affecting the future of states, but were you told that the roots of the AIDS epidemic are to be found in sexual violence against women, sexual exploitation of women, sex trafficking of women, etc.? HIV/AIDS is devastating parts of Africa and India and is on the rise in China. HIV/AIDS is disproportionately affecting women because the structural inequality of men and women in traditional cultures ensures that women have little real choice to refuse sexual relations, even when such a refusal would be an act of self-preservation. Myths such as that having sex with a female virgin will cure a man of HIV/AIDS feed into the violence against women and girls and further spread the disease. Limiting the spread of HIV/AIDS, therefore, requires a gendered perspective that includes education and emphasis on gender equality in sexual relations, rather than just treating the symptoms and making condoms available to women who have no power to make men use them.

You were taught that poor states invest little in their people and treat women badly, but were you told that states that treat women badly are more likely to be poor and invest little in their people? Certainly poor states have few resources to invest in their people—they have few social and welfare services available. What is often not seen is that women bear the brunt of the lack of such services in these states, making up for that lack through their unpaid labor. Interestingly, those states that invest in their women—for example, ensuring that girls are educated to an equal level with that of boys—are more likely to be wealthy, to be stable, and to be democratic. So taking a gendered perspective allows us to realize that foreign aid to poor states isn't enough to change the underlying inequality that leads to poor economic growth, instability, and autocracy. Policies must target societal norms of gendered inequality and violence that prevent the state from achieving the prosperity, stability, and political freedom its citizens crave.

You were taught that the security of the state rests on power (getting it, keeping it, and displaying it), but were you told that norms of equality create a more sure security for the state? What makes a state safer—power or gender equality? The answer may surprise you: both make a state more secure. Those states that foster gender equality through laws and enforce those laws are less likely to go to war. They are less likely to use force first when in conflict. They are less likely to get involved in violent crises. Once again, a gender-neutral perspective leads you to focus on military might, whereas a gendered perspective highlights the importance of gender equality to facilitate state security.

You were taught that states go to war over oil and scarce resources, but were you told that the roots of violence are even more micro-level than that? States do go to war over oil and scarce resources, among other things, but they are more likely to do so if the society has norms of violence rooted in gender inequality. Violence becomes an acceptable option when women are not considered equals. Here, too, you will find that a gendered perspective leads to different conclusions about international affairs. Oil and scarce resources are a source of conflict, but they do not necessarily lead to war. Those societies that have gender equality are less likely to resort to warfare to meet their resource needs.

You were taught that the clash of civilizations is based on ethnopolitical differences, but did you know that the real clash of civilizations may instead be based on gender beliefs? Samuel Huntington argues that people's cultural and religious identities will be the primary source of conflict in our world; in his view, the fault lines between civilizations will be the battle lines of the future. It would appear, however, that the battle lines of the future are more likely to be found between those states that treat women equally and those states that are fraught with gender inequality. The important cultural distinction is actually between societies that have greater gender equality and those that foster an environment of gender inequality and gender violence. As stated above, societies that are more gender-equal are less likely to go to war, to use force first during conflicts, or to be involved in violent international crises.

You were taught the democratic peace theory—that democratic states are much less likely to go to war with other democratic states—but were you told that democracy was rooted in the character of gender relations? As we will explore in a subsequent chapter, the historian Mary Hartman argues that the unique experience of Europe—one that included the greatest equality for women—gave rise to sustainable democracy in that continent. Democracy in this sense stands on the shoulders of gender equality. As stated above, states with greater gender equality are more likely to be democratic, stable, and prosperous.

You were taught that youth bulges would be an important demographic factor affecting the destiny of states, but were you told that the existence of such bulges depends on whether women have choices in their sexual life and choices in their reproductive life? And were you told that sex ratios are a major force that will also affect the future of the world? Youth bulges and an excess of males from skewed sex ratios lead to migration, crime, revolution, and even war. It is women's lack of reproductive freedom that is at the root of both youth bulges and the phenomenon called "bare branches," in which young adult males find themselves vastly outnumbering women in their age cohort. Whether we speak of husbands or of states that manipulate women's bodies for their own reproductive aims, these population imbalances have at their root unequal gender relations.

You were taught that loss of life in war, civil war, and genocide is a major source of suffering and a major focus of international relations (IR) theory, but were you told that most lives are lost not because of these kinds of conflict but rather as a result of societal devaluation of female life? Interestingly, more lives are lost through violence against women from sex-selective abortion, female infanticide, suicide, egregious maternal mortality, and other sex-linked causes than were lost during all the wars and civil strife of the twentieth century. From this perspective, the greatest security dilemma is, then, the systemic insecurity of women—half of the world's population. Indeed, if we want to be technical about it, the systemic insecurity of women has resulted in a situation in which women are now no longer half of humanity, with a world sex ratio of 101.3 men per 100 women on the planet.

The treatment of women is an "unseen foundation" for many of the phenomena we see as important in international affairs. What you were taught was simply the visible branches of the tree. We ask that you look beyond the obvious to see the roots that give rise to the phenomena discussed. Policymakers trying to find solutions to problems are quick to dismiss women as important actors—or do not think about women at all. Yet, as we have shown, it is imperative to take a gendered perspective to understand international issues.

In this book we take a micro-level approach to understanding international relations. We argue that gender inequality is a form of violence that creates a generalized context of violence and exploitation at the societal level. These norms of violence have an impact on everything from population growth to economics and regime type. In IR theory, we assume that our theoretical assumptions, such as the democratic peace thesis, are gender neutral. These assumptions, however, clearly take a male-centric view. We want you to see the whole picture—the tree and the roots—and to experience an approach to understanding that does not exclude but rather embraces a female perspective. It is this gendered approach that is often ignored and might be compared with the roots of the tree. In this book we will make the case that the treatment of women is an unseen foundation for many of the phenomena we see as important in international affairs.

Sex and World Peace offers three major contributions: two of them analytical and one normative. First, we hold that gender inequality, in all of its many manifestations, is a form of violence—no matter how invisible or normalized that violence may be. This gender-based violence not only destroys homes but, we argue, also significantly affects politics and security at both the national and the international levels. This linkage—empirical as well as theoretical—between gender inequality and national and international security is a new approach that has seldom if ever been considered within the discipline of international relations (and other disciplines as well). In a major shift from the conventional understanding, we suggest that efforts to establish greater peace and security throughout the world might be made more effective by also addressing the violence and exploitation that occur in personal relationships between the two halves of humanity, men and women.

A second contribution of this book is to suggest that security studies must include an account of women's security in order to fully address phenomena at the state and system levels. We hope a consideration of the situation of women will become as central to the discussion of world security as power, democracy, religion, culture, resources, and economic growth currently are. We hope that by the time you finish reading this volume, you will consider it quite odd that something so basic and so essential to peace and security is only now beginning to be recognized as such.

Our final hope is this book will be not simply an academic exercise but also a call to action. Through an examination of possible strategies to effect change in both top-down and bottom-up directions, we hope to provide information about skills and best practices that can be put to use immediately on behalf of women. In particular, our focus is on three major areas of concern: to improve the bodily integrity and physical security of women in their homes and communities, to render family and personal status law equitable between men and women, and to increase women's participation in the councils of human decision making at all levels.

Before we begin, we need to set out a few foundational definitions and concepts.

FOUNDATIONAL DEFINITIONS

Sex refers to the biological differences between men and women. For example, women can have babies; men cannot.[1]

Gender refers to the socially defined differences between men and women. For example, women are socialized to be what the society considers feminine— submissive, sentimental, nurturing, etc.—whereas men are socialized to be what the society considers to be masculine—strong, stoic, protective, etc.

Gender as an Adjective: One of the complicated aspects of the English language is that the adjective for "sex"—"sexual"—has connotations both about sexual intercourse/sexual practices and about sex as the biological difference between men and women. Thus the term "sexual beliefs" could refer to beliefs about sexual intercourse/practices or beliefs about the relationship between the sexes. Because of this inherent linguistic difficulty, when an adjective is required we will use the word "gender" in this volume to refer to both gender and sex. Thus the term "gender beliefs" refers to beliefs held within the society about the relationship between the genders as well as the relationship between the sexes. A "gendered perspective" refers to a perspective that takes into account issues of both gender and sex. "Gender equality" refers to equality between the genders and between the sexes.

Inequality is understood as an aspect of violence based on the relative power or standing a person has in society. For example, the inequality of women in some states effectively allows men to rape their wives, or it may allow employers to pay female employees less than they pay male employees. When we contrast equality with inequality, we do not define "equality" as sameness or identity. Men and women do not have to be the same to be equal. One can have equality in the context of difference. Therefore, our definition of "inequality" does not denote difference per se; rather it refers to the subordination of one who is different.

FOUNDATIONAL CONCEPTS

WOMEN AS BOUNDARIES OF THE GROUP

Jan Jindy Pettman, extending the work of Nira Yuval-Davis, has called women the boundaries of their nations.[2] What she means by this phrase is that women physically and culturally reproduce their group. While women who are not of the group may physically reproduce it, they will be inadequate cultural reproducers. Only in-group women can play both roles for the group and effectively ensure its survival.

As a result, the capture through force or seduction of women from one group by men of another is not simply a personal issue; it is a group issue. This may be codified in law. For example, take the case of a Lebanese Christian man who married a Muslim woman of the United Arab Emirates and did not convert to Islam: the government of the UAE convicted him of violating Islamic marriage laws and sentenced him to one year in jail and thirty-nine lashes for this offense against the group.[3] Similarly, women in many societies still possess only conditional citizenship, which they may not be able to confer upon their children. A woman's citizenship will be inferred from her father before she is married, and inferred from her husband after she is married. If he is from another country, she may lose her home country citizenship altogether, and her children will be considered citizens of the father's country. In cases where a woman has children out of wedlock with a man from another country, her children may actually end up entirely stateless (see WomanStats variables CLCW and CLCC).[4]

Because of the unique position of in-group women in the group's survival, the group will aim to protect the women from capture by other groups. Indeed, this is one of the reasons why the symbol of a nation is often personified as a woman, in order to elicit these deep feelings of protection. A woman becomes a "protectee" of the men of the group, especially those in her own family. However, as V. Spike Peterson has noted, over time this "protection" begins to elide into "control" and "possession."[5] "Protecting" a woman may involve practices such as purdah and infibulation,[6] which in effect lower the cost to men of protecting their female kin. Indeed, one story of how female infanticide came first to northwest India involved local patriarchs who wished to prevent the capture of their daughters by invading Aryans, who would use them as wives and concubines to cement their rule over the country. To "protect" their daughters from such capture, their fathers killed them.[7] To understand that logic more fully, we must introduce a second concept.

HONOR/SHAME SOCIETIES

Because of the unique role that in-group women play as boundaries of the group, with the resulting need of the group to protect them, the value of a woman in many cultures soon becomes associated with the state of her sexual relations. If she is chaste before marriage, and perfectly sexually faithful after marriage, her sexual relations build the group. If her sexual relations and attendant behavior, such as manner of dress, do not conform to this model, her activities are viewed as bringing chaos and instability to the group. Thus the need to protect a woman becomes more and more associated with the need to protect her chastity—not her life, not her freedom. Indeed, her life and her freedom are both subordinate to the goal of ensuring her chastity—and may even be at odds with that goal.

In this way, the honor of her family and her group becomes associated with her sexual behavior in an almost one-to-one correspondence. This is especially true for the men of her family: the chastity of their female kin *is* their honor.[8] As one of our Ecuadorean students related to us, a common saying in her country is, "The honor of a man lies between the legs of a woman." Serap Cileli, author of the book *We Are Your Daughters, Not Your Honor*, recounts,

> In many families, boys grow up as first class citizens and girls are second class citizens. Boys see their fathers hitting their mothers and learn to abuse their wives. Daughters are seen as a burden and as a possible source of social shame. The Quran says that men and women should be virgins at the time of marriage, but most men are no longer virgins by 18. Most of these young men have sex with non-Muslim girls but then want to marry a Muslim and a virgin. . . . The concept of honor is attached to the physical purity of the woman, and that's why only her blood can cleanse the shame her actions bring on a family.[9]

This emphasis on physical purity, where even the suggestion of impurity can ruin a girl, or even destroy a girl, has many far-reaching consequences for women. A girl may be withdrawn from school as soon as she hits puberty, for her sexuality cannot be assured in a context where she may have to walk long distances to school or have a male teacher. A girl may even be married well before puberty—sometimes at seven or eight years of age—to avoid any possibility that her reputation may be destroyed first. Or worse may occur, as in one horrific 2005 case in Pakistan:

> Nazir Ahmed appears calm and unrepentant as he recounts how he slit the throats of his three young daughters and their 25-year old stepsister to salvage his family's "honor"—a crime that shocked Pakistan. . . . Ahmed's actions—witnessed by his wife Rehmat Bibi as she cradled their 3 month-old baby son—happened Friday night at their home in the cotton-growing village of Gago Mandi in eastern Punjab province. . . . Bibi recounted how she was woken by a shriek as Ahmed put his hand to the mouth of his stepdaughter Muqadas and cut her throat with a machete. Bibi looked helplessly on from the corner of the room as he then killed the three girls—Bano, 8, Sumaira, 7, and Humaira, 4—pausing between the slayings to brandish the bloodstained knife at his wife, warning her not to intervene or raise alarm. . . . The next morning, Ahmed was arrested. Speaking to AP in the back of police pickup truck late Tuesday as he was shifted to a prison in the city of Multan, Ahmed showed no contrition. Appearing disheveled but composed, he said he killed Muqadas because she had committed adultery, and his daughters because he didn't want them to do the same when they grew up.
>
> "I thought the younger girls would do what their eldest sister had done, so they should be eliminated," he said, his hands cuffed, his face unshaven. "We are poor people and we have nothing else to protect but our honor." Despite Ahmed's contention that Muqadas had committed adultery—a claim made by her husband—the rights commission reported that according to local people, Muqadas had fled her husband because he had abused her and forced her to work in a brick-making factory.[10]

From Ahmed's perspective, his own little daughters were an intolerable burden to him, requiring superhuman vigilance. With his honor destroyed by something he could not control—though probably something that had never even occurred—he could not imagine continuing as the father of any daughters at all. In honor/shame societies, honor is worth more than a woman's human rights, worth more than her freedom, and certainly worth more than her life. Honor killings, and the new strategy of honor suicides (forcing a girl to commit suicide so family members can evade prosecution for honor killing), become a culturally acceptable way for families to mitigate the disaster that may reside in the body of their daughter.

The concept of honor/shame societies also helps us to understand rape as a crime of power, not a crime of sexual desire. Rape's target in such societies is not women; rape's target is men and families. Rape shows that the men could not protect the chastity of their women, hence emasculating them. And rape strips honor from a family. It is in this way that we must understand that the women who are raped are viewed not as victims to be supported but as stains to be erased. In such societies, rape victims may simply be killed, or exiled to towns that often spring up in the aftermath of war, populated solely by rape victims who must make their living through prostitution to survive.

A vivid example of this logic was recounted by Elisabeth Bumiller, who interviewed survivors of Kosovo's ethnic cleansing:

> The 22-year-old woman, married four months ago, said she was taken from this small southern village by Serbian forces, held for a day in the local police station, beaten, then threatened with death. But she was not, she said, raped.
>
> Her husband, Behan Thaqi, thinks differently. "I am 100 percent certain that they raped her," said Mr. Thaqi, 34, a farmer imprisoned by the Serbs for supplying weapons to the Kosovo Liberation Army, the Albanian guerrillas who fought Serbian forces. "I know that when women get in their hands, there is no chance to escape."
>
> Mr. Thaqi says his wife, who did not want her name published, denies the rape because "she doesn't dare tell that kind of story." If she admitted it to him, he said, "I would ask for a divorce—even if I had 20 children." As his wife listened, silent and shamefaced, in a corner of their empty home, looted of all furniture and possessions by the Serbs, Mr. Thaqi added: "I don't hate her, but the story is before my eyes. I feel very cold toward her."
>
> "Kissing her," he said, "is like kissing a dead body."[11]

It is important to recognize, as Cileli mentions, that men themselves have no honor in the same sense as women. Chastity before marriage and sexual fidelity after marriage are not expected of men in these cultures. On the contrary, men may be rewarded by their culture for promiscuous behavior. In the age of AIDS, encouraging males to be promiscuous may have deadly consequences not only for men but for women as well, as we will discuss in a later section.

PATRILOCALITY

Another important concept that we must understand in order to see the world through gendered lenses is that of patrilocality. Virtually all traditional cultures remain patrilocal, which simply means that brides relocate to the home of the groom's family upon marriage. Western societies, too, until very recently, were almost always patrilocal. Patrilocality ensures patrilineal inheritance, and patriline claim on all children produced by sons. It also ensures that all men of the clan are kin, mitigating in-group conflict. However, the family psychology produced by patrilocality may have a devastating effect on women and girls. Given concerns over the genetic consequences of inbreeding,[12] girls may find themselves married to grooms who live a substantial distance away from their natal family. Furthermore, as noted above, girls may be married off quite young, for reasons of honor. In such a context, natal families may live with their daughters for only ten to fifteen years and may possibly rarely or never see them again after marriage. In addition, the daughter's children are members of the groom's family, not her natal family.

For all of these reasons, a girl may be viewed as a "houseguest" in her own family. Proverbs testifying to the fact that daughters are not truly members of their natal family abound: "A daughter is a thief." "Raising a daughter is like watering a plant in another man's garden." A girl may come to feel profoundly alienated from her birth family, a feeling that may be reinforced by differential feeding practices and differential access to health care, education, and other resources. Her brothers may eat more, may be taken to doctors, may be encouraged to continue with schooling, and may be excused from chores to do homework. She may notice that she, as a daughter, apparently does not merit this investment from the family, and may draw some natural conclusions from that fact. Boys will draw natural conclusions as well, and will reproduce the same behaviors in their own families.

However, when a girl is married and moves to her husband's family's abode, she will find, in similar fashion, that his family does not consider her a member either. She is an outsider who will never be listed in her husband's genealogy (and will most likely not be listed in her natal family's genealogy).

Her children will belong to her husband's family, and if she were to leave her husband, he would have sole control over the children. Before she has a son, she may be considered as being at the very bottom of the household hierarchy, forced to work harder and longer than anyone else.

Where is this girl's family? Does she have one? In a sense, her true family consists of her sons, and that may be the strongest—perhaps only—love relationship in the woman's life. Son preference is thus expressed not only by fathers but also, intensely, by mothers in such cultures. No wonder that when her sons marry she will view her daughters-in-law with suspicion and alarm. As Xu Rong, of the Beijing Rural Women's Organization, put it, "In joining the new world of their husband's family, they've got their father-in-law to deal with, their mother-in-law, various uncles, sisters-in-law etc. She's got to gain everyone's acceptance. When there are conflicts, she's the weakest. So this custom of moving in with the husband's family has made many women feel helpless when they have problems. They feel very helpless."[13] Before a woman gains her family of sons, in a sense her life to that point has been lived as a commodity of men and families. It is to that concept that we now turn.

WOMEN AS COMMODITIES

In the context of patrilocality, it will be difficult not to view marriage as an exchange of a commodity—a woman—between two men, her father and her future husband (and their families). The woman's productive and reproductive capabilities are changing hands, and almost always this is accompanied by an exchange of a price in goods and/or money. The woman will provide labor and children and will serve as a means to the ends of the family of the groom. A Ugandan saying states, "The poorest man is he who does not have a wife to work for him and make his children." A wife may be seen almost as a piece of land, or as livestock, to be owned and worked by the man. As Xie Lihua of *Rural Women* magazine in China put it, "There's a saying among men: 'Marrying a woman is like buying a horse: I can ride you and beat you whenever I like.' Men feel that 'I've spent money on bringing you into my family, so I have the right to order you around.' And a man will beat a woman if she has a mind of her own."[14]

According to Brinton's Law, even the opposite of a cultural practice harming women may harm women.[15] So just as bride-price may be used as a sign of ownership over a wife justifying coercive treatment, so may the opposite of bride-price: dowry. In societies where dowry is the accepted practice, it is a sign that a woman is considered a burden and that a groom and his family must be compensated for accepting this burden from the bride's family. This intensifies son preference, for the birth of a daughter may consign a family to bankruptcy when the time comes to pay her dowry. Indeed, signs in India proclaiming, "Better 500 Rupees Now Than 50,000 Rupees Later" are posted to point out in clear economic terms why sex-selective abortion of female fetuses is desirable.[16] If women are commodities akin to livestock, then one can cull them, if necessary, to achieve one's economic ends, such as the avoidance of dowry, or to seek the birth of a son to provide social security in old age. (More on that in a later section.)

In addition, the family of the groom may pressure the bride's family for additional dowry even after the wedding. Girls may be beaten or mutilated to get her family to pay more; if none is forthcoming, the girl may be burned to death in a suspicious "kitchen fire." This frees the groom's family to keep the first dowry (since the husband was widowed, not divorced, and so is not expected to return the dowry) and then to seek a second dowry from the family of another girl. While such practices are by no means attendant in the majority of Indian marriages, they are widespread enough that the Indian government now holds the groom and his immediate family guilty until proven innocent if a young bride dies by household fire.[17]

Of course, we do not see only the wife-as-commodity situation in our world; we also see the female-body-as-commodity. The selling of women's bodies through prostitution, sex trafficking, sex tourism, mail-order brides, militarized prostitution, and even open chattel markets for women and girls in some nations demonstrates that a woman may be bought, sold, and enslaved simply as a set of orifices, with no other meaning or value to her very existence. Indeed, in keeping with a myth prevalent in several countries, that sex with a virgin cures AIDS, women's bodies are "used" in a horrifying way: according to Betty Makoni of the Girl Child Network in Zimbabwe, "The youngest girl I ever came across was a day-old baby who was raped."[18] Trafficked girls who grow too ill due to the AIDS contracted from their users are simply thrown out on the streets to die.

Also left to die are millions of women who are injured or die in pregnancy and childbirth, simply because the meager resources that would be necessary to save their lives are not allocated. Nicholas Kristof and Sheryl WuDunn tell the heartbreaking stories of Mahabouba and Prudence. Mahabouba, of Ethiopia, was sold to a sixty-year-old man when she was a young teenager and had her first stillbirth at fourteen because of obstructed labor resulting in a major fistula. She was left to be eaten by the hyenas in a hut outside her village—and relatives took off the door to make it easier for the hyenas. Though paralyzed from the waist down because of her childbirth injuries, she fended them off with a stick that night and then crawled with her arms, dragging her legs, to a nearby village, where a missionary helped her. And Prudence, of Cameroon, a twenty-four-year-old mother of three, died in childbirth after three days of obstructed labor in a hospital because no one would pay for the supplies for the C-section that she needed to live.[19] Even in reproduction, a woman's life is expendable.

WOMEN'S LABOR

Barber Conable of the World Bank once opined that women do two-thirds of the world's work, and that opinion is still supported by evidence forty years later. Of course, what counts as work is an issue at play in this statistic. Marilyn Waring shows convincingly that in the 1930s, economists planning for war defined work as only that labor that produced something sold in the marketplace—which could be reassigned to produce for the war effort.[20] Unfortunately for women, who were not consulted on this system of national accounts, this definition excludes most of the labor that women do, whether in the fields, in the informal marketplace, or in the home. All social benefits—health insurance, unemployment insurance, pensions, Social Security—were then defined around this male model of what constituted useful societal labor.

This model prevails today, despite the fact that in 1997, UNIFEM estimated—in its very first estimate of the kind—that the unpaid labor of women, if valued monetarily, would translate into about 40 percent of the world's gross product.[21] Furthermore, salary analysts in the United States consistently value the unpaid work a wife and mother does at between $120,000 and $280,000 per year, and some even offer a figure of more than $700,000.[22]

But this "reproductive" labor of making a habitat for the family, which includes gathering fuel, water, doing the cooking, cleaning, laundry, and child care, not to mention the burdens of pregnancy and childbirth, is not the entire picture. In many parts of the world, women are the primary growers of food, especially subsistence crops; according to the United Nations Food and Agriculture Organization (FAO) women produce about 80 percent of Africa's food and about 50 percent of food worldwide.[23] In addition, women are the providers of nearly all caring services, such as elder care, child care, and care for the ill, which are inevitably priced very low in the marketplace.

Feminist economists have rightly pointed out that capitalism could not even exist if women did not perform these labors with little or no remuneration.[24] Apparently, in the thinking of most economists, women are like air and water, to be used for free. And economists label women who perform these labors as "non-productive," even though the societies and economies of the world would grind to a halt if all of those "unproductive" women ceased their labors tomorrow.

Capitalism is, in a sense, parasitical upon the free labor, productive and reproductive, that women perform to keep humanity alive through time. Yet the ones on whom our very lives depend are the same ones forced to work without a safety net. Because women are "economically inactive," their caring work means they are largely excluded from social benefits such as health insurance, pensions, and Social Security—except as a woman is joined to an "economically productive" spouse. In the United States, the largest risk factor for poverty in old age is to have ever given birth to a child—that is, to be a mother.[25]

A ROAD MAP OF THIS VOLUME

With these foundational concepts in place, we are prepared to move forward. Chapter 2 lifts the veil on the invisibility of women's reality in our discussion of national and international relations. We argue that the treatment of women—what is happening in intimate interpersonal relationships between men and women—creates a context in which violence and exploitation seem natural. We show how women are disadvantaged by these norms, what wounds are thereby created, and how prevalent such practices are. More fundamentally, we look at why this inequality is invisible, what harm results, and how inequality is maintained through cultural acceptance.

In chapter 3, we provide evidence of the prevalence of inequality and describe the conditions of women. We describe in detail the situation of women across the nations of the world today. We then offer theoretical explanations and empirical evidence concerning the origins of the prevalent social structures favoring men. We explore the impact of those structures on the treatment of women, as well as the diffusion of norms of violence and exploitation throughout society.

Chapter 4 links the micro-level explanations discussed in chapters 2 and 3 to the macro or state level. We empirically demonstrate the linkage between sex and world peace and discuss the need to alter definitions of peace, democracy, and security. We examine the impact of gender civilizations on patterns of regional and international conflict and instability. We highlight the general lack of data and research in this area, and note the deleterious effects that this paucity creates for both the academic and the policymaking communities.

In chapter 5, we describe and discuss the challenges of a top-down approach to realizing greater gender equality within human societies. We note that the state is a double-edged sword, and that while it is capable of tangibly improving the situation and security of women, it is also capable of profoundly harming women with misguided policies. Nevertheless, to address the wounds inflicted upon the women of the world, the state must, at a minimum, commit to eradicating violence against women, ensuring greater equity in family law, and including women's voices in the councils of human decision making.

Chapter 6 offers a discussion of the challenges of a bottom-up approach to realizing gender equality. We focus on how alternative scripts for gender relations provide new ways of thinking and acting in families and communities— and on how these alternative scripts of gender equality may prove a more sure basis for personal happiness, security, equity, and voice. When male/female relations are changed, new social structures emerge that do not support the same level of violence as male-dominated social structures do, and that may create the roots of a more stable, prosperous, and peaceful international system, a vision that we explore further in the concluding chapter.

2

WHAT IS THERE TO SEE, AND WHY AREN'T WE SEEING IT?

IN THIS CHAPTER we examine how the foundational concepts just surveyed, such as honor and shame, patrilocality, and the devaluation of women's labor, play out in the lives of real women and girls. We argue that what is happening at the most intimate levels can be viewed as a microcosm or a mirror of the larger society—and can provide a way for us to see how violence against women within a society becomes not only pervasive but also "normal." Our contention is that what is considered normal becomes invisible to our eyes, paralyzing us from making needed changes.

THE "LITTLE" THINGS: GENDERED MICROAGGRESSION

The concept of microaggression against women is one worth defining. Gendered microaggression is composed of all those many choices and acts in the routine of day-to-day existence that harm, subordinate, exploit, and disrespect women. These "little" things, experienced day after day, year after year, ground the society in gender inequality and all of its sequelae. Given that gendered microaggression becomes entrenched in daily living, these pernicious norms are the air breathed in by children of both sexes, and they become as natural and invisible to that next generation as air itself. What is viewed as normal is not only invisible but becomes something that is not spoken about either. Silence, often self-imposed, is the sturdy ally of gendered microaggression.

Worse, gendered microaggression may warp women themselves to not only accept violence against them but perpetuate it. Women may be co-opted into voluntarily, sometimes even eagerly, participating in gendered microaggression against other women—or even themselves. For example, it is women—not men—who are, in the vast majority of cases, the perpetrators of female infanticide:

> When Rani returned home from the hospital cradling her newborn daughter, the men in the family slipped out of her mud hut while she and her mother-in-law mashed poisonous oleander seeds into a dollop of oil and forced it down the infant's throat. As soon as darkness fell, Rani crept into a nearby field and buried her baby in a shallow, unmarked grave next to a small stream. "I never felt any sorrow," Rani, a farm laborer, said through an interpreter. "There was a lot of bitterness in my heart because the gods should have given me a son."[1]

Similarly, it may in fact be girls who pressure and plead with their parents to allow them to undergo female genital cutting so that they can fit in with their peers who are also undergoing the procedure. It is also primarily women who perform the cutting. And in many traditional patrilocal societies, the person a young woman fears the most is not male but female: her mother-in-law, who may have the power to make her life a living hell. Thus, when we speak of microaggression against women, we must not overlook the fact that women may be as culpable as men.

In addition, we would be remiss if we did not point out that in every land, in every time period, there have always been people, both male and female, who refuse to either enact or submit to these norms of gendered microaggression. There were families in nineteenth-century China that refused to bind their daughters' feet; there are families in India today who refuse to pay dowry; there are women who flee with their daughters rather than let them be married against their will. There are others who have used their position of influence to attempt to change norms—we think here of the efforts of Suzanne Mubarak, the wife of the former president of Egypt, to outlaw female genital cutting in that country.[2] The social price for being so unreasonable in the eyes of society may be quite steep, indeed, including ostracism and even violence. Violating these norms may take immense courage. Therefore, when we speak in general terms of the pervasiveness of such norms of gendered microaggression, we must never forget that if we look closely, we will always find in the very same society those who have rejected those norms. Nevertheless, the insidious pervasiveness of gendered microaggression is injurious to women. We turn now to a discussion of the types of wounds women suffer as a result of such aggression.

While each specific act of gendered microaggression may seem inconsequential to human society, the cumulative impact of millions of acts of microaggression against women is enormous and, as we shall continue to argue, is one of the taproots of violence at all levels, including the international. We proceed by identifying three key wounds inflicted by microaggression against women in human society: (1) lack of bodily integrity and physical security, (2) lack of equity in family law, and (3) lack of parity in the councils of human decision making. We will rely principally on the voices of others to share examples of these wounds.

THE FIRST WOUND: LACK OF BODILY INTEGRITY AND PHYSICAL SECURITY

THE CRUELEST BLOWS: PHYSICAL AND SEXUAL ASSAULT

Sabrija Gerovic was a Bosnian Muslim woman with two children, four-year-old Samira and three-month-old Amira. Early in 1993, during the Bosnian war, she and her children were forced into a truck and driven to a house in Pilnica, where she found herself placed with many other women, Muslims like herself. Her captors were Serb soldiers, *chetniks*.

> In the next room were the women aged 15 to 19. "Every night they were taking the girls out."
>
> That night two men came into the room and took her daughter Samira. "She was gone for 24 hours, at midnight the next night a man came in and told me to come and take my child. I went into a room. It was empty and there was only a table.
>
> "They told me to take off my clothes and I was completely naked and there were seven of them. Then they all raped me. They had been drinking but only two were really drunk. One of them was biting at my breast." She pulls back the soiled cream lapels of her shabby navy toweling dressing gown and points to the purple puncture marks all around her left breast. "Here is where he bit me," she said.
>
> "There was a curtain across the room and when they had finished they said: 'Go and get your baby.' I went behind the curtain and [my 4 year old

daughter] was naked, her head was blue and she had foam on her mouth. She had no pants and there was lots of blood streaming down her legs and I knew they had raped her."[3]

Rape in war has been considered a war crime only since June 1, 1996. Before that, it was just what men did in war and was unremarkable, such as when the Red Army invaded Germany at the end of World War II, raping and literally crucifying women as they advanced. Or when women were killed by Japanese officers in Nanjing by having ceremonial swords thrust into their vaginas. Or the rape of hundreds of thousands of Bangladeshi women by Pakistani soldiers in the 1971 war of independence. Or what is happening in the Democratic Republic of Congo right now:

> "They went after my daughter [Monique, aged 20, who was engaged to be married], and I knew they would rape her. But she resisted and said she would rather die than have relations with them. They cut off her left breast and put it in her hand. They said, 'Are you still resisting us?' She said she would rather die than be with them. They cut off her genital labia and showed them to her. She said, 'Please kill me.' They took a knife and put it to her neck and then made a long vertical incision down her chest and split her body open. She was crying but finally she died. She died with her breast in her hand."[4]

Is such brutality against women merely a product of the frenzy of war? Consider this case from New York City:

> When the elevator door was finally opened it looked as though a bottle of cranberry juice had broken, on the walls, the floor, a scream of red. But it was blood. Blood where he slit her throat, blood where he broke her jaw, blood where he knocked out her front teeth.
>
> It was only after he had done all that that he told her to take off her clothes.
>
> He's still out there somewhere, the man who brutally beat a 23-year-old woman visiting New York from Eastern Europe, a woman who had come to live for a year with her sister, an actress, to study English. He is tall, perhaps 6 feet 2 inches, a black man with high cheekbones, a widow's peak and almond eyes. He was very smooth when he entered the building in upper Manhattan not far from the field where the Columbia team plays football.

He made small talk in the lobby, pleasant and unthreatening, so she got into the elevator with him.

And then . . . The man who chatted up, then beat [this woman] did his considerable damage in under 10 minutes.[5]

A horrifying new type of assault against women and girls has even been developed in our modern twenty-first century: acid attacks. For reasons ranging from opposition to a girl's desire to attend school or to her mode of dress, to revenge against a woman's refusal to have sex with or to marry a man, women may be attacked by having hydrochloric or sulfuric acid thrown into their faces. The melting of the face and destruction of the eyes that result take violence against women to a new low:

One morning two months ago [in Afghanistan], Shamsia Husseini and her sister were walking through the muddy streets to the local girls school when a man pulled alongside them on a motorcycle and posed what seemed like an ordinary question

"Are you going to school?"

Then the man pulled Shamsia's burqa from her head and sprayed her face with burning acid. Scars, jagged and discolored, now spread across Shamsia's eyelids and most of her left cheek. These days, her vision goes blurry, making it hard for her to read. . . . [I]n the months before the attack, the Taliban had moved into the Mirwais area and the rest of Kandahar's outskirts. As they did, posters began appearing in local mosques.

"Don't Let Your Daughters Go to School," one of them said.[6]

Is such brutality against women perpetrated only by depraved strangers, then, in or out of war? You know the answer to that question. The answer is "no." The war zone for women extends into the fabric of their daily peacetime lives, a realization that makes us ask sincerely, "Is there ever a true peacetime for women?" All over our world, those most likely to physically injure women are men they love or have loved: husbands, boyfriends, ex-husbands, ex-boyfriends, fathers, brothers. The FBI reports that in single-perpetrator/single-victim homicides, 89 percent of male victims were killed by males, and 90 percent of female victims were killed by males. One-quarter of female homicides are committed by husbands or boyfriends, while 3 percent of male murders are committed by wives or girlfriends. Later studies suggest the 25 percent figure may be too low and that a more in-depth investigation shows

the percentage is 50 percent or higher.[7] Turning to nonlethal violence perpetrated by intimates, women experience such violence seven times more often
than men do.[8] While home may be a safe haven for men, home may be the
most dangerous place of all for women.

Domestic violence is a global curse. Even in what many consider to be
the most enlightened societies, such as Sweden, the domestic violence rate
is still calculated to be as high as 25 percent—that is, one-quarter of Swedish
women will experience domestic violence at least once during their lifetime.[9]
In Afghanistan, the figure is 87 percent.[10]

This question of where is the safe haven for women, or where is women's
peace, is not unknown to college-aged students in the United States. There
is a secret, and very different, world of security for young women in our society, unlike that for young men. Consider some of the "tricks" shared among
young women, as discussed in this imaginary conversation:

"Now, you want to become acquainted with a woman you see in public.
The first thing you need to understand is that women are dealing with a set
of challenges and concerns that are strange to you, a man. To begin with,
we would rather not be killed or otherwise violently assaulted."

"But wait! I don't want that, either!"

"Well, no. But do you think about it all the time? Is preventing violent
assault or murder part of your daily routine, rather than merely something
you do when you venture into war zones? Because, for women, it is. When
I go on a date, I always leave the man's full name and contact information
written next to my computer monitor. This is so the cops can find my body
if I go missing. My best friend will call or e-mail me the next morning, and
I must answer that call or e-mail before noon-ish, or she begins to worry. If
she doesn't hear from me by three or so, she'll call the police. My activities
after dark are curtailed. Unless I am in a densely-occupied, well-lit space, I
won't go out alone. Even then, I prefer to have a friend or two, or my dogs,
with me. Do you follow rules like these?"[11]

Here's an activity for your classroom or circle of friends: see how many of
the items in this list are part of your world.

- I would never go jogging alone at night.
- I get on a cell phone when I am in a cab, so the driver will know that
  someone on the other end will know if I don't make it to my destination.

If I am really nervous, I say the cab company's name and the driver's name into the phone. I do this even if there is nobody on the other end of the line.

- When I leave the library or metro stop late at night, I put my keys in my fist, with the points of the keys sticking out between my fingers.
- If the elevator door opens, and I see a man in there and he doesn't get out, unless there are a lot of people around, I don't get into the elevator.
- If I have to drive home alone at night, I lock every door from the inside.
- I make sure I do not look into men's eyes when I walk down the street.
- I would never go hiking or camping by myself.
- If I am in an enclosed space with strangers, I make sure I identify a second way out.
- I find my heart beating wildly when I have to park underground, especially after dark.
- My mom made me take a self-defense class when I was in high school.

Do the answers differ by sex in your classroom or circle of acquaintances? If you are a man, you need to know that the world the women around you live in is not the same as your world. If you are a woman, have you ever stopped to consider just how constrained your life is because of concerns for your personal safety, compared to the life of the young man next to you? This is the first wound.

IT'S NOT SEXY: SEXUAL HARM

This first wound is not confined to the physical assault that we associate with murder, rape, and beatings. The lack of bodily integrity that we are referring to when we speak of "the first wound" is also closely associated with sex itself.

In a way that is not true for men, sex can be deadly for women. What is a moment's pastime for a man may well result in the death of a woman less than a year later. In Sierra Leone, the lifetime chance of a woman dying incidental to pregnancy is one in eight.[12] That's akin to taking an eight-chambered revolver, putting one bullet it, spinning the chamber, and pointing it at your head every time you have sex. Is that what men are thinking of when they have sex? That is certainly what women in Sierra Leone think about when their husbands want sex. They think about the possibility that they may die and leave their children motherless, which in most poor countries is a death sentence for those children. Not just their own death, then, but multiple deaths may result because their husband wants to have sex.

The annual global toll of maternal death is staggering. The World Health Organization estimates that about 529,000 women died in 2005 as a result of pregnancy and childbirth, and over a million more were permanently injured.[13] In contrast, the Human Security Report states that in 2005 there were 17,400 conflict deaths in the world.[14] In other words, there were thirty times more maternal mortality deaths than deaths in international or civil conflict in 2005! And yet the amount of resources allotted to conflict resolution dwarfs that allotted to maternal mortality. Maternal mortality is "normal death," and donors are interested in other, more glamorous health concerns. As Kevin Sullivan notes, "Maternal mortality rarely gets attention from international donors, who are far more focused on global health threats such as malaria, tuberculosis and HIV-AIDS. . . . 'Maternal death is an almost invisible death,' said Thoraya A. Obaid, executive director of the U.N. Population Fund."[15]

Maternal mortality is the consequence of something even more fundamental: most married women in the world have no control over whether they have sex. When a woman becomes married, cultural traditions may deny her any right to bodily integrity in sexual relations. "Marital rape" is considered an oxymoron in approximately ninety states, with no laws against such an act. It was not even considered a crime in the United States until 1976, and most states to this day consider it a lesser crime than "stranger rape." In one focus group of men in DR Congo,[16] one man commented,

> I cannot imagine a situation before now when my wife will refuse me sex. She could not, because that would result in severe beating from me. She was my property and I could use her in any way possible. Whether she enjoyed the sex or not was not even discussed. The important thing is that I enjoyed it.

Another man explained,

> I was a normal man, living with my family in a normal way. I behaved like every man within the society. My wife was a slave to me, she had no rights and had to respect me absolutely. She was always in the home, and could not go out to meet other women. She belonged to me, because at our marriage, I paid a bride-price — the dowry, which gave me all the authority to treat her as I wished. She was at my mercy for sexual activity, anytime,

anyplace, anywhere. Refusal went with punishment. I was a complete tyrant in my home.

The women's focus group concurred: "I was only a sex machine for [my husband]. He used me as he wished. I could not argue with him or refuse him sex."

Lack of bodily integrity in sex, of course, results in lack of control over fertility: "Family planning was not a topic ever discussed. It was men who decided how many children and when. Women were just 'baby producing machines.'"

Most people do not know that the United Nations produced a document in 1995 that asserts that women have the right to say no to sex, even if they are married. "The human rights of women include their right to have control over and decide freely and responsibly on matters related to their sexuality, including sexual and reproductive health, free of coercion, discrimination and violence."[17] To suggest that a married woman has the right to say no to sex is, in our opinion, one of the most important breakthroughs in the entire history of human rights. But this international right continues to be virtually unknown by either women or men.

Of course, in the age of AIDS, the right for married women to say no to sex is an important element of self-preservation. Due to the pervasiveness of double standards of marital fidelity throughout the world, where all men, even married men, are encouraged to be promiscuous as a testament to their manhood and where women may be killed even upon unfounded suspicion of sexual relations outside of marriage, a woman's assassin is often her husband, who brings home AIDS to her after visiting prostitutes. (In addition, he may kill more than one wife if the society sanctions polygamy, and may kill the children he sires by giving AIDS to their mother and through the mother to the children.) And, of course, the prostitutes themselves are assassinated by the promiscuous men who bring them AIDS. And, as we have noted earlier, even little girls may be assassinated by men who believe that having sex with a pure child will cleanse them of their AIDS. Women in these societies cannot negotiate the terms upon which they will have sex. They cannot "force" a man to wear a condom. Catherine Maternowska recounts this conversation she had with a truck-stop prostitute in Swaziland:

I met eyes with a 16-year-old named Mbali. She was thin, with close-cropped hair and a beautiful smile. I offered her a packet of crackers, which she ripped open with her teeth. After wolfing them down, she looked at me and said, "I hate having sex." Her parents were dead; she was unable to pay her school fees, had been abused by an overburdened aunt—and now, like many of the girls, she was a runaway. Nearly one in four Swazi girls is H.I.V. positive, and Mbali is one of them. Her treatment options are limited. "I have nowhere to sleep unless I find a man," she said. "Sometimes I don't have money and food for two days. A man without a condom will pay more, so obviously I say O.K. because I need money."

She continued: "I am so tired. These men are so rough."

I've been working with women and girls for over two decades now—in Haiti, in Zimbabwe, in Tanzania and in Kenya—and I have heard this story often. But this one, deep in the forest of Swaziland, seemed so desperate. I was as surprised as she was when I suddenly burst into tears.

Mbali held my face and said, "Don't cry!" She hugged me. How absurd can life be? A 16-year-old, H.I.V.-positive orphan was comforting me while I wept. It was a strange way to carry on an interview, but that's what we did. I asked her what she needed most. "Someplace safe," she said. "Someplace to be a girl. Someplace where I won't have to have sex with men anymore."[18]

Lack of bodily integrity extends also to the physical alteration of women's genitals, sometimes called female circumcision, or female genital cutting (FGC). Girls from a few months of age up to puberty may be subject to "surgery" that may inflict upon them one of four levels of modification. The first is the excision of the hood of the clitoris, practiced primarily in Indonesia. The second level is complete clitorectomy, the third is clitorectomy plus excision of the inner labia. The most invasive procedure, practiced around the lower Nile, is clitorectomy, excision of the inner labia, and cutting off the ends of the outer labia, whose stumps are then sewn together or held together by thorns, leaving an opening approximately the size of a Q-tip for the passage of urine and menstrual blood. Various reasons are invoked for the custom, including religion, Pharaonic tradition, the desire to extinguish female sexual desire in honor/shame cultures, and the need for some proof, or patent, of virginity for the girl to be marriageable in her society. While the inability to climax in sexual relations is lamentable enough, the health consequences of the fourth level of female circumcision, called infibulation, are massive. Chronic infections due to stasis of urine and menstrual blood are common, and may result in infertility. Sexual intercourse may be horribly painful, and may entail cutting open the scar tissue, or penetrating the Q-tip opening repeatedly in an effort to stretch the scar tissue sufficiently for intercourse. In some traditions, the woman must be stitched up again upon becoming pregnant, and then cut open for childbirth. Impaction of the baby's head in the birth canal is common in infibulated women, significantly heightening the risk of stillbirth and maternal death. Vesico-vaginal fistulae, where childbirth opens a passage between a woman's anus and/or her urethra and her vagina, producing an unstoppable flow of urine and feces through the vagina, are a common consequence, and women are almost always divorced and abandoned if a fistula results.

THE SIMPLE FACTS OF LIVING ARE NOT SO SIMPLE FOR WOMEN

Normal daily biological functions may be compromised in other, nonsurgical ways for women. In many areas of the world where indoor plumbing and sanitation are not available, women are able to use field latrines only at dawn and at dusk to avoid harassment and immodesty. They are expected to hold in their urine and feces during the rest of the day, and may be unable to meet their sanitation needs during menstruation.[19] One informant from Kenya told of women having to urinate and defecate in bags during the day, and then having to go out at night and throw the bags as far as they could into the fields. Girls' schooling may become sporadic if there are not adequate facilities for the girls to manage their menstruation at school, and some families may simply take a girl out of school once she begins to menstruate.

Even the basic matter of food may be compromised by gender. The World Bank reports that two-thirds of the most severely malnourished children in India are female.[20] That phenomenon is certainly not restricted to India, and in many regions girls eat last in the household, as this aid worker in Africa notes:

> I flew to Kapoeta in southern Sudan. The region was in the midst of a famine; 250,000 people had already starved to death. As is common in Africa, when we landed on the dusty runway families came from miles around to see who had arrived. They knew we were from an aid organization, so mothers held up their emaciated children to show us how much they needed our help. It didn't take me long to notice the children's distended stomachs — a sure sign of malnutrition. But it was several minutes before I realized that in this sea of humanity, the mothers were only holding up sons; there were no daughters. In the familial hierarchy, girls were the last to be fed and the first to die. By the time we arrived, they were dead.[21]

The first wound may even appear before or at birth. Especially in Asia, as we have noted, the practices of sex-selective abortion and female infanticide are altering sex ratios in alarming fashion. To have two X chromosomes is considered a genetic deformity, a situation that can be rectified before birth or at the time of birth by simple elimination of the deformed entity. Abnormal sex ratios favoring males can be found in nearly all Asian countries, including China, India, Pakistan, Taiwan, Vietnam, and others. The Chinese government estimates there will be at least forty million more young adult men than women in the year 2020, and there will be an imbalance of at least thirty million in India at that same time. In addition to direct infanticide, there is also abundant evidence of preferential feeding and medical care for sons, resulting in early childhood mortality for girls that may be three times higher than that for boys.[22]

Our world is bleeding girls and women, literally. A 2007 UNFPA report estimated that there are 163 million missing women that should be here: they are missing because of egregious maternal mortality rates, sex selection, abnormally high suicide rates, excess childhood mortality, and violence against women.[23] Lack of bodily integrity and physical security for women is the first and foremost wound that must be addressed by humankind.

THE SECOND WOUND: LACK OF EQUITY IN FAMILY LAW

The second major harm to women globally comes from inequity in family law. "Family law," sometimes known as personal status law, is law—or entrenched tradition that overrides law—concerning marriage, divorce, custody, and inheritance.[24] It is stunning to consider that for almost all of human history, family law looked very much the same across all cultures.

According to evolutionary theory, powerful males made family law in the image of their own reproductive interests. Consider the remarkable convergence of family law throughout both time and space in human history: adultery as a much greater crime for women than for men; female infanticide as a historically sanctioned practice in virtually all human cultures; polygyny legal but polyandry (multiple husbands for one wife) proscribed; divorce easy for men and almost impossible for women; male-on-female domestic violence and marital rape not recognized as crimes; the marriage of the victim to her rapist as a common legal restitution for rape; the legal age of consent and of marriage years younger for females than for males; and inheritance of resources preferentially allocated to males. Still other practices that are an expression of physical and sexual dominance of men over women, such as infibulation, chastity belts, droit de seigneur, and gender-based dress codes that inhibit the mobility of women, are also understandable in this light. The convergence in family law systems, expansively defined, through time and space leads us to the conclusion that the formation of family law is at least in part due to dominant men in all cultures having originally created family law through their political power, and having created it in the image of male reproductive interests as shaped by our evolutionary heritage. Baldly put, dominance over females by males is at the foundation of historical family law because of our common evolutionary legacy.

IT SHOULD BE THE HAPPIEST DAY OF THEIR LIVES: MARRIAGE TRAGEDIES

Each inequitable plank in family law fuels tragedy. For example, in many traditional societies, age of consent for girls may be as young as seven or eight. Given the burden of protecting a girl's virginity in honor/shame cultures, girls are typically married off at the onset of puberty, or immediately before. True consent of the bride in marriage, then, is impossible. The marriage has been arranged by her father or her nearest male relative and males from the groom's family. She has probably never met her husband before her wedding. She knows nothing about sex. But her groom is, on average, at least a decade older than she is. Her wedding night, predictably, amounts to child rape, as this memoir by a child bride in Egypt attests. She was thirteen when she was married to her twenty-five-year-old cousin:

> They held my legs apart. One of them held me firmly from behind. One woman gave my groom a clean, white gauze to wrap around his finger. He knew what to do and seemed pleased by my ignorance. . . . He inserted his finger into me, and I screamed. He did this a couple of times until he drew blood. Then he took me and threw me on the bed. I was limp. They gave me a glass of sugar water to revive me. . . . When this was done, each one went her way, and I was alone with him. He closed the door behind him. Suddenly I saw that he was undressed. He has taken off his underpants. I have drawn myself up into a ball on the bed. I was cowering like a fly against the wall. . . . Suddenly I felt myself being moved. He carried me back to the bed and was on top of me . . . I screamed . . . I said no. I was afraid. . . . I

was terrified. So it went on all night. . . . Seven or eight months after I was married, my period came.[25]

When girls become pregnant at these early ages, tragedy often looms. UNICEF notes: "Girls who give birth before the age of 15 are five times more likely to die in childbirth than women in their 20s."[26] As we wrote this chapter, Fawziya Ammodi of Yemen, married at age eleven to a twenty-four-year-old man, died at age twelve giving birth to her first child, who also died. She died of hemorrhage after three days of labor. Fawziya was murdered by the inequitable traditions of family law in her country, which amounted to outrageous negligence concerning the life and agency of another human being. While technically her marriage was illegal, it was "lawful" under tribal law.

Other aspects of family law may result in serious harm to women. Consider this case, cited by philosopher Martha Nussbaum in her book *Sex and Social Justice*:

> "I may die, but I still cannot go out. If there's something in the house, we eat. Otherwise, we go to sleep." So Metha Bai, a young widow in Rajasthan, India, with two young children, described her plight as a member of a caste whose women are traditionally prohibited from working outside the home—even when, as here, survival itself is at issue. If she stays at home, she and her children may shortly die. If she attempts to go out, her in-laws will beat her and abuse her children. For now, Metha Bai's father travels from 100 miles away to plow her small plot of land. But he is aging, and Metha Bai fears that she and her children will shortly die with him.[27]

Metha Bai is apparently being denied the right to feed herself and her children. We cannot think of a more basic human right than the right to obtain food by one's own honest labor. The exquisite horror of being forced to starve herself and her children to death because of caste rules that apply only to females seems fantastical. What higher good could possibly be achieved by the deaths of these innocents?

While the contracting of marriage may pose its own risks, the dissolution of marriage may impose others in societies where the right to divorce is not equitable between men and women, and where the fates of divorced men and divorced women may be radically different as well. In many traditional societies, men have a completely unrestricted right to divorce: they may divorce for any reason, no matter how trivial. And they may divorce easily and even impersonally: for example, in India, a Muslim man may divorce his wife through an e-mail message or an SMS text message. Men need not even register these divorces, or have a court certify them. On the other hand, a Muslim woman in India would have to prove—in court—one of a set of permissible conditions for women to divorce, which include insanity or desertion for a period of at least four years. In other cultures, the permissible reasons may include male infertility, the husband being in jail due to criminal activity, the husband bringing another woman into the marital bed, or the husband having AIDS. In short, there is but a small set of legally justifiable reasons for a woman to divorce, whereas a man may divorce his wife because she put too much salt on his dinner.[28] Alimony is very rare under such circumstances, and the woman may not be able to claim any property or assets from the marriage except for her bride-price. The woman is expected to return to her birth family to live. In turn, her family is usually hard-pressed to support their returning daughter, and they feel deep shame because of her divorce. Even in Western societies, divorce often leaves women and children in a far worse economic situation, while leaving men with greater resources.[29]

The issue of custody of minor children may be tragically inequitable as well. In most traditional societies, shared custody after divorce is an unknown concept; rather, custody of minor children may automatically devolve to the father. In many Islamic societies, for example, the rule of thumb is that custody of a boy is transferred from mother to father at the time the child is weaned, usually about three years of age. For girls, the child may be transferred at a specified time between five years of age and puberty, when it becomes the father's obligation to contract marriage for her. Indeed, the father may contract a marriage for his daughter over the disapproval of the girl's mother. If the mother were to remarry, custody of the children must be transferred to their father immediately upon that marriage. If a father dies, his widow may lose custody of her children to the father's nearest kin, especially the paternal grandparents. Because of custody considerations, women in such societies often remain in abusive marriages so as to be able to maintain a legal and ongoing relationship with their children.[30] Such considerations are not unknown even in Western societies as well, because a father's often greater economic assets may grant him a superior position in court.

And yet even that may not be enough to enable the mother to protect her children. In Afghanistan, for example, there have been numerous complaints of girls being sold into marriage to much older men as repayment for debts contracted by their fathers, even over the objections of their mothers. "Afghans readily use their daughters to settle debts and assuage disputes. Polygamy is practiced. A man named Mohammed Fazal, 45, [said] that village elders had urged him to take his second wife, 13-year-old Majabin, in lieu of money owed him by the girl's father. The two men had been gambling at cards while also ingesting opium and hashish."[31]

In addition to the use of girls as currency to pay off financial debts, girls may be given as restitution for a crime: "Some Afghans refer to the practice as 'giving *bad*,' a traditional method of conflict resolution in which a murderer, a thief, or a debtor is forced by tribal elders to give a daughter or sister as payment to the victim's family."[32] In the case of a killing, the life of the girl is exchanged for expunging the blood debt between families. The girl may be abused by the victim's family as a scapegoat. Even when a crime is not involved, brides may become hostages to the state of relations between the two families. In some cases, giving her away does not just mean giving her in marriage. It may mean the girl's death:

> Shahab told me the story of two wives who were recently killed. Two men [in Afghanistan] exchanged their sisters so they could avoid the high price of a proper bride. One of the men killed his wife the first night, accusing her of having had sexual relations before marriage. When the news arrived in the other village, the other man brought his wife—the other man's sister—and made her walk around the grave; he cut her hands and feet off and killed her on the grave of the other girl. "Why?" I asked him, and he said, "He killed my sister; I had to," Shahab told me. The government forgave the murderers because the jirga forgave them, and the jirga is higher than the law.[33]

Marriage as a form of trafficking is also evident in the legally accepted practice of marriage-by-rape. In most traditional societies a rapist will go unpunished if he offers to marry his victim, whether or not that offer is accepted. In the thinking of honor/shame cultures, it is the taking of chastity without the consent of the girl's father and not the rape of the girl herself that is the crime. As such, the honor of the girl's family may be completely restored by her marriage to the rapist. The rape is often not a random act, but a very deliberate act with a particular target:

> Harun (not his real name), the son of a rich farming family, made a proposal to the parents of a girl from the same village. The parents refused, which infuriated Harun, and a few days later he sexually assaulted the girl.
>
> Ordinarily, Harun should have been tried and sentenced—under Bangladesh law, rape carries a maximum punishment of rigorous imprisonment

for life. But . . . Harun's victim was forced with impunity into becoming his wife, in defiance of the law.[34]

This is a long-standing practice in several regions of the world. For example, in one survey of laws in Latin American countries, it was found that in fifteen of those countries the law exonerates a rapist who offers to marry his victim, and in the case of a gang rape, will exonerate all the other men who raped her as long as one offers marriage. In some countries, the law will exonerate a rapist even if the victim refuses to marry him.[35]

It is in the steppes of Central Asia that the practice of marriage-by-rape, euphemistically called "capture marriage," is most prevalent, however, and increasing in prevalence over time. It is estimated that at least one-third of all brides in Kyrgyzstan are abducted and married against their will, and in some rural villages, up to 80 percent of the women have been subject to this practice. A common saying in this culture is "Every good marriage begins in tears."[36]

Bride kidnapping, also called marriage by abduction or marriage by capture, occurs when a young woman, usually below the age of 25, is typically taken through force or deception by a group of men, including the intended groom. Sometimes the men are people she has met prior to the incident; sometimes they are complete strangers. The men are usually drunk; she is usually alone. She is taken to the home of her principal abductor, the intended groom, where his female relatives use physical force and a variety of forms of psychological coercion to compel her to "agree" to the marriage and submit to having the marriage scarf placed on her head—the sign that she consents to marry her abductor. If the kidnapped woman resists, this process can last for hours or days. Her abductor usually rapes her, sometimes prior to her coerced consent to the marriage to shame her to stay rather than go home disgraced. Rape can also occur following the wedding ceremony.[37]

Kyrgyzstan also has the dubious distinction of being the first former Soviet republic to seek to legalize polygamy. Polygamy is quite common in both the Middle East and Africa. In the Middle East, the number of wives taken may be limited by law (often to four), but in some Islamic societies, men are allowed up to ninety-nine *muta'a* marriages, or temporary marriages in which the woman provides sex to a man for a specified price and for a specified time (which may be counted in hours). In the majority of cultures in sub-

Saharan Africa, polygamy is sanctioned. Unlike Islam, there may be no limit on the number of wives that may be taken, with some men recorded as having more than twenty wives and more than a hundred children in nations such as Kenya. Anthropologists suggest that the ubiquity of polygamy in sub-Saharan African culture may derive from women's performance of most agricultural work; marrying many women is an established way for a man to increase his wealth and productivity.

In Canada, now that consensual group sex has been deemed legal, there are also some voices pressing for legalizing polygamy.[38] However, research has shown that polygamy often exploits women, is insufficiently supportive of children, and places a large economic burden on the state:

> Polygamy is exploitive of women, and is associated with high rates of spousal abuse. Rivalry is common between multiple wives, as each competes for affection and resources for herself and her children. The practice of polygamy is clearly contrary to the principle of gender equality that is fundamental to Canadian society. Polygamy also has significant negative effects on children, in large part because fathers are often distant figures. Children of polygamous unions are more likely to be abused, and—compared to children from monogamous families—they tend to have more emotional difficulties and lower educational achievement.
>
> In fundamentalist Mormon communities, young women and adolescent girls are often coerced into polygamous unions. Older boys can also be harmed by polygamy, as they are often expelled from their communities and their families so that they will not compete with powerful males for wives. Finally, polygamy also imposes economic costs on society: Polygamous families are often unable to support their many children and resort to social assistance.[39]

Polygamy complicates the support of women and children in other ways also. Resources allocated to children and also inheritance by children may be based on their mother's standing within the set of wives. Furthermore, polygamy is an acknowledged risk factor for HIV/AIDS transmission to both wives and children born of polygamous unions.[40]

Law may also discriminate against women in deadly ways. There is a special place of infamy for the *hudood* ordinances of Pakistan, which were for the most part repealed in 2006, but are threatening to make a comeback. Similar laws have also been implemented in the Islamic north of Nigeria.

Under these ordinances, a woman who had been raped could be stoned to death for adultery:

> The evidence of guilt was there for all to see: a newborn baby in the arms of its mother, a village woman named Zafran Bibi. Her crime: she had been raped. Her sentence: death by stoning. Now Ms. Zafran, who is about 26, is in solitary confinement in a death-row cell in Kohat, a nearby town. The only visitor she is allowed is her baby daughter, now a year old and being cared for by a prison nurse.
>
> Thumping a fat red statute book, the white-bearded judge who convicted her, Anwar Ali Khan, said he had simply followed the letter of the Koran-based law, known as hudood, that mandates punishments.
>
> "The illegitimate child is not disowned by her and therefore is proof of *zina*," he said, referring to laws that forbid any sexual contact outside marriage. Furthermore, he said, in accusing her brother-in-law of raping her, Ms. Zafran had confessed to her crime.
>
> "The lady stated before this court that, yes, she had committed sexual intercourse, but with the brother of her husband," Judge Khan said. "This left no option to the court but to impose the highest penalty."
>
> The man Ms. Zafran accused, Jamal Khan, was set free without charges. A case against him would have been a waste of the court's time. Under the laws of *zina*, four male witnesses, all Muslims and all citizens of upright character, must testify to having seen a rape take place. The testimony of women or non-Muslims is not admissible. The victim's accusation also carries little weight; the only significant testimony she can give is an admission of guilt.[41]

Fortunately, the federal court overturned Zafran Bibi's punishment, but only after an intensive campaign in the Pakistani media. While the worst elements of the *hudood* ordinances have been repealed, there still exists the potential for abuse, including stoning to death for false accusations of adultery.[42]

UNEQUAL BEFORE THE LAW: DOUBLE STANDARDS

These cases illustrate also that the testimony of a woman in court may not hold as much weight as the testimony of a man in court. Indeed, in certain conservative Islamic societies, the testimony of a woman is worth exactly half of the testimony of a man. And as we have just seen, in certain cases of important crime, as in the case of a rape, only the testimony of a man is considered valid.

In addition, there may be certain crimes that, when committed by a man, draw a significantly less severe punishment under the law than when committed by a woman. In many cultures, this category includes "crimes of passion" and "crimes of honor." We have already seen that certain societies view assault and murder related to questions of a woman's chastity as culturally obligatory, and hence may punish such crimes only lightly or not at all, with either no jail time at all, or three months to two years of jail time for an honor killing. Syria recently made headlines by raising the punishment for an honor killing from a maximum of one year in prison to a minimum of seven years in prison.[43]

Lest one believe that the practice of giving lighter sentences to men whose honor has been offended is limited to the Islamic world, AmericasWatch reports, "It is still possible in Brazil for a man to kill his allegedly unfaithful wife and be absolved on the grounds of honor."[44] And in Fort Worth, Texas, in 2005,

a man sentenced to just four months in prison for killing his wife, after a jury concluded he acted in a blind fury, drew a 15-year term for wounding her boyfriend. Jimmy Dean Watkins pleaded guilty Wednesday to attempted murder for shooting Keith Fontenot on December 22, 1998. Watkins' estranged wife, Nancy, was killed with multiple gunshots as she tried to dial 911 during the attack. The jury at his 1999 trial found Watkins guilty of murdering his wife but decided he acted with "sudden passion" when he discovered her with Fontenot. In a decision that provoked an outcry, the jury recommended 10 years' probation. Because of the jury's recommendation, the most the judge could have given Watkins was six months behind bars. He sentenced Watkins to four months.[45]

This double standard of criminality between men and women extends beyond murder to domestic violence as well. Despite almost (though not quite) universal laws against domestic violence, it is still a crime for which, in many countries, police will simply laugh at a woman who complains of having been a victim. Worse, police may assault or molest the victim themselves if she attempts to report the crime.[46] Domestic violence against women may be perceived as simply natural and unremarkable. Indeed, the prevalence of this attitude has led to a dramatic recent shift in U.S. asylum policy:

In an unusually protracted and closely watched case, the Obama adminis-tration has recommended political asylum for a Guatemalan woman flee-ing horrific abuse by her husband, the strongest signal yet that the admin-istration is open to a variety of asylum claims from foreign women facing domestic abuse.

The large legal question in the case is whether women who suffer do-mestic abuse are part of a "particular social group" that has faced persecu-tion, one criteria for asylum claims. In a separate asylum case in April, the Department of Homeland Security pointed to some specific ways that battered women could meet this standard.

In a recent filing, Ms. Alvarado's lawyers argued that her circumstances met the requirements that the department had outlined in April. Now the department has agreed, in practice making the case a model for other asy-lum claims.

In a declaration filed recently to bolster Ms. Alvarado's argument that she was part of a persecuted group in Guatemala, an expert witness, Claudia Paz y Paz Bailey, reported that more than 4,000 women had been killed violently there in the last decade. These killings, only 2 percent of which have been solved, were so frequent that they earned their own legal term, "femicide," said Ms. Paz y Paz Bailey, a Guatemalan lawyer. In 2008 Gua-temala enacted a law establishing special sanctions for the crime.

"Many times," she said, violence against Guatemalan women "is not even identified as violence, is not perceived as strange or unusual."[47]

A legal system may also defer to other harmful customs concerning women. In some societies, daughters and wives may by law inherit less than the male relatives of a deceased person, putting them at greater risk for poverty. In other societies, widows and their children may actually be inherited as property by the nearest male relative, usually a brother, of a deceased man. Widow in-heritance and another customary law, widow cleansing, which requires that a widow have sex with some chosen, often marginalized man in her commu-nity in order that her husband's spirit not haunt the community, puts these women at high risk of AIDS infection, in addition to all of the tragedy of nonconsensual sexual relations. In other communities, the family of the dead man has the right to evict his widow and children from the property, which is inherited by his patriline. This has led, in both India and Africa, to a vast number of AIDS widows and orphans being cast into the street as a result of the epidemic.[48]

Widows may be especially discriminated against, in that they are often considered to be the cause of their husband's death, no matter what the cause of death was. In many cases, a woman may be deemed a witch, and this label may entitle others to completely dispossess her of her home and all property, and even her life may be at risk. In other societies, elderly widows are considered unclean and/or unlucky and are reduced to begging for their subsistence.

Indeed, the entire subject of women's property rights even in the absence of spousal death is an area in which women may be at great disadvantage under traditional customs that may trump law. This is especially true in the case of land ownership. In most traditional societies, land is passed from males to male heirs, bypassing women entirely. For example, in rural China it is estimated that 97 percent of rural farmland is inherited by males, even though Chinese law gives women equal rights concerning inheritance.[49] In 2008, it was estimated that only 5 percent of registered property owners in Kenya were female.[50] This is despite the fact that women may perform up to 75 percent of all agricultural labor in such societies.[51] The inability to hold land in one's name critically affects issues such as caloric intake, ability to access credit, and many other important aspects of daily life.

That societies throughout the world have countenanced the inequality of men and women before the law, condemning women to brutality and poverty and grief as a result, is the second great wound that must be urgently attended to by humankind.

THE THIRD WOUND: LACK OF PARITY IN THE COUNCILS OF HUMAN DECISION MAKING

As we contemplate the panorama of human history, in addition to the "naturalness" of violence against women, and the "naturalness" of their unequal standing before the law, we also see something else considered "natural": the virtual absence of women's voices in the councils of human decision making at whatever level we choose to examine, from the household to the capitals of nations to the United Nations.

We have already documented in great and painful detail the voicelessness of women in their own families and marriages. But what happens in homes becomes a template for what is viewed as appropriate in the larger society. Indeed, the concept of sovereignty is based on a parallel between the state and the household. Just as men ruled their households with absolute power, even over the life and death of the members of the household, so a king was the paterfamilias of his nation, with equivalent power over its citizens. Similarly, if the governance of the kingdom began to depart from the accepted template, such as when women began to be perceived as having too much influence on the king, the government would be vulnerable to overthrow by men who saw the regime as "unnatural."[52] Whether we speak of historical figures such as Lady Yang, Marie Antoinette, and Czarina Alexandra or of more modern women who have been perceived as having too much influence on male leaders, such as the twin sister of Shah Reza Pahlavi, the daughter of Boris Yeltsin, or the wife of Bill Clinton, leaders upset the template of male governance at their risk even in the twenty-first century.[53] For example, extremist blog posts from 2007 include statements such as this one concerning Hillary Clinton:

NOTE: the survival of our Republic is threatened by two things—fundamentalist Islamic terrorists and Hillary Rodham Clinton. President Bush is leading the fight against the terrorists. It is up to those of us who know the real Hillary Clinton to lead the fight against her. We must shine the light of truth on this dangerous woman so that all Americans may know the real Hillary. . . . God help us all if this filthy socialist slut ever takes over America.[54]

Hillary and her handlers have had Bill doped up and under control for some time now. Remember the few times when he could hardly walk to the podium for a speech. . . . They let him screw whatever he wanted and he was happy while others ran things.[55]

You do not have to be a supporter of Hillary Clinton to believe that something much, much deeper than Clinton herself was being attacked here.

In a way, these deep feelings go back to what a group, a collective, a nation actually is. In evolutionary terms, as we have seen, the fundament of human groups has been the male kin group. Practicing universal exogamy, while women leave the group upon marriage, the men—all kin—stay. The group, in this sense, belongs to the men, and they perceive themselves to be its rightful rulers in many traditional societies. The ancient Greeks opined that women may give birth to babies, but men give birth to nations. Blood sacrifice in birth was viewed as trivial next to blood sacrifice in war, which is why there are thousands of monuments to brave soldiers who gave their lives in battle, but only one memorial in the entire United States to those mothers who gave blood sacrifice and lost their lives in childbirth so that their nation might have a rising generation.[56]

INVISIBLE CITIZENS

The invisibility of women's blood sacrifice in birth also explains why women for so long have not been considered full citizens of their nation. If women did not give blood sacrifice for their nation in battle, how could they claim to be full citizens? This, in fact, was the rationale given by Switzerland for not extending the right to vote to women until 1971. Along these same lines, if nation means homeland, how can women be full citizens if they are excluded by patrilineal inheritance from holding land in their own names? Tanika Sharkar, an Indian historian, comments, "Women will always be incomplete national subjects. This is because a nation is a territorial concept. Land is central. Yet women often, and most women in India certainly, have no right to land. These two things, home and land, will never belong to them. . . . Women are not only incomplete subjects, but in a permanent state of homelessness."[57]

As we will explore further in a later chapter, nationalism has an uneasy relationship with women. Women are necessary for nationalist movements to succeed, but women are also a double-edged sword, in that they can doom or subvert nationalist causes when they see common cause with women of the "enemy," such as in a desire for peace so they can raise their children in safety. As a result, while a nationalist movement may court women, the victory of the movement will almost never result in improved status for women. To the contrary, it almost always results in a rescinding of whatever rights existed for women under the previous regime.[58] While we could easily pick examples from the French Revolution, the Iranian Revolution, and many others, including the recent invasion of Iraq that resulted in significant setbacks for women in the area of human rights, we choose to highlight one from American history. From before the time of the American Revolution, women in New Jersey had the right to vote, and they exercised that right until the U. S. Constitution was adopted in 1807—which summarily disenfranchised all women in the United States for another 113 years.[59] Indeed, former black male slaves gained the right to vote more than fifty years before any American woman did. Even when race no longer mattered to franchise under American law, sex still did.

An additional rationale for this exclusion involved the idea that women were insufficiently motivated to act in the national interest, as opposed to the common human interest. This stunning anecdote from a male Cold War physicist, as recounted by Carol Cohn, summarizes the point:

> "Several colleagues and I were working on modeling counterforce attack, trying to get realistic estimates of the number of immediate fatalities that would result from different deployments. At one point, we remodeled a particular attack, using slightly different assumptions, and found that instead of there being thirty-six million immediate fatalities, there would only be thirty million. And everybody was sitting around nodding, saying, 'Oh yea, that's great, only thirty million,' when all of a sudden I *heard* what we were saying. And I blurted out, 'Wait, I've just heard how we're talking—Only thirty million! Only thirty million human beings killed instantly?' Silence fell upon the room. Nobody said a word. They didn't even look at me. It was awful. I felt like a woman."[60]

One of us has a personal anecdote in this regard, as a woman looking at this same phenomenon:

> I was sitting in the annual American Political Science Association meeting one year during the Cold War. Being a security expert, I was attending panels on that topic. I found myself sitting in on a panel discussing NATO strategy. On the panel were all bright young men in the right color and cut of suits, with glasses and briefcases, and I was the only woman in the room. After the presentations were over, a foreign scholar in the audience rose and asked, "Exactly what is NATO's Follow-On Forces Strategy? I am unfamiliar with that term." One of the bright young men said, "Oh, that's easy to understand. It's a series of swift, penetrating thrusts to the enemy's rear!" Whereupon, yours truly lost it. I started to giggle uncontrollably, could not stop to save my life, and had to leave the room under the stares of my peers. Out in the hall, I realized that I wasn't sure if I should be laughing or crying.

These patriarchal norms of dominance and control as the route to security and peace are deeply flawed, but they still permeate much of human society, even in the twenty-first century. To the extent they do, we will still hear the echo of the ultranationalist Russian politician Vladimir Zhirinovsky, who, upon hearing that Finland had appointed the first female defense minister in human history, reportedly opined, "Any country that would choose a woman for defense minister deserves to be invaded." For the initial group of women world leaders, it was almost imperative to "out-man" the men in order to be acceptable; such was the case with Margaret Thatcher, Indira Gandhi, and Golda Meir.

These norms of women leaders having to ape extreme masculinity are changing in some regions of the world. Within the last several years, almost one-third of defense ministries in South America have been headed by women. Indeed, we have now seen several female heads of state who did not achieve their position through noble or political lineage, including Michelle Bachelet of Chile and Ellen Johnson-Sirleaf of Liberia. Nevertheless, as we look out at the world in late 2009, only 18 political entities out of more than 220, or about 8 percent, have female leaders. As we look across the national legislatures, 18.5 percent of legislators are women.[61] This measure ranges from a high of 56 percent in Rwanda to 0 percent in nine nations, including Belize, several island nations, and many of the Gulf States. The United States, with about 17 percent female representation in Congress, is below the mean. If, as many contend, human government is significantly influenced by the presence of women only when at least a third of the decision makers are women, then only 17 nations in the world currently enjoy that distinction. Most nations—more than 100—have had to institute some type of quota system in order to achieve even 10 percent representation of women.[62] Ironically, the United States insisted on quotas for women in both countries it invaded, Iraq and Afghanistan, so that now there is a significantly higher percentage of women in the legislatures of those two nations than in the United States itself.

It must be recognized that in certain countries, a high level of female participation in the legislature is largely a façade, since women's seats may be controlled by men, such as husbands, behind the scenes, or political parties may seek to control women's seats by tightly controlling the women who hold them. In some countries, even dead women have "won" elections for women's seats, with male proxies sitting in for the inevitably absent women. Despite these problems, the principle of equal voice not only is requisite in terms of equity but also has the potential to be revolutionary. Preliminary research shows that sincerely equal voice does change what human collectives prioritize.

A DEFICIT OF WOMEN, A DEFICIT OF GOOD GOVERNMENT

What differences are noted when women are significantly represented in human government? Researchers are just beginning to uncover the differences, as there historically have been so few nations with significant percentages of women legislators. Political variables at the state level have also been related to the situation of women, most specifically levels of corruption. For example, a study of eighty countries found a negative correlation between indices of corruption and indices of women's social and economic rights.[63] Because a decrease in political corruption increases investment and growth, gender equity thus has additional influence on economic growth.[64] According to an Inter-Parliamentary Union survey of 187 women holding public office in sixty-five countries,[65] women's presence in politics increases the amount of attention given to social welfare, legal protection, and transparency in government and business, and 80 percent of respondents said that women's participation restores trust in government.

Ann Crittenden has authored a serious argument for taking the perspectives of women seriously in public policymaking. She quotes Ann Richards, former governor of Texas, as saying,

> "When policy is made in government or in law, when any people whose lives are going to be affected aren't at the table and in on the decisions, the reactions aren't going to be as good. For example, when I was Travis county commissioner in Austin, I had decisions to make about the hospital system. My husband had some strong opinions on the subject, and as he spoke, it dawned on me that he hadn't been in a hospital since he was a child. I'd been in a bunch more times than he had, having four children and a few other things. Now here was a strongly held opinion from someone who'd had essentially no experience being in a hospital. Someone with that experience should be the first person brought in to talk about whatever problems there are. . . . So women's presence, and especially the presence of women with children, is essential when decisions are made about child care, medical care, education, mental health, taxes, war and peace."[66]

Crittenden notes that female legislators will break party ranks on issues that are important to mothers and children, and observes that female Republican legislators often do so. And of course, in 2010, it was Republican senator

Olympia Snowe who provided a decisive across-the-aisle vote on health care reform. Crittenden notes that issues concerning the environment can also be a greater pull for women. She quotes David Suzuki, a Canadian environmentalist, as saying, "'When you look at people who start environmental organizations, who often become the leaders, but also the workhorses, invariably they are women. . . . Women think about children, and they think about the future.'"[67] Crittenden comments, women "can raise new issues, broaden the range of ideas that can be taken seriously, and extend the boundaries of accepted discourse."[68] In essence, by breaking the old molds rather than conforming to them, women can change the entire picture.

Benefits from the inclusion of women's perspectives are not limited to the governmental sphere. They extend to the nation's economy. The pioneering work in this context was arguably that of Ester Boserup, who in 1970 asserted that omission of gender aspects of development led to project failure.[69] Since then, we have seen a raft of empirical research confirming strong cross-national linkages between gender variables and variables such as national economic performance. Concrete examples of the impact of women and women's labor on development are now plentiful. The World Bank notes that in nearly all countries, women work longer hours than men, given their double day of productive and reproductive activities, and that women dominate non-market activities in all countries.[70] Studies have shown that an increase in women's income increases the share of household money spent on education, health, and nutrition, while simultaneously decreasing the share of household income spent on alcohol and cigarettes.[71] In fact, a series of striking studies showed that the effect of female income on child survival is nearly twenty times that of the effect of male income.[72] It has also been shown that the proportion of the workforce that is female bears a statistically significant relationship to the level of national economic growth.[73]

As a result of these efforts and evidences, regional and global development planners now routinely address the role of women in successful development. For example, the UN Millennium Goals include the goal of empowering women, and occasioned Women Watch 2000 (later renamed the World's Women), to undertake an effort to more closely monitor the status of women on a cross-national basis to formulate nontraditional indicators of development.[74] More recently, the Arab Development Reports of 2002 and 2005 identified the generally low status of women in Arab societies to be one of the four major variables retarding growth and advancement in those countries.

As development became more integrated with a gender perspective, other state-level phenomena also began to be seen through a gender lens, with important results. Analysis of the effects of women's education was a natural next step. For example, the World Bank has concluded that low investment in female education reduces a country's overall output. One study found that if South Asia, sub-Saharan Africa, and the Middle East and North Africa had invested earlier in closing gender gaps in education, their income per capita would have increased by 0.5 to 0.9 percent from 1960 to 1992.[75] A study of ninety nations concluded that a 1 percent increase in female to male primary enrollment rates increases GDP growth by 0.012 percent.[76] In addition, the more education a mother has, the lower her children's mortality rates, even after controlling for household income and socioeconomic status.[77] A study conducted in the Philippines concluded that a mother's education was more of a contributing factor to her children's health status than household income,[78] and another cross-national study of sixty-three nations determined that women's education was the single most important factor in levels of malnutrition over a twenty-five-year period.[79]

HALF-BRAINED DECISION MAKING

Economic prosperity and system stability in more-developed countries are also affected by the degree of women's voice. Indeed, the recent global recession has been blamed on women's lack of voice in economic decision making. John Coates and Joseph Herbert, publishing in the *Proceedings of the National Academy of Sciences,* found that testosterone levels correlated significantly with risk taking among stock market traders.[80] Victories on the stock floor led to higher levels of testosterone and higher levels of risk taking. Coates commented, "Male traders simply don't respond rationally."[81]

Over the course of time, natural selection has rewarded men who have certain characteristics with more offspring: among these reproductively successful men are men who form tight bonds with other men, men who resort to physical force to get what they want, men who lack empathy, men who are highly motivated to garner resources with minimum effort, men who are willing to take risks, men who subordinate "others," whether those others be women or strangers.[82] Cooperating with other men in "in-groups" to take resources from "others" with a mix of minimum effort, high risk, and disregard of harm done to others is a skill that men, generally speaking, possess because of our evolutionary legacy. That's how one percent of the world's population wound up as descendants of Genghis Khan.

But this skill not only has the obvious downsides of harm done to members of one's own species; it also very often backfires, according to recent research. Risk taking always eventually overshoots and crashes. Decision making becomes reckless. Preying on others without restraint undermines the entire social web, imperiling all, including the predator. Overconfidence and overcompetitiveness aggravate irrational bubbles, and when they burst, fear and humiliation can override rationality as well. Aggressiveness can produce immediate advantage for the perpetrators but also serious dysfunctionality for the entire society, which in turn ultimately harms the perpetrator.

More and more, both men and women are wondering whether the structural inequality between men and women in our societies is ensuring that human collectives are at the mercy of male sex hormones, with all that that entails. As one Icelandic man put it at the height of that island's banking crisis, caused by the utter recklessness and live-for-today approach of Iceland's all-male banking elite: "I'm so fed up with this whole system. I just want some women to take care of my money."[83] He may be onto something—researchers surveying household investment behavior in the United States discovered that single men made worse investment decisions than married men, who in turn made worse decisions than single women.[84] For some reason, the presence of females in an economic decision-making context moderated overconfidence and the pursuit of risk. Likewise, the rate of violent crime among married men is many times lower than that for single men; again, female influence on male decision making seems to temper the worst swings of the male hormonal cycle.

There is good reason to think that collective decision making between men and women might have averted some of the hormonal swings underlying the recent economic instability. Women (in the aggregate at least) tend to be less confident than males, more risk averse, less aggressive, more empathetic, less absorbed in competition, and more interested in consensual decision making. There is an evolutionary reason for these characteristics: women since the dawn of time have had to cope with the predispositions of men. Women tend to be more risk averse than men because they usually live with men who accept risk and even seek it out. Women tend to be less confident than men because they usually live with men who are overconfident. Because of this balancing effect, better decisions might be made if men and women were making them together.

Recent research has also shown that when both males and females make decisions together, all participants are more satisfied with the outcome than when decisions are the product of all-male groups.[85] Furthermore, researchers have found that mixed decision-making groups are less accepting of risk than all-male groups, and that non-zero-sum outcomes are more likely.[86] Having more women not only as significant governmental actors but also as significant economic actors may actually be good for business. Real gender equality, including a meaningful sharing of power within society, may thus be a prerequisite for optimal and rational policymaking, whether for households, countries, or the international community.

THE BOYS' WORLD OF ECONOMIC UNREALITY

However, women are systematically excluded from our conventional understanding of the economic system. Think for a moment about the fact that when male economists in the 1930s developed the national system of accounts, they decided that women in their traditional roles as housewives were economically inactive, producing nothing of value to the society. Marilyn Waring explains:

Consider Tendai, a young girl in the Lowveld, in Zimbabwe. Her day starts at 4 a.m., when, to fetch water, she carries a thirty litre tin to a borehole about eleven kilometers from her home. She walks barefoot and is home by 9 a.m. She eats a little and proceeds to fetch firewood until midday. She cleans the utensils from the family's morning meal and sits preparing a lunch of sadza for the family. After lunch and the cleaning of the dishes, she wanders in the hot sun until early evening, fetching wild vegetables for supper before making the evening trip for water. Her day ends at 9 p.m., after she has prepared supper and put her younger brothers and sisters to sleep. Tendai is considered unproductive, unoccupied, and economically inactive. According to the international economic system, Tendai does not work and is not part of the labour-force.

Cathy, a young, middle-class North American housewife, spends her days preparing food, setting the table, serving meals, clearing food and dishes from the table, washing dishes, dressing her children, disciplining children, taking the children to day-care or to school, disposing of garbage, dusting, gathering clothes for washing, doing the laundry, going to the gas station and the supermarket, repairing household items, ironing, keeping an eye on or playing with the children, making beds, paying bills, caring for pets and plants, putting away toys, books, and clothes, sewing or mending or knitting, talking with door-to-door salespeople, answering the telephone, vacuuming, sweeping and washing floors, cutting the grass, weeding, and shoveling snow, cleaning the bathroom and the kitchen, and putting her children to bed. Cathy has to face the fact that she fills her time in a *totally* unproductive manner. She, too, is economically inactive, and economists record her as unoccupied.[87]

This invisibility of the existence and the value of women's unpaid caring, productive, and reproductive labor distorts the entire system of economic policymaking. As we have noted previously, if this labor were valued even at the most minimal imputed wage, it would account for approximately 40 percent of world production,[88] and salary estimates of how much money would be required to buy the services of a full-time mother and housewife on the open market in 2009 in the United States ranged from around $125,000 to more than $700,000.[89] To exclude such a massive labor contribution toward the well-being of society from societal decision making is an invitation for economic and societal mayhem.

And mayhem is what we have reaped from this outrageous omission. If you are considered unproductive, then why should there be any resource allocation by the government to address your needs? And so we find that in the United States, the greatest risk factor for poverty in old age is to have ever been a mother—not a father, but a mother.[90] That is because the Social Security system does not count any of a mother's labor toward her Social Security check in old age. Furthermore, if you work "mother's hours" in the workplace and have taken a part-time job, then your employer has no obligation to pay you the same rate as someone doing the very same job on a full-time basis, nor any obligation to offer you health or retirement benefits. This "mommy tax," as Crittenden terms it, may well amount to $1 million or more in pay, benefits, and Social Security over the lifetime of a college-educated woman. Indeed, the gender pay gap between men and childless women in the United States is all but erased, but the pay gap between non-mothers (whether male or female) and mothers remains stubbornly at about seventy cents to the dollar in the United States.[91]

As Waring puts it, "The system cannot respond to values it refuses to recognize."[92] As long as we maintain the fantasy that women's unpaid caring labor is as free as dirt, our economic system will impoverish women and undermine their economic security, which in turn will do the same to the children who are the future of our societies. Nancy Folbre calls this labor "the invisible heart," playing off the concept of the "invisible hand" of Adam Smith.[93] But while the invisible hand is an inanimate fiction, the invisible hearts belong to real women who are performing real and absolutely necessary labor for the members of the human family—and do so without any valuation of that labor, and without any safety net. At one of the universities at which we teach, Econ 101 introduces the study of economics using a scenario involving two healthy adult men—Robinson Crusoe and Friday—alone on an island, who then end up trading palm fronds and coconuts. If this is the way we introduce young people to thinking about what an economy is, no wonder our economy has serious distortions. We have often daydreamed of beginning an Economics 101 class with this alternative scenario: "There once was a woman, and she had just given birth to a child, and was exhausted, hungry, and losing blood." What kind of economics would be taught if that were the foundational scenario? As Waring remarks concerning the "naively masculine" science of economics,

> What changes might occur in global economic policy and practice if the worth . . . of the majority of [the] human population were *valued*? . . . [T]he satisfaction of basic needs to sustain human society is fundamental to any economic system. By this failure to acknowledge the primacy of reproduction, the male face of economics is fatally flawed. We frequently hear from politicians, theologians, and military leaders that the wealth of a nation is its children. But, apparently, the creators of that wealth deserve no economic visibility for their work. . . . [I]f you have a conceptual problem about the activity of half the human species, you then have a conceptual problem about the whole.[94]

Here we see in microcosm the costs of systematically excluding women from the work of credentialed knowledge creation in our society. Because men created the science of economics—as well as many other sciences—we have a grossly distorted view of the priorities and needs of our society. Unjustified assumptions go unquestioned. Fantasies pass for sophisticated models. Pressing questions go unasked. Alternative answers go unheard. If our departments of economics had a sizable representation of mothers on their faculties, the entire science would be transformed. Consider:

> The changing pattern of layoffs is a portent of the "friction free" economy that many economists aspire to. "It's an economist's wet dream," says Roger Martin, dean of the Rotman School of Management at the University of

Toronto and a former co-head of the Monitor Consulting Group. "Economists love maximum efficiency. But people don't. We want market efficiencies to make us richer, but we don't like what an efficient market feels like."[95]

We submit that the wet dreams of male economists are not the cure for our economic ills. We choose to think that a mother who was an economist would believe that the first and foremost purpose of the economy was to provide for the material security of its members, including and perhaps especially its women and children. Her point of departure for sound economic theory would not be Robinson Crusoe and Friday trading coconuts and palm fronds; it would be a woman having just given birth to a baby, exhausted and in need of assistance so she will be able to succor her baby.

The structure of the formal workplace itself is based on male perspectives. The marketplace assumes that workers are "unencumbered" and have no equally important societal responsibilities that must be attended to while employed.[96] It assumes that workers must work away from their homes for eight to ten hours every weekday. It assumes that working a swing shift or a graveyard shift will not impede the care that children need. It assumes that workers should naturally expect that the longer hours they work, the more opportunity for advancement they will have. In short, our modern workplace is designed to force a woman to choose between being a good mother and being a good worker. And, as we have seen, that is often the choice between poverty and economic security for the woman and her children. We should note that this organization also deprives fathers from putting their children first. The expectation of the unencumbered male worker could be countenanced by assuming that mothers would perform the caring labor the fathers could not. But the question arises, What kind of society would do this to its mothers and fathers? Only a society in which caregivers, particularly mothers, are excluded from having a real voice in the organization of the most important structures of their own society.

The lack of inclusion of the perspectives of those who care for the children, the ill, and the elderly of the world hurts human perspectives on many important issues. Matthew Connelly documents how the population control movement of the early twentieth century was, in a very real way, deeply misogynistic. Women were the problem, and that problem would be solved by coercing women into sterilization as if they were things instead of human beings:

The women in these offices were amazed at how their superiors talked about their work. Adrienne Germain was one of a handful of professional women working at the Population Council, and then the Ford Foundation's population office, in the early 1970s. "It's as though women weren't human," she now recalls. Senior professional staff "could walk the corridors and be in meetings and talk about 'users' and 'acceptors' and write about users and acceptors and have absolutely no interest in who these people were." Women were excluded from discussion about contraceptive technology and the ethics of research trials. When Nafis Sadik arrived at UNFPA in 1971, she already had sixteen years of experience as a gynecologist and public health professional, culminating with her nomination as director-general of the Pakistani General Council for Family Planning. But in her new workplace, where she was the only professional woman, "it felt as if I didn't exist." Any substantive suggestions she made "fell on deaf ears." Even in the IPPF, women were underrepresented on the key budget, finance, medical and scientific committees. As for the World Bank, it did not have even one professional woman involved in population programs.

Worse yet was the sexual harassment many women experienced. "The way some women were treated by some of the topmost of the senior leaders was despicable," Germain recalls, "whether it's how they treated their graduate students, or how they behaved at the huge number of conferences . . . specially by Northern men via-a-vis women in foreign countries." One senior official bragged to the author about his escapades at these meetings, including having sex with one woman in a conference room after other participants had left. Asked whether he used protection, he replied, "I let her worry about that . . ."

A number of demographers, including Irene Taeuber, were interested in how women's access to education and paid work was correlated with lower fertility and might therefore bring down birth rates in poor countries. . . . The separation of men and women, the qualitative and quantitative, and the First and Third Worlds, meant that this crucial insight about the relationship between women's education and fertility was overlooked when it came to designing policies and programs. . . . It was not until more professional women won a place in international debates that promoting [women's] education became the solution. . . . [I]t is the emancipation of women, not population control, that has remade humanity.[97]

Again, it is hard not to gasp at the audacity of men attempting to solve population problems while excluding women from the discussion and the policymaking. But as this chapter has shown, the most important problems of our day, whether those be population problems, development problems, health problems—or even, as we shall see in chapter 4, problems of war and peace—cannot be satisfactorily addressed without the insight and knowledge of half of the world's population. That humankind ever thought otherwise will one day cause our descendants to shake their heads in utter disbelief.

Even if we were to conclude that the inclusion of significant numbers of women in collective decision making at all levels would be beneficial for families, communities, and societies, there is the question of whether female voices, even when present, can actually be heard in decision-making councils. Research has shown that men process the voices of women in the same area of the brain that processes music and noise.[98] Furthermore, research has shown that men in a group setting are much more likely to remember what other men in the group have said than what women in the group have said.[99] Furthermore, men appear to discount the objective expertise of women when comparing assertions made by men and by women in the same group. Nicholas Kristof reflects on the cumulative research in this area by commenting,

In one common experiment, the "Goldberg paradigm," people are asked to evaluate a particular article or speech, supposedly by a man. Others are asked to evaluate the identical presentation, but from a woman. Typically, in countries all over the world, the very same words are rated higher coming from a man.

In particular, one lesson from this research is that promoting their own successes is a helpful strategy for ambitious men. But experiments have demonstrated that when women highlight their accomplishments, that's a turn-off. And women seem even more offended by self-promoting females than men are.

This creates a huge challenge for ambitious women in politics or business: If they're self-effacing, people find them unimpressive, but if they talk up their accomplishments, they come across as pushy braggarts.

The broader conundrum is that for women, but not for men, there is a tradeoff in qualities associated with top leadership. A woman can be perceived as competent or as likable, but not both.

Female leaders face these impossible judgments all over the world. An M.I.T. economist, Esther Duflo, looked at India, which has required female leaders in one-third of village councils since the mid-1990s. Professor Duflo and her colleagues found that by objective standards, the women ran the villages better than men. For example, women constructed and maintained wells better, and took fewer bribes.

Yet ordinary villagers themselves judged the women as having done a worse job, and so most women were not re-elected. That seemed to result from simple prejudice. Professor Duflo asked villagers to listen to a speech, identical except that it was given by a man in some cases and by a woman in others. Villagers gave the speech much lower marks when it was given by a woman.

Such prejudices can be overridden after voters actually see female leaders in action. While the first ones received dismal evaluations, the second round of female leaders in the villages were rated the same as men. "Exposure reduces prejudice," Professor Duflo suggested.[100]

In surveying this research, it appears that the obstacles to women's having a real voice in the decision-making councils of humanity are large indeed. They may speak, but will they even be heard? If exposure actually does reduce prejudice, we can only hope that through a concerted and purposeful effort by humankind to include women in decision-making councils at all levels of society and in sufficient numbers that their distinctive perspective is supported and not quashed, over time the two halves of humanity may, finally, together guide their world. We have every reason to believe that joint stewardship would produce better results than the exclusion of half of the species from decision making. That such a true sharing of power and voice between men and women is still rare in human society is the third great wound that humanity must address.

We have spoken of what we perceive to be the three wounds caused by gendered microaggression and afflicting women in the house of humanity. The first is the lack of bodily integrity and personal safety for women; the second is the codification of unequal status before the law, especially in personal status and family law, between men and women; and the third is the lack of decision-making parity between men and women in the councils of humanity at all levels, small and great. We now turn to an empirical survey of the incidence and prevalence of these wounds, and we will make initial inquiries into the origins of gender inequality.

3

WHEN WE DO SEE THE GLOBAL PICTURE, WE ARE MOVED TO ASK HOW THIS HAPPENED

THE ANECDOTES AND EXAMPLES from chapter 2 paint a discouraging picture, a picture of a world where women, generally speaking, live without security and with little hope that the situation will change soon. Certainly, women who suffer from violence and inequality can be found in every country, region, and city, but if we were to create a mental map of where women in the world suffer in a more widespread manner, there would be some regions and countries that we might color with a darker shade than others, indicating poorer conditions overall for women. The accuracy of our personal cartographic impressions would be dependent on the accuracy of our information sources as well as our lifelong experiences and exposures. Readers in the Middle East might envision a map with darker shades over much of the Western world because of its perceived generalized debasement of women. Conversely, readers in the West may see the Islamic world in darker shades because in their minds it is a place where patriarchy prevails.

Given these divergent subjective assessments, creating a research-grade map with accurate gradients can be challenging. The status of women is so multifaceted that it would be very hard to combine every variable into just one simple map showing where women are treated comparatively well and where they are not. Finally, countries can be idiosyncratic in their treatment of women; one country may support a higher minimum age for marriage and yet not choose to prosecute for trafficking in women, while another may do just the opposite.

MAPPING THE WORLDWIDE SITUATION OF WOMEN

What follows, then, is a series of maps that we hope will better illustrate the varying patterns and the complexities of the situation of women in the countries of the world. These maps are generalizations, and so it is important to remember that the individual lives of women may not correspond to the overall condition of women in the country. Despite all of these caveats, through these maps it will become apparent that there is much work to be done and that some countries are doing better than others.

The scales used in the maps were developed by our project team and coded using the data in the WomanStats Database. These are 5-point ordinal scales, and each ranges from 0 to 4, with 0 being the best condition (often in the text called, somewhat counterintuitively, the "highest" rank) and 4 being the worst condition (often in the text called the "lowest" rank). Some of the scales are multivariate in nature, while others address a single variable. So, for example, our multivariate Physical Security of Women Scale looks at several different variables, such as murder, rape, and so forth. Our Educational Discrepancy Scale, on the other hand, looks specifically at laws, practices, and data concerning secondary education of girls, and so addresses but one cluster of variables. While we will mention the scale descriptions in the text, a fuller description of how each scale was coded can be found in the online WomanStats codebook; http://womanstats.org/CodebookCurrent.html.

PHYSICAL SECURITY OF WOMEN

Our first map, map 1, shows a surprising range and interesting patterns concerning women's physical security. It is based on a multivariate scale, the Physical Security of Women Scale, most recently assessed in 2009, that includes variables for domestic violence, rape, marital rape, and murder (MULTIVAR-SCALE-1 in the WomanStats Database). It examines not only incidence of violence against women but also whether or not there are laws against such practices and whether or not those laws are enforced.

Sadly, no country achieved the highest ranking (0), which would indicate that women are physically secure. To obtain such a ranking a country would have laws against not only murder but also domestic violence, rape, and marital rape; those laws would be enforced; and there would be no taboos or norms against reporting these crimes, which would be rare.

At the next scale point, 1, women have comparatively high levels of physical security. All ten of the countries at this scale point are Western European. Noteworthy is that the United States and Canada are coded at scale point 2, indicating that while their laws are exemplary, levels of violence against women remain relatively high. The two categories in which women are relatively physically insecure, in which they have limited or no physical security, are clustered primarily across the Middle East, Africa, South Asia, the former Communist bloc, and most of Latin America. Tunisia and Djibouti do appear to have higher levels of physical security for women than other Arab countries of the Middle East and North Africa. Regional patterns obviously exist, but there are also noteworthy regional exceptions, where some countries appear quite discrepant given their regional location.

The average Physical Security of Women score for all states in 2006 was 3.02 and in 2009 was 3.04—scores that highlight the widespread and persistent violence perpetrated against women worldwide. The majority of women live in countries where laws prohibiting violence against women are either nonexistent or unenforced and where social norms do not define domestic violence, rape, and even murder as serious and accurately reported crimes. In addition, many of these women live in ostensibly democratic states, which is a counterintuitive finding. Generally speaking, state laws either disproportionately ignore women's rights, for example, by the lack of marital rape or domestic violence laws, or create situations that may actually increase the level of violence against women, as was the case with the infamous *zina* laws in Pakistan, which were modified in 2006 but may be making an unwelcome comeback. It is difficult to fathom the global extent of violence that women experience daily—a gendered violence that permeates the personal, cultural, and state environments for half of the world's population.

SON PREFERENCE AND SEX RATIO

The Son Preference and Sex Ratio Scale, most recently coded in 2009 and illustrated in map 2, indicates the relative valuation assigned to male life and female life; in its aspect of sex ratio, it is also a supplemental indicator of violence against women. At the highest scale point (0), there is no son preference, and there is no abnormality in sex ratios, whether those be birth, childhood, or overall sex ratios. In the worst ranking (4), there is intense son preference, and there are significant abnormalities in childhood sex ratios.

We find some interesting patterns in this mapping. Catholic Ireland and Muslim Tunisia are at the same rank (4) as Hindu India and several Confucian countries (including Taiwan, South Korea, and Singapore). This worst rank also includes several Western European countries—among them Portugal and Switzerland, which were two of the highest ranked on the Physical Security of Women Scale. The general middle ranking of the Middle East in terms of sex ratio is a significant divergence from what we see with the Physical Security of Women Scale. Iceland and four Caribbean countries rank the best, with no noted preference for sons and the most normal sex ratios. In fact, a comparison of the Physical Security of Women map and the Son Preference and Sex Ratio map is perplexing: why is there so little correlation between levels of violence against women as adults and levels of violence against women as neonates?

The average Son Preference and Sex Ratio for all states in 2006 was 2.07 and in 2009 was 2.41, indicating a general, globalized son preference. This in itself is an important characteristic of our current world system that often goes unremarked. Globally, male offspring are valued more highly than female offspring. However, since the average is in the range of 2 on a scale of 0–4, this generalized son preference does not appear to necessarily result in female infanticide or sex-selective abortion in most states. Nevertheless, the comparatively low value ascribed to female life penetrates every aspect of women's daily lives, thus both perpetuating the cycle of gendered violence[1] and resulting in their own diminished sense of self.

As we have noted, Son Preference and Sex Ratio is not necessarily correlated with violent practices against adult women. This highlights the crucial importance of using a multivariate approach to assess the status of women. Just as different cultures vary in the way they perpetuate violence against women, the incidence of such violence varies across the life span from the fetus to the widow. Practices such as female infanticide and passive neglect strike women in their earliest years, whereas practices such as dowry deaths affect young adult women, and other practices such as inheriting of widows or the turning out of widows occur later in life.

TRAFFICKING IN FEMALES

Trafficking in females is inherently an act of violence that assaults women's human rights. The trafficking cluster, from which we create our ordinal

Trafficking in Females Scale, most recently scaled in 2009, includes variables measuring law, practice, and prevalence (map 3). To be scaled highest (scale point 0), a country must have laws against trafficking within that country and into or from other countries, and these laws are enforced. In addition, the country must be in full compliance (ranking of 1) with the U.S. Trafficking Victims Protection Act of 2000 and trafficking must appear to be rare, according to the U.S. State Department's Trafficking in Persons Report, which is the most comprehensive and detailed report on trafficking in persons currently available. At the worst scale point (4), there are no laws against trafficking in the country, or from or into the country; the country is not in compliance (ranking of 3) with the U.S. Trafficking Victims Protection Act of 2000; victims are not supported in any way; and the government may even benefit from and therefore facilitate trafficking.

When it comes to trafficking of females, regional patterns are less pronounced—especially at the lower end of the scale. Why is direct violence against women, captured by our Physical Security of Women Scale, more regionally defined, whereas patterns of trafficking vary quite widely within regions? At the lowest scale point (4), where trafficking is not illegal and is widely practiced, we find such diverse countries as Cuba, Zimbabwe, India, and Papua New Guinea. Sweden is the only country to achieve the highest ranking on the trafficking scale (scale point 0), with Western Europe, Canada, the United States, Australia, and New Zealand filling out the bulk of the next best scale point (1). Notable inclusions in this second tier include Colombia, Nigeria, and South Korea.

The Trafficking in Females score reflects both the economic value and the economic vulnerability of women and suggests that, generally speaking, the countries of the world are not in compliance with basic standards of international law concerning trafficking. Most women in the world live in countries that are either blind to the practices of trafficking or unwilling to take serious action to protect women from being bought and sold. Indeed, governments often facilitate the exploitation of women for financial gain.

POLYGYNY

Our scaling of polygyny, most recently scaled in 2010, differs from most of the other scales in that there are many countries in the highest ranking (scale points 0 and 1; 74 out of 170 countries—43.5 percent), meaning that, globally speaking, polygyny is illegal and its practice is relatively rare (map 4).

The global average is 1.6 on our scale. Countries where polygyny is legal and where it is more commonly practiced are primarily found in Saharan and sub-Saharan Africa. Interestingly, much of the Islamic world, where the religion allows for up to four wives if they are treated fairly by the husband, generally falls within the middle category of countries where polygyny is either legally constrained or technically legal but practiced in fewer than 5 percent of marriages. There are some Islamic countries that have more prevalent polygyny, among them Saudi Arabia and some of the Gulf States, Yemen, Afghanistan, Morocco, and Turkey.

Over time, increasing numbers of countries have moved from scale point 0 to scale point 2, as minority, usually immigrant, populations in Western nations continue to practice polygyny. While Western nations have not legalized polygyny per se, many do recognize the polygynous marriages of immigrants from countries where polygyny is legal. Other countries, such as France, insist on "de-cohabitation" of polygynous immigrant families. Given the association in the literature between polygyny and societal instability, it will be interesting to trace these trajectories over time.

INEQUITY IN FAMILY LAW/PRACTICE

As we will see in subsequent chapters, many of the top-down and bottom-up efforts to improve the status of women focus on rectifying inequities in a state's family law, and how that law is practiced on the ground. Our Inequity in Family Law/Practice Scale, most recently scaled in 2011, is a true multivariate scale, examining aspects of family law and practice such as legal age of marriage for girls, issues of female consent in marriage, polygyny, marital rape, inheritance rights of widows, rights of women in divorce, and so forth (map 5).

The eighteen countries where family law/practice is equitable for women are predictably found in Western Europe, plus Canada, New Zealand, and Australia (interestingly, neither the United States nor the United Kingdom made the cutoff; they are both at the next scale point, 1). The criteria of law and practice found in these countries of highest rank include legal age of marriage for women at least eighteen, with most women (more than 50 percent) marrying after that age. Marrying at an age younger than sixteen is virtually unknown in these countries. Polygyny is illegal and extremely rare. Women are free to choose their spouse. Women know their rights to consent and divorce and are free to exercise those rights without fear of reprisal. Marital rape is illegal and actively prosecuted. Women and men have equal rights to divorce. Women can inherit property upon the death of a parent or upon divorce. Abortion is safe and legal.

At the other end of the scale (scale point 4) are fourteen countries of sub-Saharan Africa and a few in the Middle East where family law/practice is highly inequitable. In these countries a legal age of marriage for females does not exist. In addition, girls commonly (more than 25 percent) marry around the age of twelve or even earlier. Women are rarely asked for consent before marriage, and women are often forced to marry much older men. Polygyny is legal and common (more than 25 percent of marriages). Women must overcome tremendous legal obstacles to sue for divorce, while men can seek divorce for many reasons. Women may be unaware of their right to give consent in marriage or to divorce their husbands, may not legally possess such rights, or may feel that the exercise of those rights would bring dire physical or social consequences. Women are not awarded custody and may have virtually no rights to inheritance. Marital rape is not illegal, but abortion is illegal.

The global average for inequity in family law/practice is 2.06, indicating that overall, the countries of the world have laws and practices that are at least somewhat discriminatory against women. As we pointed out in chapter 2, inequity in family law/practice is one of the three great inequities inflicted upon women in the world. When a state, such as Yemen, allows an eight-year-old girl to be sold by her father into marriage with a man four decades older, that is one of the most profound betrayals of women a state can perpetrate. When widows with their children are allowed to be cast out of their homes and left penniless by the husband's family, and the state does not intervene, that represents a true state atrocity. When a divorced woman is stripped of the custody of her children simply because she is the female parent, that is a crime against humanity. As we will discuss in chapter 5, rectification of inequity in family law is one of the most important arenas for state action to improve conditions for women, with arguably the greatest potential to transform societal and state dynamics for the better.

MATERNAL MORTALITY

The well-being, good health, and survival of a mother during pregnancy and birth are the products of strong economies, good health care systems, and sufficient nutrition. They are also the products of cultural mores that value women and mothers. Our Maternal Mortality Scale, most recently scaled in

2010, ranks countries according to maternal deaths per 100,000 births (map 6). The global average was 2.45 on our 5-point scale ranging from 0–4, meaning that most countries in the world have relatively high maternal mortality rates.

The countries with the lowest maternal mortality rates include, once again, Sweden with the highest ranking with only 2 deaths per 100,000 births. Noteworthy is that among the twenty-two other countries with death rates below 10 per 100,000 are Kuwait and Qatar. Nestled in the second tier (scale point 1) are the United States (17 per 100,000), with Saudi Arabia (23 per 10,000), and Bahrain (28 per 100,000) only slightly behind. The inclusion of four Arab states in these top two tiers might be dismissed by some as only reflective of high GDP per capita, but the fact that these Arab/Islamic countries have built hospitals and clinics and provided an education for female obstetricians and nurses suggests that woman are valued and supported as mothers in these societies.

The soberingly high maternal mortality rates among many African states should be seen as a call to arms by the rest of the world to help women through the vulnerable life stages of pregnancy and birth. It is a true devaluation of women's lives for the state to be indifferent as to whether they live or die as a result of bringing forth the next generation of citizens.

DISCREPANCY IN EDUCATION

Our Discrepancy in Education Scale, most recently scaled in 2010, examines the rates of secondary education among girls and boys, looking specifically at differences in rates of attainment of this level of education, as well as whether there are any legal or cultural restrictions on girls' education at this level (map 7).

The global average for this scale is 1.63, with an average gap of about 4.85 percent between male and female rates of secondary education. There are some clear regional patterns. Western Europe, for the most part, scores very well on this scale (with the exception of Switzerland, which scores very poorly in comparison to its neighbors). Sub-Saharan Africa and South Asia are both regions where the educational attainment of girls is significantly below that of boys, and where, in fact, there may be important barriers, legal or cultural, to girls' education. Other areas are quite diverse. For example, in the Islamic world, we have, on the one hand, nations such as Algeria, Oman, and Libya, which score very well (scale point 1), but also several countries scoring more poorly. At scale point 3, we find Islamic nations such as Egypt, Jordan, and Pakistan, and at the very worst scale point (4), we find nations such as Saudi Arabia, Syria, and Morocco. Morocco is puzzling, since it is an outlier to the good on the Inequity in Family Law Scale, but is in the worst rank for education of girls.

Latin America also contains a diversity of scores on the Discrepancy in Education Scale. Mexico, Venezuela, Argentina, Chile, and Cuba, for example, occupy the highest scale point (0), while Guatemala is coded at scale point 3. One might be tempted to correlate the score on this scale with national wealth, but we have several poorer countries that attain the highest ranking of 0, such as the Philippines, while, as noted, we have a few richer countries, such as Switzerland, that score relatively poorly.

GOVERNMENTAL PARTICIPATION BY WOMEN

Our Governmental Participation by Women Scale, most recently scaled in 2010, examines not only representation of women in parliament, but also representation of women in the cabinet or ministries of the executive branch (map 8). We hope in the future to add data on judicial posts and positions in local governments; at the time of this writing, such information is difficult to obtain for many countries.

The worldwide average is 2.74, and globally, representation of women is less than 20 percent. Patterns again emerge. South Asia and the Gulf States have, generally speaking, quite poor representation of women in government. Of course, in the case of the Gulf States, women may actually be barred legally from running for certain high offices. We also find that Russia and many former Soviet states, such as Belarus and Ukraine, have relatively poor representation of women, which is surprising because during the Cold War, these states had the best representation of women in the world. China, despite being one of the few remaining Communist countries in the world, scores in the worst rank for government participation by women.

However, other anticipated regional patterns do not hold up very well. For example, in the case of sub-Saharan Africa, while most countries exhibit poorer representation of women in government, some clear exceptions are evident. Present among the set of highest-raking nations, with the best participation of women in government, we find Uganda, Rwanda, Namibia, South Africa, and Mozambique. In the very next tier (scale point 1), we find nations such as Lesotho and Liberia. Indeed, since the United States falls in the middle rank of 2, this is a quite counterintuitive finding. Other relatively wealthy industrialized nations come in at an even worse ranking than the United States. Japan, Singapore, and South Korea are in the worst tier of nations (scale point 4) for governmental participation of women.

Anomalies abound in this category. Macedonia is in the best scale rank; Greece is in the next-to-lowest rank. Chile is in the best; Brazil is in the worst. In comparing across scales, we also find some interesting phenomena: South Africa, with one of the lowest rankings on physical security of women, is in the highest rank of nations for governmental participation of women.

Also noteworthy is that the representation of democracies in the worst ranks of the Governmental Participation by Women Scale is higher than expected. As noted previously, nations such as Japan and South Korea, as well as Brazil, all score in the worst rank on the scale. In the next-to-worst rank, we find democracies such as India, Greece, Slovenia, and Hungary.

INTERMINGLING IN PUBLIC IN THE ISLAMIC WORLD

In many of the above maps we can see that even within regions with strong cultural and religious influences, significant differences are apparent. We will now look at two maps and scales dealing with issues concerning women specifically in the Islamic world: the intermingling of women and men in society and required dress codes for women. Both maps show a wide variance in the rankings and belie the view of many a mental map that all women of the Islamic world are subject to the same rigid requirements.[2] Furthermore, given the massive transformation of the Arab world in 2011, that variance may well expand. The first map, showing our assessment of intermingling in public in the Islamic world, most recently evaluated in 2008, addresses the practices of separating men and women in public places and of limiting the movement of women in public when they are not accompanied by a male relative (map 9).[3]

The map shows that most of the Islamic countries do not have legal restrictions on women's freedom of movement within public spaces. Social restrictions, however, are extremely common, and in many instances are just as limiting. The prevalence of patrilocality in the Middle East lends legitimacy to beliefs that a woman is the property of her husband's extended family and therefore does not have the right to travel without permission of a husband or male guardian. Most Islamic countries can be characterized as honor/shame societies, in which the perceived sexual purity of women is a direct reflection on the honor of male family members. Thus, limiting a woman's ability to interact with men protects the family's honor. Social pressure accounts for why many women choose not to travel alone or leave the country, even if they have legal protection to do so.

Limitations on the ability of men and women to intermingle in public can take many forms, depending on the particular country. In Kuwait, the state has spent millions of dollars on a program to completely segregate men and women at the university level. Some Turkish cinemas have separate showings for men and women. In almost all Islamic countries there are regional and urban/rural differences between practices of sex segregation, and in some countries this contrast is starker than in others. Women may even support such segregation as affording them greater personal protection in public spaces.

Despite the lack of legal restrictions upon women's freedom of movement, law enforcement frequently follows the norms of society. In Egypt, for example, married women do not legally need the permission of their fathers in order to obtain passports and travel, but they require it in practice nonetheless. Similarly, Moroccan government passport authorities may require unmarried women to produce a "certificate of good conduct," although no legal stipulation requires it. In the United Arab Emirates and Lebanon, women are guaranteed freedom of movement by law, but a man can prevent a wife or unmarried daughters from leaving the country by contacting immigration authorities. In Yemen, although it is against the law to do so, a male guardian can prevent a woman from obtaining education or employment outside the home, and law enforcement officials often obey a husband's wishes.

There have been a number of recent legal changes in Islamic countries regarding segregation. Turkey repealed a law in 1990 that required a woman to obtain permission from a husband to work outside the home. In 1996 Palestinian women obtained the right to obtain passports without the consent of male guardians after age eighteen. Bangladesh lifted the ban on female travel in 2005. In the past few years Lebanon, Jordan, and Bahrain have dismissed the law that required a woman to have a husband's permission before obtaining a passport. Despite all these legal improvements, some nations still lag behind their peers in repealing these laws or they enforce segregation in a way that is cause for concern. Syrian law actually gives a man the right to prevent a wife and daughters from leaving the country, and Omani law requires a male guardian's permission for a woman to travel outside the country.

As the map shows, Iran and Saudi Arabia are two countries where the segregation of the sexes and the systematic restriction of women's movements are part of the legal code and are enforced by state police. In Saudi Arabia, boys and girls are generally segregated beginning at puberty, and sex segregation is enforced in schools, restaurants, banks, and other public buildings. The labor code prohibits the intermingling of men and women in work settings. Everything a woman does is subject to the approval of a *mahram*, or male relative. Women must have the permission of a male guardian to obtain a passport or travel abroad, and in fact are not even supposed to be out in public without a *mahram*. Additionally, "visible and invisible spatial boundaries also limit women's movement. Mosques, most ministries, public streets, and food stalls (supermarkets not included) are male territory. Furthermore, accommodations that are available for men are always superior to those accessible to women, and public space, such as parks, zoos, museums, [and] libraries."[4] The Saudi Committee for the Promotion of Virtue and the Prevention of Vice is the organization charged with enforcing segregation laws. It is the almost universal enforcement of these laws that separates Iran and Saudi Arabia from neighboring countries that may not have the means or manpower to enforce them. In recent years Saudi Arabia's laws have come under international condemnation as a result of high-profile news events. In 2002 fourteen school-aged girls died in a fire at their school when the virtue and vice police prevented them from leaving the burning building because they did not have *mahrams* to accompany them home, and actually prevented rescue workers from entering the building because unrelated men and women are not supposed to intermingle. And in 2006 a gang-rape victim was sentenced to an unbelievable ninety lashes for being in a taxi with an unrelated man right before her rape.

Laws and the enforcement of laws in the Islamic Republic of Iran are likewise comparably strict. The 1979 Islamic revolution in Iran brought about many changes for the country's women. Coed schools are now banned by the Ministry of Education, and women are required to have a husband's permission to work outside the home. Women are restricted from riding in specific sections of buses and from using the main entrances in public buildings. They are also banned from attending sporting events.

REQUIRED CODES OF DRESS FOR WOMEN IN THE ISLAMIC WORLD

Some societies enforce required dress codes for women; this practice is most prevalent in Islamic societies, taking the form of certain garments and/or veils (map 10, which reflects our most recent assessment, in 2008). Veiling acts as a barrier between the sexes, and some have suggested the veil is akin to having a woman bring her home with her, because it is a way for her to stay protected from the gaze of unrelated men and to remain respectable. Again, such dress may be perceived by the woman as affording her greater personal protection in public spaces, and also as an outward sign of piety, which should be respected by men.

In some Islamic countries, the possibility of women mingling with men in the public sphere may be determined by their dress. In some countries, women will not be harassed if they are out at night and are wearing the *hijab* (a scarf that covers all of the head but the face). Women are thus allowed to participate in society and interact with others, but only if they are covered and behaving themselves properly. If women are perceived as not behaving well or dressing properly, they may be subject to verbal abuse and/or physical violence from both family members and strangers. Thus the veil becomes a protection against such abuse and as much a symbol of the powerful reach of fear as it is a symbol of piety.

In some areas the threat of violence is so bad, and women may be threatened to such a great extent by militant groups in society, that they are essentially forced into wearing the veil. Such is the case in Afghanistan, where despite the fact that President Karzai declared that women can choose whether or not to wear the burqa (a garment that covers the whole body, with a mesh opening for the eyes), Islamist groups and even government officials enforce veiling in many regions of the country. Religious vigilantes have also enforced veiling in south Iraq in recent years. Women who do not dress in what these groups perceive as a modest way can be beaten, abused, and even murdered. In the Shi'ite south of Iraq, even Christian women are forced to veil, although no such law in Iraq requires them to do so.

In the past half century, as Islamist movements and Islamic fundamentalism have spread, veiling has become increasingly common. Islamization is in part a reaction to globalization and the spread of Western values. Veiling is thus seen as a way not only to express piety but also to combat what is perceived as the loose morals of the West, a solution exemplified by the increase in veiling in North Africa after the colonial period of the early 1900s.[5] A fear of Western morality reaches across the Islamic world, even as far as Comoros, where parents are turning toward a strict interpretation of Islam and are forcing their daughters to veil in order to combat moral laxity. There are many additional examples of increasing Islamization and its effect on women's dress codes. The Malaysian *tudong* (similar to the Middle Eastern *hijab*) became popular about fifteen years ago as part of an Islamic revival. Islamist movements in the Gaza Strip began pressuring women to veil in the 1980s. Although Indonesia is a secular nation, there has been a trend toward Islamization and as a result headscarves are now very common.

At the same time, however, Islamization and the spread of fundamentalism are causing political unrest in many other countries. In Kuwait, the use of the *niqab* (covers all of the face but the eyes) has shifted from a distinct dress associated with Bedouin women to a political symbol associated with fundamentalism and has consequently sparked debate between liberals and conservatives in the country. In Libya under Gaddafi, a woman wearing a *niqab* would be suspected of Islamism, and therefore antigovernment activity.

Because many of the secular governments in Islamic countries fear Islamization and the popularity of Islamic fundamentalism, they attempt to enact laws or policies that restrict women's right to wear a veil. This limitation is manifested differently depending on the country. In Libya under Gaddafi schoolteachers were not allowed to wear the *niqab*. As in most central Asian countries, the wearing of a headscarf in official photographs is prohibited in Azerbaijan. Secondary schools in Kyrgyzstan will not allow girls who wear veils to attend school. The Education Ministry in Tajikistan has likewise banned Islamic headscarves at schools and universities. Female students have been expelled from universities in Uzbekistan for wearing Islamic veils. In Egypt (before the revolution of 2011), where 80 percent of women veil, government-sponsored newspapers discouraged the *niqab* and state-run television networks prohibited wearing the veil on air. Morocco has recently removed references to and pictures of veils in its textbooks.

Elsewhere, opposition to veiling is even stronger. In Tunisia (speaking of conditions before the revolution of 2011) it is against the law to wear a *hijab* in public office buildings, and government ministers frequently denounce the wearing of veils as foreign to Tunisia's traditions. The original decree against *hijabs*, which has since been repealed, "led to an oppressive campaign against veiled women in public institutions, in the streets, on public transport and in hospitals. It included violence against the women, the tearing of their clothing and their removal to security centres."[6] In recent years government policies against veiling have led to violent clashes between the police and Islamist rebels. As noted previously, no one yet knows how the uprisings of 2011 will affect dress codes for women.

Turkey, where more than 60 percent of women veil, also has banned wearing veils in schools and universities, and many women have been deprived of an education as a result. In February 2008 Turkey passed a law allowing women to veil in public buildings, but only with a loosely tied headscarf and not with an Islamic veil that covers the whole head. The ruling party would like to lift these restrictions entirely, but it has not been successful in those efforts.

For as many countries that have laws and policies that prohibit veiling, there are even more countries that have laws and policies that encourage or enforce veiling. Women in government-run institutions such as schools must wear the *tudong* according to law in Brunei. Female employees of the state in Turkmenistan must adhere to an unofficial dress code that includes veils and long cloaks. Police officers in Aceh, Indonesia, can stop women pedestrians or drivers if their heads are uncovered.

As was the case with segregation, Iran and Saudi Arabia are the most extreme cases of government enforcement of veiling restrictions. In order to fight moral corruption, Iranian police have cracked down in the past year on women who are not adhering to the country's strict dress codes. Among the prohibitions are tight clothing, hats instead of scarves, Western haircuts, and hair that is not fully covered by a veil. Women who are repeat offenders may be subject to forty lashes. In Saudi Arabia, women are required to wear an *abaya* (long dark cloak) and a *hijab*, while native Saudi women are also expected to wear a *niqab*, although this is not always enforced. The religious police can stop, beat, and/or arrest those who do not comply with the dress code.

WOMEN'S GLOBAL SITUATION

As these maps have hopefully shown, one cannot simply look at one aspect of women's lives in order to evaluate the condition of women. The forms of subordination of women may vary dramatically across cultures and states, and a more holistic examination is required. For example, government participation by women in South Africa may be relatively high, but so is violence against women in that country. Conditions for women may be starkly different even between neighboring countries of arguably similar cultures. Such differences may also be found between subnational regions.

Nevertheless, despite the variety of forms of subordination of women, we can say as a result of this empirical investigation that the overall situation of women in the world is one of insecurity and oppression. How is it possible that this is the normal condition for one-half of the human species? What are the origins of this global predicament?

HOW DID MALE-DOMINATED SOCIAL STRUCTURES DEVELOP THROUGHOUT HUMAN CULTURES?

To establish the theoretical linkage between the security of women and the security of states, we synthesize insights from several disciplines, including evolutionary biology and psychology, which provide an account of basic tendencies of human behavior in terms of natural selection; biological, developmental, and social psychology, which provide an account of more proximate causal mechanisms of diffusion in terms of cultural selection through social learning; and social psychology and political sociology, which offer an account of the social diffusion of both naturally selected and culturally selected traits.

EVOLUTIONARY BIOLOGY AND PSYCHOLOGY

Evolutionary biology and psychology have been underutilized by social scientists, leading political scientist Bradley Thayer to comment that "this leads to an artificially limited social science" using assumptions about human behavior that may be "problematic, or fundamentally flawed."[7] Evolutionary theory provides explanations in terms of ultimate cause, not proximate cause, framing the context within which individual creatures strive to increase their fitness (survival and reproductive success). Differential fitness levels, then, drive natural selection: if one survives to reproduce (or if one can facilitate the reproduction of close kin, a concept termed "inclusive fitness"), natural selection will move in the direction of one's genotype. Changes in rates of survival and reproduction among individuals and kin groups will therefore eventually change the genotype of the overall population.

Evolutionary theory suffers from two common misconceptions. The first is that evolutionary predispositions are intractable. No evolutionary theorist believes this. Richard Dawkins explains, "It is perfectly possible to hold that genes exert a statistical influence on human behavior while at the same time believing that this influence can be modified, overridden, or reversed by other influences."[8] The second misconception is that evolutionary theory posits static and essential characteristics for males and females. In debunking this myth, Theodore Kemper notes, "Across the spectrum of the social sciences, the results show that females are not essentially pacific, retiring, unaggressive, lacking in motives and psychological need for power and dominance. While successful ideological socialization may persuade many women that this is true of themselves, it is not biologically true."[9] Laying those two misconceptions aside, we turn to the insights that evolutionary theory can provide into the relationship between the physical security of women and general traits and behaviors of human collectives, including nation-states.

SOCIAL STRUCTURES ARE SHAPED BY NATURAL SELECTION FOR MALE DOMINANCE OVER BOTH SEXES According to evolutionary theory, human social structures are profoundly—even predominantly—shaped by natural selection for reproductive fitness. Anthropologist Richard Alexander writes that culture can be seen as a "gigantic metaphorical extension of the reproductive system. . . . [There is] a reasonably close correspondence between the structure of culture and its usefulness to individuals in inclusive-fitness-maximizing."[10]

Sex differences across animal species produce a dazzling diversity of male-female interaction. Anthropologists Richard Wrangham and Dale Peterson note, however, that out of "4,000 mammals and 10 millions or more other animal species" only two species (humans and chimpanzees) live in "patrilineal, male-bonded communities wherein females routinely reduce risks of inbreeding by moving to neighboring groups [to mate with these communities] . . . with [these communities having] a system of intense, male-initiated territorial aggression, including lethal raiding into neighboring communities in search of vulnerable enemies to attack and kill. . . . The system of communities defended by related men is a human universal that crosses space and time."[11] While noting this universality in human systems, they also note that "we quickly discover how odd that system really is, [making] humans appear as members of a funny little group that chose a strange little path."[12]

In this section we will highlight the work of anthropologist Barbara Smuts on the evolutionary origins of patriarchy.[13] Smuts asserts that "[h]umans exhibit more extensive male dominance and male control of female sexuality than is shown by most other primates."[14] Furthermore, she (somewhat controversially[15]) believes that patriarchy's beginnings are to be found long before the development of agriculture.

Male reproductive success centers on control of female sexuality; without the intensive labor provided by females in gestation, lactation, and nurture of the young, males cannot reproduce. Robert L. Trivers's 1972 theory argues that the more competitive (or in Darwin's language, the more "eager") sex is usually the sex that invests less in reproduction, in terms of both gamete production and parental investment in offspring survival.[16] As Archer explains, "the sex showing higher parental investment becomes a limiting resource, the other sex competing for reproductive access."[17] In a similar manner, differences in the reproductive success of males and females further drive competitive processes of sexual selection. Whereas females are not able to mate again immediately after producing offspring, males do not experience any interruption and can therefore move on to mate with other females to increase their reproductive success.

While there are a wide variety of male-female interactions that result in reproduction, one of the most common in nonhuman primates is sexual coercion by the male of the female, according to Smuts. Such coercion lowers males' costs of reproduction, compared to strategies such as assisting females in the care of the young. Such sexually coercive strategies involve not only forced copulation (usually on pain of physical violence), but also infanticide by males of nonrelated offspring of the female with whom he seeks copulation. Smuts explains that the females typically do mate with these males who have killed their infants, thereby reducing the females' reproductive success, in order to receive protection for their future offspring.[18] They may also have little choice in resisting mating with a violent male who could potentially kill the female as well as her infants. Sexual coercion, then, can be effective as a male mating strategy.

Indeed, evolutionary biologist Patricia Adair Gowaty suggests that even sexual dimorphism can be better explained if we place relations between the sexes as the most influential factor in its development: "Female-male competition over control of female reproduction is an untested, viable alternative to the male-male competition explanation for 'males larger' in sexually dimorphic species."[19] Interestingly, Gowaty's own research demonstrates that in contrast to the typical "coy" behavior of females in a typical group setting, when males and females have been reared separately (and thus females have never witnessed male-on-female violence), females do not exhibit "coyness" or choosiness when introduced to the males, suggesting that they have not yet learned to fear male aggression.[20]

The first conflict among humans, then, was the clash of reproductive interests between males and females. This leads Rosser to assert, "Women's oppression is the first, most widespread, and deepest oppression,"[21] and Gowaty to opine, "[S]exist oppression is fundamental to—is 'the root' of—all other systems of oppression."[22] This is why Smuts believes that patriarchy predates agriculture. Smuts concludes that "men use aggression to try to control women, and particularly to try to control female sexuality, not because men are inherently aggressive and women inherently submissive, but because men find aggression to be a useful political tool in their struggle to dominate and control women and thereby enhance their reproductive opportunities."[23] Smuts adds that "male use of aggression as a tool is not inevitable but conditional; that is, under some circumstances coercive control of women pays off, whereas under other circumstances it does not."[24]

Why is human male dominance so much more pervasive and elaborate than male dominance in other primate species, then? Smuts theorizes that the differences have to do with how effective or ineffective female resistance to control by males is within a given collective. The more ineffective that resistance, the deeper and wider male dominance will be—and social structures and processes that systematically decrease the effectiveness of female resistance will, in general, be chosen by males for just such purposes.

MALE DOMINANCE HIERARCHIES ORGANIZE MALE PROTECTION OF THE GROUP, REDUCE IN-GROUP MALE CONFLICT, AND PROMOTE GENDER INEQUALITY Smuts hypothesizes that several near-universal social structures and processes in traditional human societies preclude effective female resistance: patrilocality (female movement from their natal group to another group when sexually mature; also present in chimpanzees) is, first and foremost, a practice that deprives a woman of female kin networks that could potentially prohibit sexual coercion. Anne Campbell claims that hunter-gatherer societies adopted patrilocal mating patterns in which women left their natal families to mate with males outside their kinship system, thereby weakening natal bonds.[25] This is the first example Smuts offers of how "male aggression has influenced not only female behavior but also the form of the social system itself."[26]

The second strategic development is the formation of male-male alliances, which aid males in the primary conflict with females. Because of patrilocality, most males in a particular area are kin, which forms a natural foundation for alliances. A primary function of these alliances is to protect the group from the predations of other male kin-bonded groups. But perhaps their most important function is to generate specific effects within the kin group. Smuts notes, "[M]ale reproductive strategies came to rely increasingly upon alliances with other males. . . . Male reliance on alliances with other males in competition for status, resources, and females is a universal feature of human societies."[27] Again, male reproductive advantage appears to be the root. Anthropologist Napoleon Chagnon's research into hunter-gatherer societies demonstrates that individual men who are aggressive have a higher status in the village and greater reproductive success.[28] Simply put, "Better fighters tend to have more babies. That's the simple, stupid, selfish logic of sexual selection."[29]

As such fraternal alliances developed, the male dominance hierarchy structure was increasingly selected as a way to dampen male-male competition within the group. Indeed, pair-bonding in human societies may have developed as a social structure to that very end—that is, to produce "male respect of the mating privileges of their allies."[30] With amelioration of in-group conflict among males, such male dominance hierarchies were more effective in coercing women, as well as in facing threats from out-group male coalitions. These male coalitions also formed the foundation for male control of economic resources important for female reproduction. Male hunting parties would control division of game; male raiding parties would control division of spoils. Smuts notes, "[M]en may use their alliances with other men to prevent actions that may benefit the women, but at a cost to the men."[31]

Male dominance hierarchies can, however, become extremely hierarchical, with some men controlling a vastly disproportionate share of the resources and power. Smuts hypothesizes that in such inegalitarian contexts, women will be subject to the most extreme forms of coercion, as the fear of powerful men over "the problem of imperfect monopolization of the mate" increases.[32] Powerful men with greater resources have much more to lose than poor men if their control over women is ineffective, and so they will use their resources and power to ensure that they will not be losers. Smuts suggests, "[T]he degree to which men dominate women and control their sexuality is inextricably intertwined with the degree to which some men dominate others."[33]

This has important ramifications for the development of the political system. In environments where resources are distributed more equitably, males will exhibit less aggressive behavior toward one another. This holds in contemporary studies of violence: "evidence indicates that relative deprivation (as indexed by income inequality) is typically a more powerful predictor of variation in male violence than other socioeconomic measures such as percent below the poverty line or average income."[34]

This increasing male monopoly over the economic resources needed by females for reproduction is not mirrored in nonhuman primates, where females collect their own food. It is in human societies, especially after the development of agriculture and animal husbandry in which land and animals belonged exclusively to men, that the complete economic dependence of the female could be effected.[35] As Smuts notes in a survey of empirical results produced by various researchers, the lower the share of female contribution to subsistence, the higher the level of wife beating and rape within the society.[36]

In such a state of relative economic prostration of human women, more effective and less costly means of sexual coercion were developed that did not require constant one-on-one violence. Indeed, Smuts argues that "gender ideology" was the first product of human speech.[37] Men created codes of conduct for women, including marriage patterns, that would favor their control interests over female autonomy interests. Furthermore, they can easily coerce women to adopt and enforce such codes: "women's adoption of cultural values that appear to go against their own interests may in fact be necessary for survival."[38]

Male aggression is, then, in the first place, a strategy in the battle of the sexes, as are male alliances and other social structures and practices. Smuts suggests, "[I]n many primates, hardly an aspect of female existence is not constrained in some way by the presence of aggressive males."[39] Furthermore, she asserts, "Evolutionary analysis suggests that whenever we consider any aspect of gender inequality, we need to ask how it affects female sexuality and reproduction in ways that benefit some men at the expense of women (and of other men)."[40]

This is not to say that all men are aggressive, or that all men coerce females, or that such oppressive social systems are inevitable or biologically determined. Far from it. While selected, these phenomena are not genetically determined: "[C]ulture affects phenotype, and the phenotypes of individuals in any one generation can, in turn, affect the culture encountered by the subsequent generation. Thus, an individual's phenotype is the result of dynamic interactions among an individual's genotype (genetic makeup) and the biotic, abiotic, social, and historical environment in which the individual develops and lives."[41] We are seeing a complex and varying interplay between genetic, epigenetic, and extragenic influences, and the result thereof is subject to change by, among other things, altered cultural values. Nevertheless, we would be remiss if we did not notice that there is a strong evolutionary component to violence, and that its origin is male-female conflict over reproduction. Wrangham and Peterson write,

Patriarchy is worldwide and history-wide, and its origins are detectable in the social lives of chimpanzees. It serves the reproductive purposes of the men who maintain the system. Patriarchy comes from biology in the sense that it emerges from men's temperaments, out of their evolutionarily derived efforts to control women and at the same time have solidarity with fellow men in competition against outsiders. . . . Patriarchy has its ultimate origins in male violence.[42]

As we have noted, given the natural selection of sexual dimorphism in humans, violence and coercion are an effective male mating strategy. Women accede to dominance hierarchies because of "the one terrible threat that never goes away"[43]—the need of females to have protection from killer males, who will injure or kill not only females but also the children that females guard. The battering that women suffer from the males they live with is the price paid for such protection, and occurs "in species where females have few allies, or where males have bonds with each other."[44] Indeed, among humans, sex differences trump the blood ties associated with natural selection for inclusive fitness. As anthropologist Barbara D. Miller notes,

> Human gender hierarchies are one of the most persistent, pervasive, and pernicious forms of inequality in the world. Gender is used as the basis for systems of discrimination which can, even within the same household, provide that those designated "male" receive more food and live longer, while those designated "female" receive less food to the point that their survival is drastically impaired.[45]

The sex with physical power also dominates political power, so that when law developed in human societies, men created legal systems that, generally speaking, favored male reproductive success and interests—with adultery as a crime for women but not for men; with female infanticide, male-on-female domestic violence, and marital rape not recognized as crimes; with polygyny legal but polyandry proscribed; with divorce easy for men and almost impossible for women.

FEMALE ADAPTIVE CHOICES MAY HELP PERPETUATE VIOLENT PATRIARCHY The development of male dominance hierarchies may also alter female evolution, and females apparently begin to make adaptive choices that serve to perpetuate this system. Primary among these female choices that entrench violent patriarchy are a general preference for the most dominant men (who are able to provide superior protection, though also increased domestic violence and control) and female-female competition for these males (which reduces the opportunity to form countervailing female alliances to offset male violence against women). Male dominance hierarchies also appear to change women emotionally, and as a result change them endocrinologically. The experience of chronic, intimate oppression, exploitation, and violence shapes women hormonally, molding them into creatures more easily persuaded by coercion to yield and submit—predispositions that Kemper asserts may be inherited by their daughters through placental transfer of specific ratios of hormones in utero.[46] As biologist Malcolm Potts and his coauthor, Thomas Hayden, note, "Speaking very broadly, one of the themes through much of human history is men laboring to keep women under control, and benefiting from their success in achieving this."[47]

PATRIARCHY USES POWER AND VIOLENCE TO OBTAIN RESOURCES

The entrenchment of patriarchy also leads to aggression against out-groups. Males in dominance hierarchies quickly discover that resources may be gained with little cost and risk through coalitional violence; and these resources include women. The form of exogamy practiced among humans and chimpanzees (where daughters leave the group to mate) means that males of the group are kin. As a result, blood ties provide the necessary trust to engage in such violence as male-bonded gangs. Coercion of out-groups becomes relatively inexpensive in this context, with potentially great payoff. Dominant males in coalitions with male kin are able to adopt a parasitical lifestyle based on physical force: with very little effort, but with a willingness to harm, kill, and enslave others, they can be provided with every resource that natural selection predisposes them to desire—food, women, territory, resources, status, political power, pride. As Kemper puts it, "The dominant are not dependent for their sense of well-being on the voluntary responses of others. The dominant simply take what they want."[48]

Contemporary human societies do not inhabit the evolutionary landscape of hundreds of thousands of years ago. We would be remiss, however, if we did not note how primal male coalitionary violence and the resulting patriarchy are, and what influence those forces still have today. Thayer notes that humans are only about four hundred generations removed from that landscape, and only eight generations have passed since the Industrial Revolution:[49] the past still bears heavily on our behavioral proclivities. The men among us have certain behavioral proclivities induced by the "strange path" our ancestors took; Wrangham and Peterson argue:

> Men have a vastly long history of violence [which] implies that they have been temperamentally shaped to use violence effectively, and that they will therefore find it hard to stop. It is startling, perhaps, to recognize the absurdity of the system: one that works to benefit our genes rather than our conscious selves, and that inadvertently jeopardizes the fate of all our descendants.[50]

In other words, the foreign policy of human groups, including modern states, is more dangerous because of the human male evolutionary legacy:

> Unfortunately, there appears something special about foreign policy in the hands of males. Among humans and chimpanzees at least, male coalitionary groups often go beyond defense [typical of monkey matriarchies] to include unprovoked aggression, which suggests that our own intercommunity conflicts might be less terrible if they were conducted on behalf of women's rather than men's interests. Primate communities organized around male interests naturally tend to follow male strategies and, thanks to sexual selection, tend to seek power with an almost unbounded enthusiasm.[51]

Thayer concurs, noting that "war evolved in humans because it is an effective way to gain and defend resources."[52] Moreover, because the evolutionary environment produced egoism, domination, and the in-group/out-group distinction, "these specific traits are sufficient to explain why state leaders will maximize their power over others and their environment, even if they must hurt others or risk injury to themselves."[53] Indeed, the title of Thayer's book speaks to the point: *Darwin and International Relations*. He finds ultimate cause for such observable modern state-level phenomena as offensive realism and ethnic conflict in natural selection.[54] Potts and Hayden note, "[M]ale Homo sapiens . . . have an inherited predisposition to team up with kin—or *perceived kin*—and try to kill their neighbors" (emphasis added).[55] It is important to note, then, that nationalist identity can substitute for biological kin ties in the perverse logic of male aggression.

Might there be selection within certain types of states for such "evolutionary" leaders? Political scientist Stephen Rosen believes so, and postulates a concrete explanatory linkage between the logic of small clan aggression and the logic of state aggression. He notes that particular societal arrangements and cultural beliefs will bring clan-minded men to positions of highest authority:

> [S]ome societies do embody values that reward strong responses to perceived challenges. This means not only that men with a higher predisposition to react strongly to challenges will be rewarded, but also that, as these men interact with each other, a cycle of reinforcing behavior would emerge that could explain . . . high levels of aggression that are provoked and sustained by perceived affronts among habitually interacting males. . . . Once established, the culture might survive its . . . origins because of institutions that inculcated and reinforced those patterns of behavior. The biological argument suggests that, in addition to those cultural factors, the ways in which members of such cultures would tend to interact with each other would produce elevated testosterone levels that would also create a self-sustaining cycle, producing individuals who are prone to [dominance behaviors]. . . . [A]re there societies and institutions that we would expect to select for and reinforce the behavior of high testosterone males? The answer, in theory and empirically, is that there are and have been societies and political structures that do just that.[56]

Rosen is explicit in his predictions for such states: "[A] population of states run by groups of men who are prone to react to perceived challenges by punishing the challenger should see more conflict. Such systems will be prone to war."[57]

MALE DOMINANCE IS NOT INEVITABLE IN HUMAN SOCIETY Patriarchy and its attendant violence among human collectives are not inevitable, however; and this is not simply a politically correct view—it is the view of evolutionary theorists. As Wrangham and Peterson note, "Patriarchy is not inevitable. . . . Patriarchy emerged not as a direct mapping of genes onto behavior, but out of the particular strategies that men [and women] invent for achieving their emotional goals. And the strategies are highly flexible, as every different culture shows."[58]

We offer three reasons why male dominance is not inevitable in human society. First, other primate groups, such as bonobos, avoided it by developing strong female alliances—male dominance is not order-wide among primates.

Second, cultural selection modifies natural selection through engineering of social structures and moral sanctions. Examples include how socially imposed monogamy, posited as leading to the depersonalization of power through democracy and capitalism, helped to open the way for improved status for women.[59] Another example is offered by the historian Mary Hartman, whose research has demonstrated that when northwestern Europe began in the twelfth century to break traditions of patrilocality and the marriage of pubescent girls to grooms ten years older, this unprecedented one-two punch to the traditional male dominance hierarchy that structured society created equally unprecedented changes in societal attitudes about many things, including governance. Indeed, Hartman believes that it was the more egalitarian marriages of northwestern Europe that set the stage for the rise of sustainable democracy (and capitalism) in human society.

> Long before the contingent nature of the marital contract was recognized in law, marriages were conducted in northwestern Europe as joint enterprises by the two adult members, each of whom had recognized and reciprocal duties and obligations. In circumstances that required both members of an alliance to work and postpone marriage until there was a sufficient economic base to establish a household, individual self-reliance was a requirement long before individualism itself became an abstract social and political ideal. A sense of equality of rights was further promoted by such arrangements long before notions of egalitarianism became the popular coin of political movements. These later marriages, forged now through consent by the adult principals, offered themselves as implicit models to the sensibilities of political and religious reformers grappling with questions of authority. Experience in families, which were miniature contract societies unique to northwestern Europe, offers a plausible explanation for popular receptivity to the suggestion that the state itself rests upon a prior and breakable contract with all its members. And if this is so, the influence of family organization on the ways people were coming to conceive and shape the world at large can hardly be exaggerated. The lingering mystery about the origins of a movement of equal rights and individual freedom can be explained. Contrary to notions that these were imported items, it appears that they, along with charity, began at home.[60]

In a sense, then, the companionate marriages of the late marriage system were a training ground for sustainable participatory democracy. To live domestic parity day in and day out, year after year, allowed the majority of individuals in society to appreciate the virtues of voluntary association in larger collectives, including the state. As Hartman puts it, "More important than [class and religious divisions] for the appearance of equality as a popular political ideal was the shared domestic governance most people had experienced from the Middle Ages."[61] When you mitigate the social structure of the male dominance hierarchy, especially through family and personal status law, the effects cascade outward in unforeseen and felicitous ways.

A third reason to be optimistic that male dominance hierarchies are not our fate as a species is that cultural selection for improved female status in many human societies also changes females in both emotional and endocrinological ways, and these changes have a good chance of being passed to their female offspring, making them less likely to submit to male coercive violence.[62] This in turn may serve to make female alliances against males more likely within such societies, providing an effective countervailing force to violent patriarchy. For example, Clarice Auluck-Wilson reports how one female village organization in India, the Mahila Mandal, was able to reduce domestic violence by having all the women run as one to the home of any woman who was being beaten by her husband and protect her from further abuse.[63] The Mahila Mandal was also able to force domestic abusers to temporarily leave the home for a cooling-off period, rather than the victim having to leave her home. Through such collective action, levels of domestic violence against women decreased.

BIOLOGICAL, DEVELOPMENTAL, AND SOCIAL PSYCHOLOGY

Evolutionary theorists recognize that predispositions are not inevitably manifested in human society, which is where psychologists begin their analyses of various influences that shape social behavior, including violence against women. John Archer and Sylvana Côté argue that a full explanation of any form of behavior involves its historical antecedents and its survival value, as well as its causes within the individual, its development in a social context, and its immediate impact.[64] Identification of early genetic expressions nested in social behavior along with the developmental consequences of reciprocities in children's social interactions is needed in order to predict violent behavior later in life[65] Rape, for example, if explained solely by principles of evolution that emphasize an adaptive genetic basis, would not include the interacting influences of male privilege, social power, and the status of women—social and cultural dimensions of rape.[66] Instead of conceptualizing rape within a singular theoretical framework, rape and all violence against women should be understood within a contextual developmental model that integrates factors across several levels of analysis, examining not only individual differences but individual behavior in the context of intergenerational patterns and traditions as well as social-political objectives, including war.[67] Certain intrapersonal variables predict violence against women, but only in specific historical and sociocultural environments. Embedded in networks of families, peers, and work are characteristics of the personal relationships in which individuals commit microaggressive acts.

THE ENVIRONMENT IS CRITICALLY INVOLVED IN SHAPING MALE VIO-LENCE AGAINST WOMEN Archer's meta-analytic review of sex differences in aggression between heterosexual partners in Western societies found that women were slightly more likely than men to have used physical aggression and to have used it more frequently.[68] Men were more likely to inflict injury because of their greater physical strength. However, these findings are based on studies of modern Western societies where men are taught that they should use restraint when it comes to physical aggression toward women. The results would likely not be replicated in countries with substantially different cultures, where violence against women is condoned, where patriarchal beliefs that men are responsible for controlling their wives' behavior are predominant, or where traditions inhibiting men from hitting women are absent. John Archer reports that ethnographic records further show that aggression by men toward women is more common where male alliances are strong and where men have power over resources. In addition, Archer's comprehensive meta-analyses of sex differences in aggression from real-world studies found that men used more dangerous acts of physical aggression. These sex differences were consistent across those nations for which there was evidence.[69]

Social role theorists, such as Alice Eagly and Wendy Wood, argue, however, that sex differences in human behavior do not lie mainly in evolved dispositions, but in the differing placement of women and men in the social structure.[70] Both positions focus on a functional analysis of behavior that emphasizes adjustment to environmental conditions. Here social role theory purports that sex differences emerge primarily from physical sex differences in conjunction with influences of the social constraints under which men and women carry out their lives. Despite their acknowledgment of the importance of some evolved genetic influences on the behavior of women and men, "social change emerges, not from individuals' tendencies to maximize their inclusive fitness, but instead from their efforts to maximize their personal benefits and minimize their personal costs in their social and ecological settings."[71]

These same theorists reviewed the cross-cultural evidence on the behavior of women and men in nonindustrial societies, especially the activities that contribute to the sex-typed division of labor and patriarchy.[72] They concluded that "the origins of sex differences are best understood from a biosocial perspective that gives priority to the interaction between the bodily specialization of each sex and the attributes of societies' economy, social structure, and ecology."[73] Although they recognize that "men's political and economic power in patriarchal social structures is perpetuated through male privileges that are incorporated into family structures, organizational practices, and political processes," they still believe that women and men are sufficiently malleable that individuals of both sexes are potentially capable of effectively carrying out roles at all levels.[74]

It is this malleability of human behavior that is the crucial point. While inherited tendencies toward becoming violent may be present, it is the interaction of the individual with other individuals and social structures that results in violence against women. Social learning theory dissects the specific learning processes that are at the core of the socialization that enables men to inflict the wounds women suffer as outlined in chapter 2. Understanding these processes of socialization also ignites hope that social engineering can bring about changes that will reduce the suffering of women.

BOTH BIOLOGICAL AND SOCIAL RISK FACTORS ARE INVOLVED IN INCREASING VIOLENCE There is growing evidence that both child-specific and social factors contribute to antisocial behavior.[75] Adrian Raine documents thirty-nine empirical examples of biosocial interaction, demonstrating that when both biological risks and psychosocial risks are present together, they account for a greater number of antisocial behaviors than either of these two factors alone.[76] Furthermore, twin and adoption studies find that genes make a small contribution to various forms of antisocial behavior compared to environmental factors. While having an antisocial biological parent increased the risk for antisocial behavior to be seen in an adopted child, having a disrupted home environment contributed more significantly to the risk of a child's engaging in antisocial behavior.[77] Significant increases in antisocial behaviors occur when an adopted child has both a genetic factor and an adverse environmental factor present. Again, the number of antisocial behaviors attributable to the presence of both genetic and environmental factors is far greater than the predicted increase from either factor acting alone.[78] Kenneth Dodge and Michelle Sherrill review findings that provide robust support for a person-environment interaction effect and argue that because maltreatment of children also alters biological processes in neural brain development, biology and the environment do not merely interact but transact across development.[79]

After further analyses, Raine concludes that environmental influences may even alter gene expression to trigger the cascade of events that translate genes into antisocial behavior.[80] Furthermore, according to Steve Cole, the relationship between genes and social behavior has historically been construed as a one-way street, with genes in control.[81] Recent analyses have challenged this view by discovering broad alterations in the expression of human genes as a function of differing socio-environmental conditions. Thus it appears that "the experience of environment not only 'gets inside the body' but 'stays there' in a concrete molecular way that propagates through multiple gene-transcriptional responses, physiologic systems, and time epochs."[82] Frances Champagne and Rahia Mashoodh also argue that there is evidence of the inheritance of environmentally induced effects, reflected in the findings of the new field of epigenetics, which provides further support for the notion that the transmission of traits across generations is not limited to the inheritance of DNA.[83]

These findings underscore the importance of the environment, not only because it is a critical determinant of whether violence against women will occur, but also because it is involved in perpetuating this type of violence over generations. Thus, an analysis of the social learning processes contributing to such gender-based violence as infanticide and sex trafficking provides a more complete explanation of how these heinous practices have come about, as well as a blueprint for designing strategies that will decrease them.

INDIVIDUALS ARE ACTUALLY TRAINED TO BE VIOLENT AGAINST WOMEN Although many studies have concluded that among preschool-age children, boys are more physically aggressive than girls,[84] when the stimulus of gender is removed[85] there is no difference between the amount of aggression boys display against girls and the amount girls display against boys.[86] This finding emphasizes the need to focus on deciphering the sequence of long-term training that results in children's learning aggressive skills.[87]

Evidence of training children and adolescents to use violence to accomplish their own purposes covers several key points. First, the emergence of gender differences favoring males in their susceptibility to the reactions of others starts very early in life.[88] From the beginning, this may influence long-term training in which violent individuals are inadvertently trained by parents and siblings who reinforce their coercive behavior but provide little positive reinforcement for their prosocial behavior.[89] Such parenting practices are carried on over generations. Second, as time goes on, the child who has learned antisocial behaviors in his family is likely to be rejected for aggressive behavior by less violent peers.[90] This creates a situation in which the antisocial child seeks companionship among other antisocial children, and these aggressive peers then become the primary determinant for the metamorphosis of childhood forms of violent behavior to more complex adult forms of violence, including violence against women.[91]

Characteristics of environments where children are most likely to be trained in the use of violence include those where there is poor parental supervision, primarily because of large families and broken homes; where harsh discipline and physical abuse occur; where the child is exposed to violent parents, siblings, and peers; and where children are exposed to violence and violent individuals portrayed in film and other media.[92] If a toddler, for example, is subject to harsh discipline, emotional neglect, or lack of teaching from parents, he or she is likely to experience conflicts with siblings that may contribute to early antisocial behavior and launch the child on a trajectory toward further involvement with violent peers and violent behavior. Intimate-partner violence has specifically been associated with close peer groups supporting the sexual maltreatment of girls and abusive male role models.[93] While these conditions fostering violence, particularly among men, have been identified in Western cultures, the same conditions are prevalent in societies where violence against women is common. The key point here is that children are taught to be aggressive, but they would not use aggressive behavior if it did not have functional value and provide the outcome they seek.[94]

VIOLENCE IS USED WHEN IT IS FUNCTIONAL AND ITS REWARDS ARE IMMEDIATE AND FREQUENT In concordance with evolutionary theory, psychologists believe that the key to training an individual to become violent, both within the family and in peer groups, is the functionality of violence.

Violence and coercion must "work" for these behaviors to be perpetuated or, in the parlance of evolutionary theory, "selected for." The reactions of parents, siblings, and peers train children to select actions that work and to ignore those that do not, to repeat responses that are functional and drop responses that are nonfunctional. For example, Thayer notes, "[c]ulture allows warfare to be either suppressed or exacerbated. . . . It is difficult to overstate the significance of educational systems, popular culture, and the media, among many [proximate] causal mechanisms."[95] It is the environment that determines the nature of the fittest response.[96] Here we glimpse the proximate causes of cultural selection in the very act.

The simple fact is that behavior is not regularly engaged in unless it is serving some purpose important to the individual. Furthermore, as the magnitude of the reinforcement increases, the acquisition of the behavior is faster, the rate of responding is higher, and resistance to extinction is greater. Individuals would not commit violent acts against women unless such violence benefited the perpetrators in some way. Sometimes the consequences solve a problem,[97] or alleviate an adversity.[98] The selling of a child bride, for example, might protect the family from the possibility of dishonor that would come should the child become promiscuous as a teenager, or perhaps such a transaction would provide income for a starving family. Many wife batterers have reported that they are violent in order to control their partners and assert themselves as powerful and in charge.[99] Child molesters, rapists, and serial sexual killers consistently reveal erotically charged violence, with sexual satisfaction obtained either overtly or symbolically.[100] Other reported rewards for violating women include the use of rape as revenge, with women viewed as collectively liable for the perpetrators' problems, or as a particularly exciting form of impersonal sex, in which women are viewed as sexual commodities to be used rather than as human beings with rights and feelings.[101]

While peers play a key role in reinforcing violent behavior, often the reinforcement comes directly from the victim in the form of submission, crying, or pain.[102] Under these circumstances, violence against women is immediately reinforced. Sexual coercion and marital rape are almost always related to fulfilling the emotional or physical needs of men.[103] Such violence provides immediate and intense gratification. Sex, itself, is a powerful reinforcer that fulfills a basic physical need for survival of the species. Furthermore, the selfish satisfaction inherent in this type of male domination is often justified by cultural and religious traditions that are themselves results of social diffusion, and that in turn offer additional social rewards for the perpetrator's aggression.

Although individual differences clearly exist,[104] male children who imitate the violence they observe against women in the home are likely to perpetuate it as long as it gets them what they want.

In cultures where violence against women is allowed to persist, male perpetrators arc continually committing numerous daily acts of microaggression and violence. Extrapolating from Patterson's model,[105] the relative rate of reinforcement is a significant predictor for the relative rate of aggressive behavior. Given the multitude of degrading acts and demeaning innuendos constantly being made against girls and women, the rate of reinforcement for violence against women is extremely high, resulting in over-learned automatic violent behaviors.

Furthermore, Patterson also states that boys who engage in high frequencies of antisocial behavior are at a significantly greater risk to commit violent acts within their communities. This strongly suggests that violence at different levels of analysis are connected, in that states that allow violence against women to persist are allowing men—the half of society that holds both physical and political power—to engage in frequent antisocial acts, perhaps even on a daily basis. This increases the likelihood that they will experience low barriers to engaging in violence on an even larger scale, up to and including intrasocietal and interstate conflict. Societal expectations of benefits from violence at every level of analysis will almost certainly be higher if men—who are dominant in political power in virtually every human society—have received many rewards from committing high frequencies of aggressive acts toward women. Unless aggression toward women becomes less rewarding to men, and less frequently engaged in, and prosocial skills become more functional within families, communities, and societies, violence against women will continue.

IMITATION OF AGGRESSION AGAINST GIRLS AND WOMEN BEGINS EARLY IN LIFE Nielsen and Tomaselli found that children as young as eighteen months of age engage in over-imitation, the universal trait of routinely copying even arbitrary and unnecessary actions.[106] Furthermore, this trait was exhibited by both children from a large, industrialized city and children from remote Bushman communities in southern Africa, a finding the researchers believe reflects an evolutionary adaptation that is fundamental to the development and transmission of human culture. As such, imitation likely prolongs constructive as well as destructive human practices.

The first instances of abuse that children observe closely are those within their own homes. When little girls are made to go hungry in order for little boys to have access to more food, the message is immediately sent that female children are of less value than male children and that little girls should not be given the same opportunities that are given to little boys. The discriminatory act against girls is followed by boys obtaining more food, which serves as a powerful reinforcer in any situation but particularly where food is scarce. As time goes on, boys are continually inundated with examples of adults' demonstrating their lack of value for female life and female work, with each example followed by reinforcing advantages given to boys and men. These adult models that children first observe imposing such gender inequities are usually their parents or other caregivers of the children. As such, these adults are the sources of affection and protection for their children and therefore have enormous influence on them.

In homes where interparental violence occurs, children who witness such violence are susceptible to adopting the aggressive behavior patterns they observe.[107] Children who witness violence between their parents are more likely to be violent with their peers and with their partners in future relationships; this is particularly true for males.[108] Those children found to be most violent are sons of abusers, following in their fathers' footsteps by becoming violent in the same types of conflicts that trigger their fathers' violence.[109] Sons' imitation of their fathers' aggression toward their mothers may be the first step in perpetuating patterns of violence against women across generations.

MALE AFFILIATION LEADS MEN TO PREFER MALE COMPANY AND TO ASSOCIATE WITH OTHER MEN In concert with findings of evolutionary biology concerning male coalitions, studies of children have repeatedly found evidence that boys prefer to play with boys.[110] Bonnie Ballif-Spanvill and her coauthors found that when three-year-old boys play with other three-year-old boys, the amount of prosocial behavior between them significantly increases.[111] Findings show that as early as six years of age, males form more durable bonds than females do with unrelated same-sex individuals.[112] This male camaraderie may be not only the foundation for same-gender preferences observed in children at play, but also the dynamics observed in everyday anecdotal activities of athletic teams and male-only clubs.

Clear evidence has demonstrated that when compared to females, males exhibit a higher threshold of tolerance for genetically unrelated same-sex individuals.[113] Across diverse cultures, males form larger, more inclusive, and more interconnected networks than females and exhibit greater cooperation among unrelated males. The authors conclude that their studies provide evidence that compared with females, males should be able to cooperate with more individuals for lengthier periods of time. It has also been observed that male bonding occurs in small and select groups where men reaffirm their solidarity partly by degrading the male-female bond through stag parties, fraternity activities, and the like.[114] Some even explain gendered war roles by reference to biologically rooted group dynamics that prevent women from taking part in male bonding, which is necessary for military units to fight successfully.[115]

AS MALES GROUP TOGETHER THEY DEVELOP SOCIAL IDENTITIES THAT DISTINGUISH THEM FROM FEMALES At the heart of the social-psychological approach to intergroup conflict is the notion that people categorize their social worlds into "us" and "them." Identification with social groups shapes attitudes and behaviors in intergroup contexts and determines the nature of intergroup relations.[116] Individuals establish social identities as members of collectives with characteristics that are shared with other group members. Furthermore, Forsyth points out that as groups influence and alter their members' attitudes, values, and perceptions, norms develop gradually over time and tend to be consensual, implicit, and stable.[117]

Beginning with very young children, girls' and boys' groups develop different peer cultures and socialize one another in different ways.[118] At first, children are attracted to others who are similar to them, but they are likely to become more similar as they interact with each other. These children who play in same-sex peer groups are socialized in predictable ways and develop sex differences consistent with gender-stereotyped expectations for boys' and girls' behaviors.[119] Gender stereotypes then become a lens through which behaviors are viewed and interpreted, with people automatically relying on gender stereotypes when perceiving others.[120] Children assume that boys and girls will share similar gendered activities, and as young as four, they admonish their peers for gender role nonconformity.[121] Eleanor Maccoby believes that the fact that boys are more interconnected may mean that males are more accustomed to functioning as a unit with clearer group identity.[122] Once a social category becomes activated, a process of depersonalization occurs whereby individuals self-define as interchangeable representatives of their group. This cognitive alignment with the in-group prototype results in a shift from personal- to group-based perceptions and behaviors.[123]

In addition, a meta-analysis of the relationship between measures of masculinity and sexual aggression found that when the male stereotypes included acceptance of aggression against women as well as negative, hostile beliefs about women, the associations were stronger.[124] Groups of men who accept violence in relationships, believe that women deserve violence, and think that it is men's place to be dominant are much more likely to be violent against women.

THE MALE IN-GROUP VIEWS FEMALES AS AN INFERIOR OUT-GROUP

Although there is overwhelming evidence that young children favor their in-group, they do not engage in out-group derogation. When it does occur, it appears that children are simply reproducing attitudes held by adult members of particular national contexts.[125] Evidence does exist that men respond more strongly than women to intergroup threats.[126] When conflicts become more intense or circumstances more dire, adult in-group members display more extreme misperceptions and distorted judgments of the out-group. According to Ervin Staub, persistent difficulties of life also disrupt the relationships among members of the group because people focus on their own needs and compete with others for resources.[127] Threats and frustrations give rise to hostility, but the appropriate targets of this hostility usually cannot be identified or are too powerful to be reached; hence the hostility is displaced and directed toward substitute targets, often women who are already devalued and whose suffering is viewed as deserved. Goldstein believes that men adhere more strongly than women do to an in-group versus an out-group psychology and are, therefore, inherently more hostile toward outsiders, more able to demonize and dehumanize an enemy, and hence more willing to be violent and even kill.[128]

Particular attention should be paid to Donelson Forsyth's discussion of groups and power.[129] He says that individuals vary in their desire for power, but power holders who are very secure in their position may overstep the bounds of their authority and become preoccupied with gaining more. Further evidence has been found that shows that higher-power individuals have less compassion in response to another person's suffering.[130] In addition, violence among the powerful has been found to be a result of a threatened ego.[131] In these studies, individuals with power became aggressive when they felt incompetent in the domain of their power. Here the behavior of the powerful is not unlike the behavior of men involved in domestic violence who compensate for their lack of marital power with physical aggression.[132]

WHERE MALE GROUPS CONDONE VIOLENCE AGAINST WOMEN, THEY PERCEIVE WOMEN AS ENEMIES AND THUS JUSTIFY VIOLENCE AGAINST THEM

In terms of deviant behavior and partner violence,

differential association is the most predictive variable because it provides the environment in which individuals are influenced.[133] When particular groups of men do not value women and condone treating them poorly, their solidarity, cemented by their affiliation for each other, constitutes a closed system of constant modeling and reinforcing of such behavior. Indeed, it has been found that men's aggression toward women can be accounted for, in part, by engagement in hostile talk about women with male peers.[134] The group identity of such male collectives is often strengthened by various initiations and rituals often dehumanizing nonmembers and enhancing willingness to use violence against them.[135] Furthermore, these characteristic in-group behaviors are used to train new recruits to carry on the dynamics of the group, often perpetuating violence against women across generations. Same-sex groupings of men may also accentuate their views of women as different, a view that is reinforced when men do not feel the same positive interactions with women as they experience when in the presence of other men. Some men may also interpret these dynamics as evidence of the inferiority of women and as justification for objectifying and dehumanizing them.[136] Indeed, enemies are often constructed as feminine, using terms that describe the adversary as a woman, and such terms are taken to be derogatory.[137]

Individual aggression against a woman is thus best explained through an examination of larger group contexts.[138] Social networks change across developmental years and these changes are predictive of subsequent changes in types of violence against women. For example, there is some evidence that bullies in their young teenage years become perpetrators of sexual harassment during their later teen years and are likely to become sexual assault perpetrators in adulthood. While different cultures may express violence against women in different ways, it is likely that some developmental sequence could be traced that would show progressively more violence against women socially sanctioned at different ages.

In addition, Jeffry Fagan, Deanna Wilkinson, and Garth Davies argue that social contagion suggests that individuals are likely to mutually influence the behaviors of others with whom they are in frequent contact.[139] Accordingly, the social interactions underlying violence toward women are most likely spread by social contact and specific forms of social interaction. "The dynamics of social contagion . . . suggest an endogenous process, in which the spread of social norms occurs through the everyday interactions of individuals within networks that are structurally equivalent and closely packed."[140]

LACK OF FEMALE AFFILIATION RESULTS IN WOMEN'S ALLEGIANCE TO MALE AUTHORITIES Female children or adults do not appear to have as positive same-sex compatibility, comparable to that found among males. Even at three months of age, both sexes preferred to attend to the male peers.[141] These findings, coupled with the fact that in most societies, women are structurally organized in patrilocal families under the direction of men, could explain why even when women associate with other women, their allegiance is primarily to the male heads of their households. As previously discussed, this may also be a tragic by-product of human evolution as it pertains to female choice.

SOCIAL ENGINEERING OF THESE PROXIMATE CAUSES CAN COUNTERACT VIOLENCE AGAINST WOMEN The special contribution of psychology to the women and peace thesis is the identification of the discrete proximate causes that can be manipulated to counteract and even undermine violent patriarchy. Very young boys are not demonstrably prone to aggression against girls; it takes active modeling, reinforcement, and rewarding of gendered violence to make it appear functional to boys. If it is not modeled, if it is not reinforced, if it is actively punished, its incidence can be severely limited. These are proximate causes that humans can consciously control. If gendered microaggression and violence can be undermined at its taproot—domestic violence within the home—the effects, as we have shown with violent patriarchy, should cascade outward to affect many social phenomena, including state security and behavior. Furthermore, if institutions can be created that depersonalize political power, thus severing its connection to power within a male dominance hierarchy, then legal systems and political institutions that allow females to live free of violence from males, and therefore free to form countervailing female alliances to prevent male violence and dominance, will also have a profound effect on state security and behavior. To the extent that the security of women is a societal priority, the security and peacefulness of the state will be significantly enhanced. State security rests, in the first place, on the security of women.

POLITICAL SOCIOLOGY AND SOCIAL DIFFUSION

From the view of evolutionary theorists that the primal character of violent patriarchy ensures that it becomes a template for broad classes of social behavior that concern social difference, and from the contributions of social psychologists' and political sociologists' analyses of subtle but strong environmental influences on individuals, male-female relationships, and bonded groups of males, we turn to a discussion of the more proximate causal mechanisms in the diffusion of these templates and processes leading to domination and control.

NORMS OF PEACEFUL SOCIAL RELATIONS ARE POSSIBLE ONLY WHERE MALE-FEMALE RELATIONS HAVE UNDERGONE FUNDAMENTAL TRANSFORMATION Theories of social diffusion are not alien to security studies. Scholars in the field have investigated the relationship between the spread of new forms of social relations, such as democracy, and resulting observable differences in state security and behavior.[142] Interestingly, several theorists believe that the rise of democracy is rooted in the amelioration of violent patriarchy. For example, as we have seen, some scholars have posited that the social imposition of monogamy and later marriage for women (leading to a lessening of gender inequality) were necessary, though not sufficient, conditions for the rise of democracy and capitalism in the West.[143] Breaking key elements of male dominance hierarchies—polygyny, patrilocality, early to mid-teen marriage for females—may have been the first, critical steps to eventually breaking the political power of such hierarchies. Although in the initial stages the rise of democracy did not facilitate women's political power, without an adjustment in the fundamental character of male-female relations, these scholars assert, democracy may never have been a historical possibility for humans. And as norms of democracy arose, the stage was set for women to achieve political power. If these theorists are correct, then levels of violence against women should be more predictive of state security and peacefulness than levels of procedural democracy. In other words, in states where democracy arose from within through amelioration of gender inequality, we should find greater state security; but where democracy was imposed or veneered over systems where male-female relations did not undergo fundamental transformation, we should not find as significant differences in state security and peacefulness.

Just as a proclivity toward international peace in democratic societies is based, in part, "on tolerance and a respect for the rights of opponents,"[144] so scholars might also contemplate that norms of gender-based violence have an inflammatory impact on domestic and international behavior. For example, studies have shown that if domestic violence is normal in family conflict resolution in a society, then that society is more likely to rely on violent conflict resolution and to be involved in militarism and war than are societies with lower levels of family violence.[145] A vicious circle may result, in which such state violence may in turn lead to higher levels of gender violence.[146] Indeed, lower levels of gender inequality hinder the ability of societies to mobilize for aggression through the denigration of women.[147]

PERVASIVE STRUCTURAL VIOLENCE AND SYSTEMATIC EXPLOITA-TION DESCRIBE THE MEANS BY WHICH GENDER INEQUALITY IS TYPICALLY MAINTAINED WITHIN A SOCIETY Johan Galtung, a political scientist specializing in political sociology, offers two concepts that help explain how a generalized ideological justification for violence is formed and diffuses throughout society: structural violence and cultural violence.[148] Galtung's conceptualization of structural violence paints a picture of pervasive and systematic exploitation that makes open violence in the public sphere unnecessary: "The amateur who wants to dominate uses guns, the professional uses social structure."[149] According to Galtung, structural violence has at least four manifestations: exploitation based on a division of labor wherein benefits are asymmetrically distributed; control by the exploiters over the consciousness of the exploited, resulting in the acquiescence of the oppressed; fragmentation, meaning that the exploited are separated from each other; and marginalization, with the exploiters as a privileged class who have their own rules and form of interaction.[150]

The concordance between this list and the means by which gender inequality is typically maintained in human societies is clear. Gender roles lead to highly differential possibilities for personal security, development, and prosperity, even in today's world. An example of this kind of exploitation occurs when women "naturally" receive less pay than men for equal work, or when domestic violence is considered "normal." The second component, manipulation of consciousness to ensure acquiescence, is maintained through socialization, gender stereotyping, and a constant threat of domestic violence—all of which insidiously identify women as inferior. The perpetrators of female infanticide, for example, are virtually all female. The third component, fragmentation, is easily effected from women's circumstances of patrilocality, economic prostration, and greater family responsibilities (and in some cases, a physical purdah may be used), thus minimizing social access that could otherwise be used to build networks with other women. And finally, marginalization serves to clearly distinguish men and women, with no doubt as to the relative status of each sex.

STRUCTURAL VIOLENCE IS BASED ON CULTURAL VIOLENCE—THAT IS, OPEN OR IMPLICIT VIOLENCE IN PRIVATE SPHERES Galtung posits that structural violence arises from cultural violence—the day-to-day use of overt or implicit force to obtain one's ends in social relations. Thus, while structural violence may obviate the need for open violence in the public sphere, it is based on open or implicit violence in the private sphere of the home. Norms of cultural violence diffuse within religion, ideology, language, and art, among other aspects of culture. "Cultural violence makes direct and structural violence look, even feel, right—or at least not wrong," writes Galtung.[151] Violent patriarchy is the primary basis of cultural violence in human collectives: although women have become active agents with notable success in the struggle for equality in many states, violence remains an enduring component of relations between men and women in the private sphere the world over, providing a natural wellspring for social diffusion.[152]

GENDERED HIERARCHIES ARE THUS AT THE ROOT OF STRUCTURAL INEQUALITY, GROUP IDENTITIES, AND PATRIARCHAL NATIONALISM

Gendered hierarchies also help explain the violence associated with nationalism, for the hierarchized difference between men and women that is at the root of structural inequality and violence diffuses to become an integral aspect of nationalism. Evolutionary theory tells us that clan or national identity is almost exclusively male-defined, for in the evolutionary landscape, it was males who defined who was a member of the in-group and who belonged to outgroups, determined on the basis of male reproductive and resource concerns. "Gender relations are a crucial, not peripheral, dimension of the dynamics of group identities and intergroup conflicts,"[153] thus helping to explain the inherent nationalist antipathy toward feminist goals. Given this linkage between violent patriarchy and nationalism, any reforms of the cultural distribution of power between men and women will be viewed as a threat to nationalist efforts to protect or unify the community.[154] Legitimized by gendered structural and cultural violence, patriarchal nationalism provides justification for advancing state interests through the use of force.

In that light, we would expect that neither a meaningful decrease in societal violence nor a sustainable peace among nations is possible in human society without a decrease in gender inequality.[155] Is that in fact what the empirical evidence shows? It is to that topic that we turn in chapter 4.

4

THE HEART OF THE MATTER

The Security of Women and the Security of States

What are the roots of conflict and insecurity for states? Attention turns to differences in state attributes when the international system is relatively stable. Some scholars argue that civilizational differences, defined by ethnicity, language, and religion, are an underlying catalyst for conflict and insecurity.[1] Others have spoken of the importance of differentiating between democratic and nondemocratic regime types in explaining conflict in the modern international system.[2] Still others assert that poverty, exacerbated by resource scarcity in a context of unequal access, is at the heart of conflict and insecurity at both micro levels and macro levels of analysis.[3]

In this chapter, we argue that there is another fundamental and powerful explanatory factor that must be considered when examining issues of state security and conflict: the treatment of females within society. At first glance, this argument seems hardly intuitive. How could the treatment of women possibly be linked to matters of high politics, such as war and national security? The two realms seem not to inhabit the same conceptual space. Yet in 2006, Secretary-General of the United Nations Kofi Annan opined, "The world is starting to grasp that there is no policy more effective in promoting development, health, and education than the empowerment of women and girls. And I would venture that no policy is more important in preventing conflict, or in achieving reconciliation after a conflict has ended."[4] It is possible that views such as Annan's are just a nod to political correctness, which can be ignored without consequence by security scholars and policymakers. Yet it is also possible that security scholars are missing something important by overlooking the situation of women in the study of security. In this chapter, we wish to examine the question, Is there a significant linkage between the security of women and the security of states?

When a coauthor of this volume raised that question in a departmental research meeting, the answer was swift and certain: "No." Violence wrought by the great military conflicts of the twentieth century was proof that security scholars would do best by focusing on larger issues such as democracy and democratization, poverty and wealth, ideology and national identity. Along a scale of "blood spilt and lives lost" as the proper location of concern for security studies, colleagues queried, Why would one ever choose to look at women?[5] Taken aback by such professed certainty that we were on the wrong course, it took some time for us to articulate an answer. How to explain, for example, that the death toll among Indian women as a result of female infanticide and sex-selective abortion from 1980 to the present is almost forty times the death toll from all of India's wars *since and including* its bloody struggle for independence? Perhaps, we reasoned, it would be instructive to consider the scale upon which women die from sex-selective causes. Using overall sex ratios as a crude marker for a host of causes of death by virtue of being female (female infanticide, sex-selective abortion, egregious maternal mortality rates, disproportionate childhood mortality, and murder/suicide rates), we would find ourselves contemplating the results shown in figure 4.1 in comparison with the great slaughters of the twentieth century.

Because the death tolls for the wars and conflicts listed above include deaths of women as both civilians and combatants, it would not be an exaggeration to suggest that the "blood spilt and lives lost" over the last century have been, in the first place, those of females. When thinking of war and peace and national security, many people picture a uniformed soldier—male—lying dead on the field of battle, gendering these important issues male. Perhaps a fresh vision, such as that offered in figure 4.1, would turn thoughts to the girl baby drowned in a nearby stream, or the charred body of a young bride burned in a "kitchen fire" of her in-laws' making. To pose the question more conceptually, might there be more to inquire about than simply the effect of war on women—*might the security of women in fact affect the security of states?*

Theoretically, as we saw in chapter 3, there is a strong rationale for asserting a relationship between the security of women and the security of states. Gender serves as a critical model for the societal treatment of difference between and among individuals and collectivities. A long tradition in social psychology has found three basic differences that individuals notice immediately when they encounter a new person almost from infancy: age, gender, and

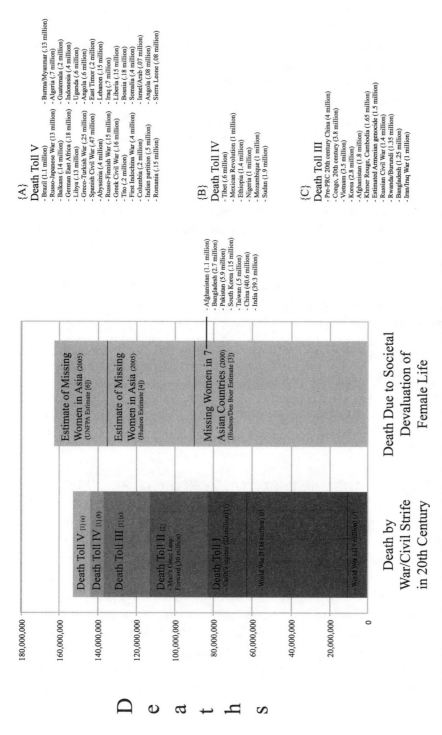

FIGURE 4.1 Comparison of Conflict Deaths in the Twentieth Century and Deaths Resulting from Devaluation of Female Life at the Turn of the Twenty-first Century

{A}
Death Toll V
- Brazil (1.1 million)
- Russo-Japanese War (13 million)
- German East Africa (.18 million)
- Libya (.13 million)
- Greco-Turkish War (25 million)
- Spanish Civil War (47 million)
- Abyssinia (.4 million)
- Russo-Finnish War (.15 million)
- Greek Civil War (.16 million)
- Tito (2 million)
- Columbia (.2 million)
- Indian partition (.5 million)
- Romania (.15 million)
- Burma/Myanmar (13 million)
- Algeria (.7 million)
- Guatemala (.2 million)
- Indonesia (.4 million)
- Uganda (.6 million)
- Angola (.6 million)
- East Timor (.2 million)
- Lebanon (.15 million)
- Iraq (.7 million)
- Liberia (.15 million)
- Bosnia (.18 million)
- Somalia (.4 million)
- Israel/Arab (.07 million)
- Angola (.08 million)
- Sierra Leone (.08 million)

{B}
Death Toll IV
- Tibet (.6 million)
- Mexican Revolution (1 million)
- Ethiopia (1.4 million)
- Nigeria (1 million)
- Mozambique (1 million)
- Sudan (1.9 million)

{C}
Death Toll III
- Pre-PRC 20th century China (4 million)
- Congo, 20th century (3.8 million)
- Vietnam (3.5 million)
- Korea (2.8 million)
- Afghanistan (1.8 million)
- Khmer Rouge, Cambodia (1.65 million)
- Estimated Armenian genocide (1.5 million)
- Russian Civil War (1.4 million)
- Rwanda/Burundi (1.35 million)
- Bangladesh (1.25 million)
- Iran/Iraq War (1 million)

- Afghanistan (1.1 million)
- Bangladesh (2.7 million)
- Pakistan (5.9 million)
- South Korea (.15 million)
- Taiwan (.5 million)
- China (40.6 million)
- India (39.3 million)

race.[6] Although there is some preliminary evidence that recognition of racial differences can be "erased" when such differences are crossed with coalitional status, no one has shown a similar disabling of gender recognition.[7] Indeed, the psychologist Alice Eagly asserts, "Gender stereotypes trump race stereotypes in every social science test."[8] In this way, gender, like age, becomes a basic category of identification and a profound marker of difference.[9]

Gender and age categorizations play variant roles in society. Everyone will someday move into another age group; in general, however, this kind of change does not occur with regard to gender groupings. Gender difference is arguably the primary formative fixed difference experienced in human society,[10] and sexual reproduction is the strongest evolutionary driver of human social arrangements.[11] Concurring with these insights from psychological and evolutionary research, French philosopher Sylviane Agacinski reflects, "It is always the difference of the sexes that serves as a model for all other differences, and the male/female hierarchy that is taken as a metaphor for all inter-ethnic hierarchies."[12] Societally based differences in gender status beliefs, reflected in practices, customs, and law, may well have important political consequences, including consequences for nation-state security policy and for conflict and cooperation within and between nation-states.

Utilizing the theoretical framework that we call the "women and peace thesis," presented in chapter 3, we first survey the existing empirical literature linking the situation of women to the situation of states, and then present an initial empirical investigation of the framework's propositions.

WOMEN AND THE STATE: EXISTING EMPIRICAL FINDINGS

There is a substantial literature linking the treatment of women to important state-level variables. Scholarly attention to the link between women and the state arguably began in the field of development. As early as 1970, Ester Boserup argued that omission of gender aspects of development led to project failure. Since her pioneering work, we have seen waves of successive research concerning the role of women in economic development and quality of life.[13] As noted in chapter 2, the empirical literature in this field has contributed to the establishment of strong cross-national linkages between gender variables and economic variables, including GDP per capita, global competitiveness ranking, and economic growth rates.[14] State-level health variables, especially child survival/mortality and malnutrition, are also significantly correlated to female status and education.[15]

Besides the linkages between the situation and status of women, on the one hand, and economic and health variables on the other, we are now beginning to see research on political variables also. We have already noted the negative correlation between indices of corruption and indices of women's social and economic rights.[16] Women's rights thus offer an added economic benefit: because decreases in political corruption increase investment and growth, gender equity additionally promotes economic growth.[17] Furthermore, the priorities and perspectives of the government may change as women become more visible and audible within its ranks. Remember the research that we surveyed in chapter 2: studies show that the more women in government, the greater the attention given to social welfare, legal protection, and transparency in government and business. In one survey, 80 percent of respondents said that women's participation restores trust in government.[18] All in all, then, the world is beginning to recognize that the status of women often substantially influences important aspects of the states in which they live. This recognition, in turn, has led to innovative policy initiatives to capitalize on these insights.[19]

Despite this impressive array of empirical findings, when one turns to questions of women and national security defined in a more traditional sense, questions still remain. Although there are theoretical reasons for believing that the security and behavior of a state is linked to the situation and security of its women, does the evidence support this proposition? And what is the form of that linkage? These questions have not been as exhaustively researched as has the linkage between the situation of women and the prosperity/health of nations.

There are two primary strands of inquiry that have brought this linkage into sharper focus: academic theory and policy exposition. A strong foundation in the rich theoretical literature of feminist security studies emphasizes the relationship between women's status and international relations, and we urge our readers to begin an enlightening journey of discovery by delving into these works.[20] In addition to academic endeavors, noteworthy is the formal articulation of the need to include women in peace negotiations as codified in the 2000 UN Security Council Resolution 1325, the 2008 recognition in UN Security Council Resolution 1820 of the need to punish those who commit rape in conflict, a broader IGO/NGO advocacy program called Women,

Peace, and Security, which has resulted in stronger gender mainstreaming in areas such as UN peacekeeping operations, and a new Gender Architecture (GEAR) for the United Nations, which resulted in the creation of UN Women in July 2010.[21] Of course, words without implementation and institutions without power may not be effective, and all of these initiatives have been criticized on those grounds, but words and institutions are the first steps that must be taken.

The empirical literature linking the security of women to the security of states does not, however, generally conform to accepted (though contested) social science norms of standard statistical hypothesis testing. Important theorists in feminist security studies have argued that such methodological norms are either an uncomfortable fit with feminism or antithetical to a feminist stance.[22] Using in-depth ethnographic case studies, process-tracing, and post-structuralist discourse analysis, researchers have penned many fine empirical works in feminist security studies.[23] Nevertheless, their insights remain at the margins of mainstream security studies, because the initial hurdle after theoretical assertion—acceptable conventional empirical warrant—has not been cleared.

We agree with those who lament this marginalization.[24] At the same time, we believe that the hurdle can certainly be cleared. Indeed, it is possible that the marginalization of feminist insights derived from unconventional methodologies would decrease as a result. We do not believe that conventional empirical methodologies are antithetical to feminist research; indeed, extremely valuable insights can be gained from feminist use of conventional methodology.[25] Here we survey several examples of how this may be done, noting that there are similar small literatures linking women and state security that we do not examine here, in fields such as comparative politics, geography, and psychology.

In a recent empirical analysis of Muslim societies, M. Steven Fish finds that predominantly Muslim nations do not disproportionately suffer from political violence, but they do disproportionately suffer from authoritarian rule.[26] He explores why Islam appears to disfavor democracy, and after controlling for many variables, including economic development, economic growth, ethnic fractionalism, and others, he finds that indicators related to the subordination of women, including literacy rate gap and sex ratio, account for a substantial proportion of the relationship between Islam and authoritarianism. He hypothesizes that the oppression of females—one of the earliest social acts observed by all in the society—provides the template for other types of oppression, including authoritarianism, in Islamic nation-states. Treatment of women, then, may affect societal propensity to adopt a particular governance system, such as authoritarianism or democracy.

Another primary question of interest is how the treatment of women at the domestic level has an impact on state behavior internationally. This question is important to show the linkage between gender and security because it shows those with decision-making power that the treatment of women has far-reaching consequences well beyond that of social justice. The international system may be more or less secure depending upon the situation of women within its units. A body of conventional empirical work spearheaded by Mary Caprioli links measures of domestic gender inequality to state-level variables concerning conflict and security, with statistically significant results. Caprioli uses four measures of gender equality—political equality (percentage of women in parliament and number of years of suffrage), economic equality (percentage of women in the labor force), and social equality (fertility rate)—to show that states with higher levels of social, economic, and political gender equality are less likely to rely on military force to settle international disputes.[27] In other words, Caprioli found that higher levels of gender equality make a state less likely to threaten, display, or use force, or go to war once involved in an interstate dispute. Caprioli argues that foreign policy aimed at creating peace should focus on improving the status of women.

Caprioli and Mark Boyer examine the impact of gender equality on a state's behavior during international crises, which is a situation in which there is a high probability of violence. They wanted to find out whether gender equality has an impact on state behavior when violence is highly likely. They show that states exhibiting high levels of gender equality measured by the percentage of women in parliament also exhibit lower levels of violence in international crises and disputes.[28] Examining aggregate data over a fifty-year period (1954–1994), they found a statistically significant relationship between level of violence in crisis and the percentage of female leaders. In general, states with higher levels of political gender equality are less likely to have minor clashes, serious clashes, or war in the high-stakes environment of international crisis. As did Caprioli's inquiry, the research by Caprioli and Boyer finds that gender equality has an effect on a state's foreign policy behavior in terms of decreasing violence during international crises.

Thus far, we have examined the literature showing that gender equality matters when states are involved in interstate disputes and when they are involved in international crises. This literature does not examine the process of escalation during conflict, however. Are states with higher levels of gender equality likely to use force first when involved in militarized interstate disputes? In other words, are they likely to throw the first punch in the conflict environment? Caprioli extends this literature and finds a similar relationship: states with the highest levels of gender equality display lower levels of aggression in these disputes by being less likely to use force first.[29] So states with higher levels of gender equality are less likely to throw the first punch during interstate disputes, and even when attacked they are less likely to escalate the use of violence.

Virtually the same pattern was found with respect to intrastate incidents of conflict.[30] Because war is rare, and civil war and conflict are more prevalent phenomena, Caprioli studied the impact of gender equality on domestic conflict. She found that states with higher levels of gender equality are less likely to experience domestic conflict. M. Steven Fish has commented, "[T]he repressiveness and unquestioned dominance . . . of the male in relations between men and women replicate themselves in broader society, creating a culture of domination, intolerance, and dependency in social and political life."[31] This suggests that while it is surely not the only important factor, the promotion of better treatment for women would help ensure greater social justice and peace, and would help prevent domestic conflict within a nation.

In an attempt to examine domestic human rights abuses as a whole, Caprioli and Peter Trumbore created a measure capturing gender inequality, ethnic inequality, and political repression. They found that states characterized by norms of gender and ethnic inequality as well as human rights abuses are more likely to become involved in militarized interstate disputes and in violent interstate disputes, to be the aggressors during international disputes, and to rely on force when involved in an international dispute.[32] David Sobek and his coauthors confirm Caprioli and Trumbore's findings that domestic norms centered on equality and respect for human rights reduce international conflict.[33] Here, too, the lesson appears to be that norms of inequality and violence at the domestic level, including between the sexes, may help "replicate" violence at the international level.

In sum, this body of empirical work demonstrates that the promotion of gender equality goes far beyond the issue of social justice and has important consequences for international security. International security cannot be attained without gender equality, for gender inequality is characterized by norms of violence that permeate society and have a negative impact on foreign policy by making states more likely to become involved in militarized disputes, to use violence during militarized disputes, to use force first during militarized disputes, to increase the severity of violence during international crises, and to become involved in civil conflicts. The status of women, it seems, is a taproot of international security.

Furthermore, the relative absence of women's perspectives and voices in the society's decision-making councils may also have a negative effect on prospects for peace. Rose McDermott and Jonathan Cowden examine sex differences in aggression with the context of a simulated crisis game.[34] In these experiments, all-female pairs proved significantly less likely than all-male pairs to spend money on weapons procurement or to go to war in the face of a crisis. In further research, McDermott and her coauthors found that in simulation, males are more likely to display overconfidence prior to gaming, and are more likely to use unprovoked violence as a tactic.[35] These types of simulations, despite their constraints, permit the inclusion of sex-based psychological variables in theories concerning the micro processes by which gender differences might affect resulting state security processes and outcomes.[36]

Indeed, perhaps Samuel Huntington's reflections on the clash of civilizations between nations would be better viewed as a clash between gender civilizations, with treatment of women being an important marker of civilizational divide.[37] Ronald Inglehart and Pippa Norris, though not researching nation-state behavior per se, examined psychological attitudes toward women across "civilizations" defined more traditionally in terms of religion or ethnicity. They found that contrary to popular impression, beliefs about democracy and other political values are not very different between, say, Islamic and Christian cultures. Beliefs about gender equality, however, differ markedly, which they take to be evidence that conceptualization of culture, or the nation-state, or civilization must be redefined to include a gender component. Furthermore, they find strong associations between psychological attitudes about women and indicators such as the percentage of women elected to the national legislature.[38]

These findings are encouraging: using conventional methodologies, we can glimpse aspects of the relationship we would expect to find between the security of women and the security of states. We have subjected the women-and-peace thesis to further empirical testing, specifically including a examination of levels of violence against women as a predictor of state peacefulness. After surveying our sources of information, we will present our research findings to date.

COUNTRY-SPECIFIC DATA ON WOMEN, OR THE LACK THEREOF

As scholars and politicians have begun to recognize the importance of the situation of women to political and economic stability as well as to peace, indices on gender equality have likewise assumed greater importance. Despite the many differing cultural conceptions of women and women's lives, certain underlying aspects of their lives can be assessed to determine the security and status of a woman in her society, and that status may, justifiably, be compared cross-nationally. According to Martha Nussbaum, observable variables such as highly abnormal sex ratios in favor of males, or restrictions that deny girls the legal right or the access to education, can be applied cross-nationally to determine gender status beliefs and the security and status of women.[39] We apply the same logic to create cross-national scales capturing various aspects of women's security as a prelude to investigating hypotheses derived from the "women-and-peace thesis."

To create scales one needs data. One of the most striking features of the research agenda we are pursuing, however, is a paucity of meaningful indicators with which to investigate its propositions.

Several useful compilations of statistics concerning women do exist: the UN's Woman's Indicators and Statistics Database (WISTAT; approximately seventy-six statistics), GenderStats (twenty-one statistics), and the World Economic Forum's Gender Gap Project (thirty-three statistics), for example, though a significant degree of overlap exists among these data sources. Because of issues of missing values, comparability, and longitudinality, however, most scholars have in practice relied on one or a small handful of statistics to measure women's status. An informal survey of the empirical literature revealed that the overwhelming majority of gender statistics used in cross-national empirical analysis came from a quite limited list: female representation in parliament, female literacy rates, female enrollment in education, female life expectancy, female representation in the formal economy, and female suffrage/political representation. Though these are important statistics, even taken as a whole they do not capture the nuanced differences of women's status across nation-states. Perhaps more importantly, none of these variables directly addresses issues concerning the physical security of women (though life expectancy is an indirect indicator).

Beyond single statistical measures, some laudatory attempts have been made to create multivariable indices of women's status. Two of these indices, developed in 1995, are the United Nations Development Programme's Gender Empowerment Measure (GEM) and Gender Development Index (GDI). These oft-used indices, though pioneering, still leave much to be desired in light of the research agenda we wish to pursue, because they rely on less than half a dozen of the most often used statistics, primarily those cited above, and they omit measures of violence against women. The newly announced GII (Gender Inequality Index), is set to replace both GDI and GEM, but still shares some of its predecessors' problems. In addition to GEM and GDI, the CIRI Human Rights Dataset has also developed three indices of women's rights.[40] These include four-point indices of women's political rights, women's economic rights, and women's social rights, and CIRI is to be commended for its attempt to include gender-sensitive indicators in its dataset. At the same time, the CIRI index seeks to capture the stance taken by the government, not the actual situation of women in the country.

The Gender Gap Index (GGI) of the World Economic Forum (WEF) is the most ambitious project to date in efforts to more fully capture the situation of women. The WEF has developed eight scales. The coding for four of the scales is obscure (paternal versus maternal authority, polygamy, female genital mutilation, and the existence of laws punishing violence against women). The coding for the other four scales, however—economic participation and opportunity (five statistics), educational attainment (four statistics), political empowerment (three statistics), and health and survival (two statistics)— contains the usual half dozen statistics, as cited above, plus variants; for example, educational attainment looks at gaps not only in female-to-male literacy but also in enrollment figures at the primary, secondary, and tertiary levels. This is an impressive achievement, but we cannot help but notice that once again important variables concerning the status of women—for example, rates of violence against women—are not compiled. All of the scales evidence a persistent reliance on easily quantified information, to the exclusion of qualitative information that could provide a more nuanced view of the situation of women. The United Nations Economic Commission on Africa's AGDI (African Gender and Development Index) comes much closer to our ideal of multifactorial, qualitative-plus-quantitative measures used as the foundation for a richer scaling of the cross-national status of women, but it was scaled for only twelve sub-Saharan African nations.[41]

Researchers seeking to study the impact of gender inequality on state security and behavior are thus faced with a serious challenge. There are approximately six to ten variables concerning women that are easily quantified and that form the basis for most analysis of the situation of women in the world today. But in order to advance a research agenda linking the security of women and the security of states, scholars must develop more robust capabilities. They must expand beyond the confines of the most easily obtainable information, and they must incorporate not only statistics but also more detailed qualitative information. The empirical research agenda we wish to advance, then, requires creation of the means by which it could effectively be pursued. To address this need, we created the WomanStats Database, which compiles data on more than 320 variables concerning the security and situation of women for 175 states, and currently contains more than 125,000 data points.[42] Additional data points are added every day.

Realizing that discrepancies often exist among rhetoric, law, and practice, we seek data on three aspects of each phenomenon in which we are interested—law, practice/custom, and statistical information. This approach allows researchers to access useful and reliable data regardless of their preferred method of inquiry, whether quantitative or qualitative. Quantitatively oriented researchers can find statistics on the prevalence of particular practices as readily as qualitatively oriented researchers can locate narrative information on the experiences and lives of women. We are thus able to provide a richer data source for researchers who are dissatisfied with relatively superficial indicators, and to empower researchers to create their own indices. For example, when examining the phenomenon of domestic violence, we collect data not only on the incidence of domestic violence and laws concerning domestic violence but also on custom and practice concerning domestic violence. For example, is domestic violence generally reported? Why or why not? What is the level of societal support for victims of domestic violence, such as the existence of shelters and hotlines? How is fault decided in legal cases concerning domestic violence? What is the range of punishment for this offense? Is violence sometimes sanctioned by the culture, such as in cases of "disobedience" by a wife or daughter? Are there regional, religious, or ethnic differences in the incidence of domestic violence within the society? Are there other barriers to enforcement of the law, such as low arrest and/or conviction rates? In the WomanStats Database, there are seven variables on domestic violence alone; eleven on rape; fifteen on marriage practice, and so on.[43]

HYPOTHESES ON WOMEN AND SECURITY

If the women-and-peace thesis elucidated in chapter 3 is valid, the proposition follows that measures of women's security should be strongly associated with state-level phenomena related to security. Furthermore, the degree of association should meet or exceed that of established alternative hypotheses.

What state-level phenomena related to security might be related to the security of women? The literature has already confirmed a linkage to state-level variables indicating the relative health and prosperity of nations. Though these are certainly related to the concept of security, here we wish to use variables that are traditionally associated with "national security." These would include data on whether the state was involved in intrastate or interstate conflict, whether the state demonstrated an aggressive foreign policy, whether the state used force first in an interstate dispute, whether the state was compliant with international norms as set down in United Nations treaties and covenants, whether the nation had friendly or unfriendly relations with its neighbors and other members of the international system, and so forth.

Although this discussion suggests many possible indicators of state security, in this empirical analysis we focus primarily on three measures as dependent variables. First, we examine a general measure of state peacefulness (the Global Peace Index, or GPI). The GPI score incorporates twenty-four indicators, including external conflicts, civil conflicts, and military expenditures. Second, we investigate a general measure of the degree of behavioral deviancy of the state in light of international norms (the States of Concern to the International Community, or SOCIC scale). This scale, which overlaps in conceptualization with the GPI, also includes information, absent in the GPI, on whether the state has violated certain security-related international treaties and covenants, such as the Nuclear Non-Proliferation Treaty, or the Convention Against Torture. Third, we analyze one of the GPI subcomponent indicators, Neighbouring Countries Relations (RN). Dominance hierarchies rooted in the domination of one sex by the other should manifest their dysfunctionality in relations with neighboring countries, even if they do not possess the capabilities to project dominance in a global sense.

In this exploratory empirical analysis, we examine the following hypotheses that probe the linkage between the security of women and the security of states:

THE PHYSICAL SECURITY OF WOMEN H1. Higher levels of women's physical security will exhibit significant and positive statistical association with the Global Peace Index, the States of Concern to the International Community Scale, and the Relations with Neighbors subcomponent of GPI.

H2. As measured by polytomous logistic regression pseudo-R-squared values in both bivariate and multivariate analysis,[44] measures of the physical security of women in society will be better predictors of the above dependent variables measuring state security than indicators related to more established explanations based on state attributes, such as level of democracy, level of wealth, or prevalence of Islamic civilization.[45]

H3. Democracies with poor physical security of women will be less peaceful than democracies with good physical security of women.

INEQUITY IN FAMILY LAW AND POLYGYNY H4. The higher the prevalence of polygyny, the higher will be the level of intrastate conflict and the lower the level of state peacefulness, compared with nations without prevalent polygyny.

H5. The more inequitable family law is in a society, the lower the level of overall state peacefulness.

DISCREPANCY BETWEEN STATE LAW AND SOCIETAL PRACTICE CONCERNING WOMEN H6. States that are uninterested in enforcing laws that protect women will be less compliant with international norms to which they have committed their nations.

METHODS AND RESULTS

THE ISSUE OF CAUSALITY

Before we present our empirical analysis, a word on what we can and cannot aspire to say through this effort. At this stage, we seek only to clear the initial hurdle of conventional empirical warrant for further investigation of a theoretical stance linking the security of women and the security of states. The question of causality is complicated by data concerns, theoretical concerns, and philosophical concerns. Data concerns are obvious: our scales, being new, have not been applied longitudinally. Without temporal variance, no conventional statistical causal analysis is possible. Second, when evolutionary theory is used, ultimate evolutionary causes are shrouded in very ancient prehistory. If violent patriarchy resulting from male dominance as a reproductive strategy is indeed primal in human society, then one might have to contemplate interspecies comparison even to be capable of seeing contrast—which raises so many issues as to make recourse to such a strategy quite problematic. Third, there are philosophical concerns: many scholars in the field of feminist security studies believe that conventional notions of causality do not apply when phenomena are co-constitutive and that violence against women and state violence may well be co-constitutive. In this view, if scholars must confine themselves to an arbitrary temporal separation to show causality, co-constitutive phenomena will defy the logic of conventional empirical investigation—perhaps ruling out the very notion of a gendered analysis.[46]

We do aspire one day to conventionally ascertain causality through temporal extension of the Physical Security of Women (PSOW) Scale, but here we must content ourselves with assessing the significance of association in the context of what we think are strong theoretical reasons to believe that dominance hierarchies rooted in evolutionary human male reproductive strategies do create templates of violence that diffuse through society widely, affecting even state behavior in relation to internal and external entities. In a sense, what we are probing for is whether the degree of mitigation of the primal templates of violent patriarchy (measured as variation in the prevalence and level of violence against women) is reflected in mitigation of state insecurity and violence. The greater the mitigation of the first, the greater we should find the mitigation of the second to be. This stance does not rule out the possibility that state insecurity and violence in turn exaggerate the insecurity of women.

OPERATIONALIZATIONS

To test the hypotheses listed above, each variable must be operationalized. Information on all variables utilized, with their associated operationalizations, is available in appendix A. Briefly, the variables used in the analysis include PSOW (Physical Security of Women; WomanStats), PSOWSP (Physical Security of Women including Son Preference, WomanStats), PSOWMMR (Physical Security of Women Minus Marital Rape; WomanStats), GPI (Global Peace Index; Economist Intelligence Unit; used as a dependent variable); SOCIC (States of Concern to the International Community, Carl Brinton; used as a dependent variable), RN (Neighboring Countries Relations (Economist Intelligence Unit; used as a dependent variable), Level of Organized Intrastate Conflict (Economist Intelligence Unit; used as a dependent variable), Level of Democracy (Freedom House; used as a control variable), Level of Wealth (GDP per capita quintile; CIA World Factbook; used as a control variable), Prevalence of Islamic Civilization (Stearmer and Emmett; used as a control variable), IFL (Inequity in Family Law/Practice; WomanStats), Prevalence of

Polygyny (WomanStats), Huntington's Classification of Civilizations (Huntington; used as a control variable), and Discrepancy Between State Law and National Practice Concerning Women (WomanStats).

RESULTS

THE PHYSICAL SECURITY OF WOMEN   The first cluster of hypotheses (H_1, H_2, and H_3) inquires as to whether there is a statistically significant relationship between our measures of the physical security of women (PSOW) and three dependent variables: GPI, SOCIC, and RN. Table B.1 in appendix B summarizes our results from chi-square testing.

The observable relationships for this first cluster of hypotheses are highly statistically significant. The physical security of women, whether that is measured including or excluding the enactment of son preference through female infanticide and sex-selective abortion, is strongly associated with the peacefulness of the state, the degree to which the state is of concern to the international community, and the quality of relations between the state and its neighbors.

However, the other three alternative explanatory variables (democracy, wealth, Islamic civilization) are also significantly associated with these same security measures (with one exception: prevalence of Islam is not significantly related to GPI at the 0.01 level). Therefore, our second set of hypotheses concerns the relative explanatory power of our measure of the physical security of women as it relates to the dependent variables of interest. Does our measure of the physical security of women explain as much of the variance in state peacefulness and the degree to which a state is of concern to the international community as other, more conventional explanatory variables? Specifically, how does the physical security of women compare as an explanatory variable to standard measures of level of democracy, level of wealth, and prevalence of Islamic culture? Because of the ordinal nature of the data, we used polytomous logistic regression, with pseudo-R-squareds computed. For simplicity of display, we used only the measure of the physical security of women that did not incorporate son preference enactment, except when needed in the case where the original scale failed the test of parallel lines that renders the pseudo-R-squared measure unreliable. Table B.2 in appendix B lays out the Cox and Snell pseudo-R-squareds for the bivariate polytomous logistic regressions performed.

These results indicate that the prevalence of Islamic culture is not, comparatively speaking, an important predictor of the level of peacefulness of the state, or of the degree to which a state is of concern to the international community, or of the quality of relations between the state and its neighbors. The pseudo-R-squared values for level of democracy, wealth, and the physical security of women are all much higher than those for Islamic culture, and in multivariate analysis this variable is not a significant discriminator (see table B.2 in appendix B for full multivariate results).

In comparing bivariate regression results for the three alternative independent variables, the highest pseudo-R-squareds are obtained for the measure of the physical security of women. In three of the four possible comparisons (level of democracy/physical security of women in reference to GPI; level of wealth/physical security of women in reference to SOCIC; and level of democracy/physical security of women in reference to RN), the physical security of women obviously outperforms the other explanatory variables. In the fourth possible comparison (level of democracy/physical security of women in reference to SOCIC), the pseudo-R-squareds are too close to represent a meaningful difference, though technically the pseudo-R-squared for the physical security of women measure is higher than that for level of democracy.

Multivariate regression is a critical next step, as it allows us to control for the alternative independent variables. Though space does not permit all three tables of multivariate results to be included, table B.3 in appendix B presents the multivariate regression of GPI on all four independent variables. In this analysis, the best significant discrimination is also obtained with the PSOW scale, as compared to the other three variables. Especially noteworthy in the multivariate analysis is that the discrimination afforded by PSOW obviously dwarfs that provided by level of democracy.

An additional test of the importance of the security of women for state peacefulness is to ask whether democracies, in particular, see their level of state peacefulness fall if their level of physical security of women worsens. The answer is yes. Tables B.4, B.5, and B.6 in appendix B examine the subset of full democracies (not "partially free" but fully "free" in the Freedom House terminology), dichotomized according to whether their PSOW score is low (0 or 1) or higher (2, 3, or 4). (Note: Full cross-tabulation is provided only for GPI.) Does the first group enjoy greater state peacefulness (GPI), better compliance with international norms (SOCIC), and better relations with neighbors (RN)? Yes, and the relationship is both strong and highly significant.

These results indicate that if a scholar or policymaker had to pick one variable—level of democracy, level of wealth, prevalence of Islamic culture, or the physical security of women—to assist him or her in predicting which states would be the least peaceful or of the most concern to the international community or have the worst relations with their neighbors, the physical security of women would be the best choice.

INEQUITY IN FAMILY LAW AND POLYGYNY The second cluster of hypotheses (H4 and H5) inquires into the relationship among family law, the security of women, and the security of the state. Family law, and practice dealing with matters such as marriage, divorce, custody, inheritance, and other intimate family issues, may well act as a marker describing to what extent a society has been able to mitigate the evolutionary male dominance hierarchy.[47] Whereas inequitable family law favoring males was for the most part universal until the twentieth century, we see now in the twenty-first century a real spectrum of family law systems. Systems range from almost completely equitable, de jure if not de facto, to being virtually intact from a millennium ago.

There is a special place for polygyny in this analysis. Anthropologists have noted the inherent instability and violence of societies where polygyny is prevalent. As Robert Wright puts it, "Extreme polygyny often goes hand in hand with extreme political hierarchy, and reaches its zenith under the most despotic regimes."[48] Laura Betzig, in an intriguing empirical study of 186 societies, found the correlation between polygyny and despotism to be statistically significant.[49] Anthropologists have found significant correlation between polygyny and the amount of warfare in which societies engage;[50] Boone even suggests that polygynous societies are more likely to engage in expansionist warfare as a means of distracting low-status males who may be left without mates.[51]

What do our data show? Tables B.7, B.8, B.9, and B.10 in appendix B show polygyny's association with GPI, SOCIC, RN, and Level of Organized Conflict (Internal), respectively. (Note: The full cross-tabulation is provided only for GPI.) Our results do bear out the findings of the anthropologists: prevalent polygyny is associated with worse outcomes for the state in terms of peacefulness and internal stability.

In H5, we examine more broadly whether inequitable family law favoring men is associated with reduced levels of state peacefulness. Table B.11 in appendix B indicates that the association between IFL, on the one hand, and PSOW (MMR), on the other, is highly statistically significant using Pearson's r and Gamma, with significance measuring at $p < .0001$. Table B.12 in appendix B lists the Cox and Snell pseudo-R-squareds for *bivariate* regression of PSOW (MMR) on IFL, and also on the control variables, democracy, wealth, and prevalence of Islam. The results presented in table B.12 indicate that IFL clearly outperforms both democracy and prevalence of Islam in explaining the variance in PSOW. The desultory results of prevalence of Islam indicate that apparently there are several legal systems that encode inequitable evolutionary family law other than those found in Islam, and scholars would be remiss in focusing their attention solely on the inequities manifest in shari'a law. Furthermore, the Islamic nations are not uniform in their adherence to shari'a law, introducing a real spectrum of IFL scores within that group of nations.

Given that IFL is much more readily observable than physical security of women from a data collection standpoint, can we use IFL in the place of PSOW as a predictor of state peacefulness? Unsurprisingly, but importantly, 98 percent of the nations with nationally inequitable family law systems (IFL scale points 3 and 4) have high levels of societal violence against women (PSOW scale points 3 and 4), so this direction may be justified. Table B.13 presents bivariate Cox and Snell pseudo-R-squareds for each variable. These results indicate that IFL is a much better predictor of state peacefulness than either level of democracy or prevalence of Islamic civilization. In multivariate analysis (table B.14 in appendix B), we are able to see that level of wealth discriminates at only the highest scale point, not at any other scale point. Level of democracy provides no significant discrimination of state peacefulness at all, and neither does prevalence of Islamic civilization. However, the discrimination provided by IFL is impressive: by far the best predictor of state peacefulness in this analytic set is actually level of inequity in family law and practice.

DISCREPANCY BETWEEN STATE LAW AND SOCIETAL PRACTICE CONCERNING WOMEN If a state is indifferent about enforcing laws that protect the women in its society, is it also less likely to be compliant with international norms to which it has committed? We can examine this question by examining the association between the discrepancy between state law and societal practice concerning women variable on the one hand, and the SOCIC scale on the other. Table B.15 in appendix B shows that the results are very strong and quite significant. If a state does not care about its women, it also tends not to care about the international commitments it has made.

CONCLUSIONS

We find conventional empirical warrant for hypotheses linking the security of women and the security of states. There is a strong and statistically significant relationship between the physical security of women and three measures capturing the relative peacefulness of states. Furthermore, in comparative testing with other conventional explanatory factors assumed to be related to such measures of state security—factors including level of democracy, level of wealth, and prevalence of Islamic civilization—the physical security of women explains more of the variance in the same three measures of state security in both bivariate and multivariate analysis. In addition, we can show that other practices indicating a low level of security for women, whether that be prevalent polygyny, inequitable family law and practice favoring men, or a high level of discrepancy between state law and societal practice concerning women, are also associated with lower levels of state peacefulness in a strong and significant manner.

This is not to say that gender equality is the only important factor to consider or to address. But what would be possible to say is that inattention to gender inequality is not likely to produce sustainable results in peace or security. In her TEDWomen speech in 2010, Secretary of State Hillary Clinton stated, "The United States has made empowering women and girls a cornerstone of our foreign policy because women's equality is not just a moral issue, it's not just a humanitarian issue, it is not just a fairness issue. It is a security issue, it is a prosperity issue, and it is a peace issue. . . . [I]t's in the vital interests of the United States of America." On the basis of our own and others' research findings, we would agree with this assessment.[52]

We hasten to add that we view these results as a very preliminary excursion into a methodologically conventional research agenda linking the security of women and the security of states. Much more in the way of empirical analysis must be undertaken before these results can be considered authoritative; in addition, we believe that unconventional methodologies also offer important insights that must not be overlooked in the quest for conventional warrant. Nevertheless, even in preliminary form, these are challenging and provocative results.

WHAT IS SECURITY?

The results described above lead us to ask anew, What constitutes security? And how is security to be obtained? An account of security that does not include gender-based violence is an impoverished account of security. This is not so for reasons of political correctness; it is so on the basis of fairly robust, though preliminary, empirical findings. We find a strong and significant relationship between the physical security of women and the peacefulness of states. Furthermore, we believe there are sound theoretical reasons to expect this relationship to obtain. We assert that when evolutionary forces predisposing to violent patriarchy are not checked through the use of cultural selection and social learning to ameliorate gender inequality, dysfunctional templates of violence and control diffuse throughout society and are manifested in state security and behavior. Combining our present results with those of previous research efforts,[53] not only do we fail to falsify that theoretical assertion by using conventional aggregate statistical hypothesis-testing methodologies, but we find greater empirical warrant for that assertion than for several well-established alternative hypotheses.

We can now envision new research questions for security studies, which are possible to raise only if the linkage between the security of women and the security of states is taken seriously in that field. For example, terrorism is a topic that may profit from a gender analysis: Does polygamy lead to marriage market dislocations, which also heighten the allure of the terrorism among young adult males with no hope of eventually marrying?[54] Does the subjected status of women feed into the development of terrorist groups offering a promise of greater equality to women, such as we see in Sri Lanka and Nepal? Similarly, security demographics is a nascent subfield that, we argue, must incorporate gender lenses: for example, is enactment of son preference through female infanticide and sex-selective abortion a predisposing factor for state instability and bellicosity?[55] And what would Huntington's map look like if we re-drew it along the lines of differences in the security of women? Would we see a new type or definition of "civilization" by looking at that map, and would it give us greater leverage on questions of identity, conflict, and security than Huntington's original map? Are alliance patterns associated with membership in the same "gender civilization"? Is the recently noted ability of populations to increase their happiness set point over time linked to the improving security of women in those nations,[56] and what ramifications will that have for state behavior? In the subfield of foreign policy analysis, are there identifiable differences in processes and outcomes of foreign policy decision making in nations with higher levels of gender equality? Does the average psychological profile and foreign policy orientation of national leaders differ between countries with higher versus lower levels of security for women?

WHAT ARE STATES FOR?

If security is the aim of the state, then our research indicates that the purpose of the state includes assuring the security of women, for their security profoundly affects state security. Our results suggest that to both understand and promote national and international security, the situation and treatment of women cannot be overlooked. Security is a garment that must be woven without seam: if we are not paying attention, the loose threads of women's systemic insecurity will unravel peace for all.

Now, there are some who recall the words of Russian nationalist Vladimir Zhirinovsky, and wonder if the world can "afford" security for women. As we noted in chapter 2, upon hearing of a precedent-setting government appointment in Finland back in the mid-1990s, he was quoted as saying, "Any country that would choose a woman for defense minister deserves to be invaded." Of course, since that time there have been many female defense ministers appointed; at one point there were three serving at the same time in different countries in South America. But the point that must be addressed is whether a state that has mitigated the worst of the human evolutionary legacy would also be prey for those states that have not. Are the old dysfunctional and violent ways of patriarchy a bulwark against enemy states that embrace these old ways?

We believe not. States that have improved the status of women are as a rule healthier, wealthier, less corrupt, more democratic, and more powerful on the world stage in the early twenty-first century. It is almost as if fortune smiles most broadly on those states where women are most secure. We do not believe this is a coincidence. As Malcolm Potts and Thomas Hayden note:

> [W]arfare, terrorism, and their attendant horrors are based on just this sort of inherited predisposition for team aggression which, whatever its origins, has become a horribly costly and counterproductive behavior in the modern world. . . . The original survival advantage enjoyed by individual males with a predisposition for team aggression has long since been replaced by

a major, verging on suicidal, disadvantage for our species as a whole. . . . [T]o a very large extent . . . the natural tendencies of men are not consistent with the survival and well-being of their sexual partners, their children, and future generations to come.[57]

These questions will not subside in importance, but rather will grow in importance over time. We see in the current international system the rise to great power status of states in which the security of women is severely compromised. We cannot help but think of the rise of India and China, where almost a hundred million women are missing from the population as a result of sex-selective abortion, high suicide rates among young women, and other symptoms of a profound lack of security for women. We take this to mean that the true clash of civilizations in the future will not, in fact, be along the lines envisioned by Samuel Huntington but along the fault lines between civilizations that treat women as equal members of the human species and civilizations that cannot or will not do so. Furthermore, we expect to see much more prevalent conflict between and within nations of that second group.

FROM THEORY TO ACTION

In addition to these fresh new questions in the academic field of security studies, we must not overlook that women's status may actually be an integral element of any proposed solutions for international conflict. Though the treatment of women is written deeply in the culture of a society, it is amenable to change. Women have recently received the rights to vote and stand for office in countries where they have not had those rights before; UN Security Council Resolutions 1325 and 1820 have changed peacekeeping and conflict resolution practices on the ground; stricter enforcement of laws against sex-selective abortion is making a dent in abnormal birth sex ratios in some countries. There is no reason to shrug helplessly if we identify the insecurity of women as an important factor in state insecurity and conflict. To the contrary, the recognition that the security of women affects the security of states offers policymakers an inestimably valuable policy agenda in the quest for greater peace and stability in the international system.

In the view of Potts and Hayden, "Empowered women tend to counterbalance the most chaotic and violent aspects of men's predisposition for brutal territoriality and team aggression. . . . [I]n the human species, the empowerment of women and the possibility of peace and freedom . . . are united in important and genuine ways."[58] This is a significant insight, and is worthy of further investigation by scholars and policymakers alike. They continue:

> [O]ne way to reduce the risk of violence is to empower women and maxi-mize their role in society. This is perhaps the most profound insight to come from taking an evolutionary perspective on war: empowering women reduces the risk of violent conflict. Far from being a politically correct no-tion of feminist philosophy, women's role in reducing the risk of war is borne out by rigorous study and historical experience. . . . [C]ontemporary Western nations have a great opportunity to make the world more secure and reduce terrorism by doing everything they can to empower women who live in countries where they currently enjoy few choices and wield little or no political power. . . . Overseas, the US preaches democracy and free markets, but is slow to challenge the traditional restraints so cruelly heaped on women in many developing countries—restraints that keep women from participating as equals in political and economic life.[59]

Much blood and treasure have been spent on the export of democracy or free-market capitalism in the pursuit of less conflictual international rela-tions, with less success than hoped for. Is it possible that the export of norms of greater gender equality may prove a more promising and effective strategy? "Peace needs strong allies to persist, and the ally that has been most consis-tently overlooked is the one that makes up slightly [under] half of the human race—women."[60] Such norms of gender equality would include not only high levels of physical security for women, but also equity under the law (especially family law), and parity in the councils of national decision making, addressing all three important elements of gender inequity that we have identified. It is to the issue of action that we now turn in the final chapters of this book.

5

WINGS OF NATIONAL AND INTERNATIONAL
RELATIONS, PART ONE
Effecting Positive Change Through Top-Down Approaches

THE ENORMITY OF THE THREE great inequities between men and women —
the physical insecurity of women throughout the world, the gross inequity in
family law in many parts of the world, and the relative absence of women in
councils where the important decisions concerning human collectives are
made — is daunting. Humankind has been likened to a bird with one strong
wing (men) and one wounded wing (women), a bird that has never flown.
How should human societies move to heal these wounds?

Contemplating this question, some think to pit top-down approaches
against bottom-up approaches, asserting that one is more efficacious than the
other. We view that discussion as a red herring: both approaches are necessary
and must be used together in a pincer movement to effect lasting change. In
this chapter, we will begin our examination of the dynamics of change by
investigating the potential and the pitfalls of top-down policies to improve the
security and situation of women.

WHY THE TOP MATTERS

The state possesses resources and capabilities that are simply not shared by
other actors in society. Among these is the legitimate use of coercive violence.
The power to detain, imprison, and even execute is capable of changing social norms, even those concerning women. The state can also coerce through
nonviolent means, such as through its powers to impose fines or taxes upon
activities that it wishes to discourage. Carrots are also available to the state,
for it has the power to craft regulations, including tax and benefit codes, and

to fund programs to encourage and facilitate behavior that it deems desirable. Law itself is pedagogical in nature, lauding some behaviors and censuring others in the most public of displays. To suggest that the state is somehow powerless against existing social norms concerning women is, in the end, unsupportable.

However, it is possible to make the argument that states often purposely choose not to involve themselves in issues concerning women. Numerous feminist philosophers point out that the state often asserts its legitimacy over its citizens by referring to the "natural" hierarchy of the patriarch over his family, particularly the women of his family.[1] Just as the father's word is "naturally" law in his home, so the sovereign, being the patriarch of the state, is "naturally" the legitimate lawgiver within the nation-state. In a way, the leaders of such states strike an implicit bargain with the men of the society: don't mess with our authority over you, and we won't mess with your authority within your home. Seen in this light, any effort by the state to improve the security and situation of women risks betraying that bargain and losing the support of the micro-level patriarchs. According to this theory, the state must keep the men of the society happy. Whether the women are happy or not is of little importance.

As we write this volume, we see this logic playing out in Afghanistan. On the eve of his "reelection" in 2009, Hamid Karzai was willing to throw the interests of Shi'ite women to one side by enshrining the most oppressive interpretation of shari'a family law for Shi'ites, practically sanctioning marital rape and making a Shi'ite wife the virtual prisoner of her husband. Though this law was in obvious conflict with the Afghan constitution, written in concert with Americans, as well as Afghanistan's accession (with no reservations) to CEDAW, Karzai's political logic makes sense theoretically. But it is not just illiberal leaders to whom this logic appeals. The Americans themselves, even under President Barack Obama, began to see issues of women's rights and security as disposable. As President Obama moved in the direction of a plan to reintegrate "moderate" Taliban into the Afghan government pursuant to an eventual American exit, all rhetoric concerning U.S. commitment to the women of Afghanistan vanished. And no one asked the women of Afghanistan how they felt about this newly created concept of "moderate Taliban."

If anyone had asked, he or she would have heard an earful, as in this story told by Patricia Leidl:[2]

One day in November 2009, in Helmand Province's capital city of Lashkar Gah, a group of widows and divorcees met with a reporter commissioned to write a series of success stories for USAID. All of them were in their 20s, 30s and 40s but looked to be in their 60s. Until very recently, none of them could work outside the home because they possessed no marketable skills, could neither read nor write and were unable to leave their homes for fear of being killed. Not one of them had less than five children and three of the seven had more than nine. A number of women mentioned that, prior to taking part in the programme—which focused on tailoring and basic literacy—their children used to weep at night from hunger.

As the reporter prepared to leave, the women fluttered around her like fragile moths, touching her sleeves and speaking all at once. "What are they saying?" asked the reporter to the young Pashto-speaking interpreter. "They are telling you to go back to your country and to ask your people not to abandon them," she replied.

"The women of Afghanistan don't want you to leave. They will quite literally die if the Taliban return," she said. Said the young interpreter as the reporter climbed back into the armoured SUV, "They will be killed or starved to death. Their [daughters] will be treated like dogs. They want you [to] return to your country and tell your leaders that the Coalition is their only hope." Importantly, every female foreign aid worker in Afghanistan I have met shares this view.[3]

In a recent question-and-answer period at one of our universities[4] (on his tour of sixty American universities), General David Petraeus was asked bluntly whether anyone thought to ask the women of Afghanistan how they felt about American hopes to incorporate "reformed" Taliban into governance struc- tures as the Americans leave.

In an answer that carefully sidestepped the most important noun— "women"—the general assured the questioning student that only "moderate" Taliban would be eligible for such rehabilitation. Left unaddressed was the definition of "moderate," which clearly depends on where you sit: if you sit in a burqa, perhaps there is no such thing as a "moderate" Taliban. In fact, in talks with Hizb e-Islami, a Taliban group, one of its conditions for being "rehabilitated" is a return to its hard-line interpretation of shari'a law for all of Afghanistan.

Apparently, for the Americans, women (and by extension, as we have seen, prospects for peace) have taken a backseat to realpolitik and the exi- gencies of a Coalition exit strategy. Make no mistake: the decampment of the West will spell an end to efforts to bring equal rights to one-half of the Afghan population—and hope to a younger generation of moderates. Though

Secretary of State Hillary Clinton has forthrightly and correctly stated, "The subjugation of women is a direct threat to the security of the United States,"[5] the United States cannot credibly be said to be acting to meet that threat now in Afghanistan, or indeed in any of the nations in which the United States has intervened.

It is not only states that fall prey to this false notion of a misogynist strait-jacket; nationalist movements are also not immune to this logic.[6] To overthrow an existing government, a nationalist movement may need to claim greater legitimacy on all fronts, including the sociocultural. In traditional, gender-hierarchical cultures, this claim may involve suggesting that the government has become "effeminate," and thus illegitimate. Not only does the nationalist movement promise to restore the proper relationship between the government and the people, but such movements often emphasize that they would also restore the proper hierarchical relationships within the household. This pattern explains why most mass revolutions are accompanied by a substantial regression in women's rights. The extension of greater rights to women by the former regime is one of the evidences noted by the nationalist movement as proof of the government's illegitimacy. Even if the nationalist movement seeks the support of women during the struggle, women will be told that the first and foremost battle is the nationalist struggle, and women's aspirations must wait for later. What women find, in nearly every case, is that "later" never comes. Consolidation of legitimacy after an overthrow precludes any extension of greater rights to women. In fact, the quest for legitimacy may mandate the opposite. This will be an important factor to monitor with regard to the 2011 revolutions of the Arab Spring.

The history of revolution is a history of nationalist movements wooing women to their side, only to strip them of what few rights they have after the revolution is successful. Whether we speak of America in 1776, or India in 1947, or the Palestinian movement today, nationalist leaders and revolutionaries are happy to have women's support and material assistance, as long as women acquiesce in the denial of their rights afterward. Gilbert and Cole note, "Many women who participated actively in the French Revolution did not know that by 1793 the revolution would to all intents and purposes ban them from political life. Many women who participated in the Iranian Revolution did not know that the end result would be a conservative backlash against them."[7]

In a remarkable move, the 2009 public demonstrations against the current Iranian regime featured male dissidents wearing headscarves. While the backstory on this was complex, one dissident asserted, "We Iranian men are late doing this. . . . If we did this when *rusari* [the headscarf] was forced on those among our sisters who did not wish to wear it 30 years ago, we would have perhaps not been here today."[8] This is a profound and poignant statement. Men who see women as beings who must be subjugated will themselves be forever subjugated. Men who see women as their equal and valued partners are the only men who have a true chance to win their freedom and enjoy peace. Indeed, as the empirical results of the previous chapter have shown, the most unstable societies are those that allow a high level of violence against women and control over women by men.

Furthermore, even from the point of view of the government, it is simply harder and more dangerous to rule a society where male-dominance hierarchies are not only condoned but actively promulgated. The alpha males of today will be the preferred targets of these hierarchies tomorrow. Who, then, wins from this system of "natural" hierarchy?

CEDAW

In concert with considering the power that states have to improve the lives of women in their society, it is important also to consider the broader international context. While there are many instruments that speak about human rights, such as the International Covenant on Civil and Political Rights, it has also been noted that unless a right is said to expressly belong to women, it may not in fact be assumed to do so. For this reason, in 1979 the Convention on the Elimination of All Forms of Discrimination Against Women was adopted by the UN General Assembly. CEDAW now has 186 state parties.[9] Indeed, the aforementioned Covenant on Civil and Political Rights has only 165 state parties. The International Covenant on Economic, Social, and Cultural Rights has only 160 state parties. In other words, more nations have become party to CEDAW than to the two oldest and most universal covenants on human rights.

CEDAW endeavors to be a bill of human rights for all women across the globe. It sets forth principles that embody equality, and it also defines what discrimination against women is. Nations acceding to the treaty agree to end discrimination against women in their laws and punish those who do not abide by these laws. Each state party is asked to present a report every four years that documents what actions the government is taking to implement CEDAW, and in what areas progress still needs to be made. These state reports are reviewed by the CEDAW Committee, which issues observations about the truthfulness and rigor of the state reports. Indeed, the committee also welcomes the submission of "shadow CEDAWs," CEDAW reports written by nongovernmental organizations within the nation, in order to seek non-state opinions on the status of women within a particular society. (One state has signed the treaty but not ratified it: the United States, which signed the treaty in 1980.)

It is important to note, however, that the list of countries stipulating reservations to CEDAW is not insignificant, as table 5.1 reveals.

Nevertheless, the number of countries raising objections to the reservations of these states' parties is also not insignificant. Austria, Belgium, Canada, the Czech Republic, Denmark, Estonia, Finland, France, Germany, Greece, Hungary, Ireland, Italy, Latvia, Mexico, the Netherlands, Poland, Portugal, Romania, Slovakia, Spain, Sweden, and the UK have all raised numerous objections to the reservations of the Islamic states and Korea. It gave these authors a profound sense of gratitude to read these, and we offer two as examples,[10] so that readers may understand our feelings on this matter:

With regard to the reservations made by Saudi Arabia upon ratification:
　　The Government of Denmark has examined the reservations made by the Government of Saudi Arabia upon ratification on the Convention on the Elimination of All Forms of Discrimination Against Women as to any interpretation of the provisions of the Convention that is incompatible with the norms of Islamic law.

　　The Government of Denmark finds that the general reservation with reference to the provisions of Islamic law are of unlimited scope and undefined character. Consequently, the Government of Denmark considers the said reservations as being incompatible with the object and purpose of the Convention and accordingly inadmissible and without effect under international law.

　　The Government of Denmark furthermore notes that the reservation to paragraph 2 of article 9 of the Convention aims to exclude one obligation of non-discrimination which is the aim of the Convention and therefore renders this reservation contrary to the essence of the Convention.

　　The Government of Denmark therefore objects to the aforesaid reservations made by the Government of the Kingdom of Saudi Arabia to the Convention on Elimination of All Forms of Discrimination against Women.

　　These objections shall not preclude the entry into force of the Convention in its entirety between Saudi Arabia and Denmark.

TABLE 5.1 Countries Posting Non-technical Reservations to CEDAW*

Algeria
Australia
Austria
Bahamas
Bahrain
Bangladesh
Brunei
Chile
DPRK (North Korea)
Egypt
France
India
Ireland
Israel
Jordan
Kuwait
Lebanon
Lesotho
Libya
Liechtenstein
Malaysia
Maldives
Malta
Mauritania
Mexico

(continued)

TABLE 5.1 (*continued*)

Micronesia
Monaco
Morocco
Niger
Oman
Pakistan
Qatar
ROK (South Korea)
Saudi Arabia
Singapore
Spain
Switzerland
Syria
Thailand
Tunisia
UAE
UK

* "Technical" here meaning reservations to Article 29, which prescribes a particular mode of adjudication between state parties in conflict over treaty obligations under CEDAW.

The Government of Denmark recommends the Government of Saudi Arabia to reconsider its reservations to the Convention on the Elimination of All Forms of Discrimination against Women.

21 February 2002

With regard to the reservations made by Saudi Arabia upon ratification:

The Government of Finland has examined the contents of the reservations made by the Government of Saudi Arabia to the Convention on the Elimination of all Forms of Discrimination Against Women.

The Government of Finland recalls that by acceding to the Convention, a State commits itself to adopt the measures required for the elimination of discrimination, in all its forms and manifestations, against women.

A reservation which consists of a general reference to religious law and national law without specifying its contents, as the first part of the reservation made by Saudi Arabia, does not clearly define to other Parties to the Convention the extent to which the reserving State commits itself to the Convention and therefore creates serious doubts as to the commitment of the reserving State to fulfill its obligations under the Convention.

Furthermore, reservations are subject to the general principle of treaty interpretation according to which a party may not invoke the provisions of its domestic law as justification for a failure to perform its treaty obligations.

As the reservation to Paragraph 2 of Article 9 aims to exclude one of the fundamental obligations under the Convention, it is the view of the Government of Finland that the reservation is not compatible with the object and purpose of the Convention.

The Government of Finland also recalls Part VI, Article 28 of the Convention according to which reservations incompatible with the object and purpose of the Convention are not permitted.

The Government of Finland therefore objects to the above-mentioned reservations made by the Government of Saudi Arabia to the Convention.

This objection does not preclude the entry into force of the Convention between Saudi Arabia and Finland. The Convention will thus become operative between the two States without Saudi Arabia benefiting from the reservations.

5 March 2002

One of the most exciting recent developments in the area of CEDAW is the No Reservations Movement.[11] This movement, spearheaded by Muslim women, attempts to remove the reservations to CEDAW stipulated by many Islamic nations, particularly concerning articles 9–15, which address women's rights within the family, under what is variously termed "family law" or "personal status law." As anthropologist and noted Islamic feminist Ziba Mir-Hosseini said in a 2010 interview, "I think the issue of gender relations within the family—which is what personal status laws are all about—actually relates to the core of power in society at a broader level. Since the family is the basic unit of society, only if there is justice and democracy within the family can you possibly have justice and democracy in the wider society. In other words, the key to democratizing the whole society is to democratize its basic unit, the family, and for this legal reform is crucial."[12] Equality Without Reservation, the name of the Arab coalition seeking these changes, includes more than six hundred organizations in the Arab world and in 2008 launched a regional campaign and an online petition drive.[13] We wish the coalition well, for this is a very significant and important work.

As we have mentioned, in addition to CEDAW's formal system of accession and reporting, there is also a "shadow CEDAW" process. Since the periodic official reports to the CEDAW Committee are authored by the national governments, these reports can be a site for misinformation and whitewashing. For example, the official CEDAW report of North Korea describes a virtual paradise for women. Indeed, according to the latest report (2002), "In the DPRK, discrimination against women has been eliminated and sex equality realized. . . . Equality between men and women has been realized in such a degree that the word 'discrimination against women' sounds unfamiliar to people now."[14] As a result of such national misinformation, the CEDAW Committee welcomes "shadow" CEDAW reports penned by nongovernmental sources, particularly in-country NGOs when possible, at the time the committee is reviewing that nation. Several transnational NGOs, such as IWRAW, the International Women's Rights Action Watch, facilitate the creation of shadow CEDAWs by providing guidance and advice.[15]

In our own experience working on the WomanStats Database, these shadow CEDAWs can be an invaluable source of information about what is actually happening on the ground concerning women. Indeed, it is crucial to the effort to heal the three great wounds, to document cultural practices and not simply document laws. First, as we well know, laws concerning women are often neither honored nor enforced. Sex-selective abortion, as we have seen, is strictly illegal in China, and yet the birth sex ratio is officially over 118 boy babies being born for every 100 girl babies. Second, in some cases opponents of greater opportunities for women have pointed to what they claim is long-standing tradition in their nation, which tradition must be respected. What we find in many such cases is that the "long-standing" tradition turns out to be a recent invention by those desiring, as we have seen, to shore up their support among the micro-patriarchs they believe are key to obtaining political power.

This is perhaps best illustrated by the experience of Afghanistan itself. As Leidl notes, "More than thirty years ago, Afghan women were attending universities, teaching, working as doctors, nurses and professors—some of them in mini skirts (this point has been exaggerated) but many of them unveiled. Far from being a black hole of gender apartheid, Afghanistan, although impoverished and backward, was still more progressive than many of its Muslim neighbors."[16] The fiction that cultural practices concerning women are immutable and untouchable is simply farce. The dynamic nature of gender practices must be monitored and archived, so that those who seek power by subjugating women cannot claim the legitimacy they crave.

THE STATE AS A DOUBLE-EDGED SWORD FOR WOMEN

In addition to the potential of CEDAW accession to make an important contribution to improving the status of women worldwide, the arena of state law is perhaps even more critical. While we have seen that laws on the books for women do not always translate into action on the ground, without the laws grassroots activities (detailed in chapter 6) will never ultimately succeed. As one Nepalese activist put it, "If we wash with a bucket of water and start from our feet, the water is wasted washing only our feet. But if we pour the water over our heads, we can wash our whole body."[17]

For women, the state is a double-edged sword: it can hurt them or it can defend them. Often, it does both; in fact, the record of the state concerning women is quite mixed. As we have seen, regimes struggling to gain legitimacy in traditional societies based on male dominance hierarchies will betray women, no matter how instrumental those women were in helping the new regime gain power. Other regimes are guilty of a studied neglect concerning women, even if fairly decent laws are on the books. The choice—for it is a choice—to not enforce equitable laws concerning women is also a betrayal of women by the state.

However, the crowning betrayals of women by the state must be identified as those that make women's bodies a tool of the state, overruling their inalienable human right to control their own bodies. The most salient examples of this are extreme pro-natalist and anti-natalist policies. Now, all regimes have some pro-natalist or anti-natalist policies; for example, the U.S. child tax credit can be seen as a pro-natalist policy. These mild policies are not what we have in mind; here we speak of forced childbearing and forced abortion/sterilization policies implemented by the state. To hijack women's bodies for the ends of the state is probably the most egregious harm a state can inflict. Some states, such as Japan during World War II and Romania during the Cold War, set a quota of five children to be borne by every woman. Both nations stubbornly refused the manufacture or import of birth control. Romania even went so far as to implement monthly mandatory gynecological exams for women, at their workplaces no less, which would ensure that the regime would know when a woman was pregnant. This was done so that the state could monitor the woman and make sure that she did not procure an illegal abortion.[18] (Ironically, the Chinese government does the same today, to the opposite purpose.) That the orphanages were packed with badly neglected children whose parents could not afford to feed them was apparently inconsequential to the Ceausescu regime. In the late 1980s, HIV from dirty and reused syringes appeared in the orphanages and spread like wildfire, infecting approximately ten thousand orphans.[19]

Extreme anti-natalist policies exact a similar toll of human suffering. Forced sterilization campaigns and forced abortions mandated by the state can be found in many areas of the world, including Europe, Latin America, Central Asia, and East Asia.[20] Even the United States once upon a time countenanced forced sterilization of poor black, Puerto Rican, and Hispanic women. These procedures, whose sterilizing nature was not revealed to the women involved, were called "Mississippi D and C's."[21] Forced sterilization in India under, ironically, Indira Gandhi, was promoted through "vasectomy and tubectomy camps." As Matthew Connelly reports, "Sterilization became a condition not just for land allotments, but for irrigation water, electricity, ration cards, rickshaw licenses, medical care, pay raises, and promotions. Everyone, from senior government officials to train conductors to policemen, was given a sterilization quota."[22]

Forced abortion (and attendant sterilization) has been repeatedly reported in connection with China's one-child policy. One case from 2008 concerns a young woman who, though married, conceived before her marriage and thus was without a birth permit:

> On October 5 of 2008, an article appeared in the *South China Morning Post* about a young woman, Jin Yani, who was drifting off to sleep one night when the family planning police smashed the lock to her front door and dragged her out of her house in her nightclothes, screaming and terrified. Her crime: getting pregnant without a birth permit. Her punishment: forced abortion, even though she was nine months pregnant, and this was her first child. Jin Yani knelt on the floor of the family planning center and begged the police to let her keep her baby. They dragged her crying and screaming, and five people held her down on the hospital bed as they ripped off her clothes and injected saline solution with a long needle through her womb

and into the full-term fetus to terminate it. The dead baby was extracted on September 9, 2000. When her husband, Yang, returned from his business trip, he rushed to the hospital to find Jin Yani purple and near death from blood loss. She spent 44 days in the hospital because of severe hemorrhaging. Now, she is infertile. . . . This incident is exceptional because Jin Yani and her husband, Yang, sued the Chinese government for the loss of their child and fertility. For the first time, a Beijing court agreed to hear the case. Later, a court in Qinhuangdao, Hebei province, ruled that certain officials should be replaced. This has not happened. Nor did the court offer any monetary compensation to Jin Yani or her husband. As of October of 2008, Jin Yani and Yang were living in hiding—not even their mothers know where they are. They cannot return to their village for fear that the cadres there will retaliate for the lawsuit.[23]

When we say that the state is a double-edged sword for women, this statement must be taken seriously. Unleashing the power of the state in the lives of women can have devastating consequences.

However, it can also not be denied that the state can be a powerful force for good for women. In the often very unequal balance of power within a household, the state, in some cases, can protect and nurture women in a manner that would otherwise never occur. In the language of the male dominance hierarchy, the state can become like a father or older brother to a woman—an extremely powerful father or older brother who is willing to hold her family, the woman's husband, and the men in the society accountable for what happens to her. The state can serve as a counterweight to the wishes and desires of her family, the husband and his family or, more generally, to the men of the society—and in some unmitigated male dominance societies, that counterweight can make an enormous and positive difference in the lives of women. The state has an important role in banking the incontinence of men, whether that incontinence manifests itself in household tyranny, financial sector recklessness, violent crime, unsustainably high fertility rates, or even imperial overreach. As we shall see, parity for women's voices in government is an important element in the state's ability to perform that role well.

STATE STRATEGIES

The diversity of strategies used by states to improve the status of women is impressive (table 5.2). The means by which state actors can create meaningful

TABLE 5.2 State Strategies for Effecting Positive Change for Women

STATE STRATEGY	VARIANTS
Information Strategies	■ Document women's situation ■ Provide gender disaggregation for all national statistics ■ Protect Women's Human Rights Defenders ■ Educate women about their rights under state law ■ Include women's unpaid caretaking labor in national economic statistics
Rhetorical Strategies	■ Rename previously accepted practices to reflect their true reality (example: "forced marriage" termed "a crime against humanity") ■ Sponsor ads, slogans, signs, radio spots encouraging gender equity ■ Sponsor gender equity plotlines in popular media programs, such as soap operas
Harvest Low-Hanging Fruit	■ Ban dying practices harmful to women ■ Legally preempt new or imported practices harmful to women that have not yet taken root ■ Increase punishments for crimes against women previously seen as "natural"
Tap the Power of State Personalities	■ First ladies ■ Monarchs ■ Esteemed historical or media figures ■ Esteemed religious figures ■ Material inducements used by leaders to facilitate change
Put Women's Priorities on the State's List of Priorities	■ Maternal mortality ■ Access to family planning ■ Education of girls
Engage Formal and Informal Judicial Bodies at All Levels	■ Disentangle religious rulings from state law, and make the latter preeminent ■ Use the appeal system to reach higher and higher courts ■ Involve informal judges, such as tribal elders, leaders of madrassas, etc. ■ Involve household powers, such as mothers-in-law
Prohibit Development of Inequitable Family Law Enclaves	■ Prohibit their establishment ■ Prohibit what is illegal in your country, even if the practice is legal in the immigrant's home country ■ Criminalize illegal behavior committed abroad by citizens ■ Establish a system of protective orders for vulnerable young people

TABLE 5.2 (*continued*)

STATE STRATEGY	VARIANTS
Make National Family Law Equitable	■ Establish a minimum age for marriage, preferably 18 ■ Grant equal right to divorce and access to custody for men and women ■ Prohibit polygyny ■ Equalize inheritance laws and property rights within marriage
Enact Pro-Women Legislation	■ Femicide laws ■ Asylum laws ■ Media image laws ■ Laws focusing on concrete enforcement measures
Change the Incentive Structures	■ Offer scholarships for girls ■ Pay for vaccinations for girls ■ Target development assistance to girls ■ Enforce pro-women laws, thus significantly increasing costs for those who would harm women
Include Women in Decision Making	■ Establish quotas for political representation ■ Facilitate greater access for female judges and attorneys ■ Create standards for gender composition of executive boards in private industry ■ Involve women in peace negotiations, *jirgas*, etc. ■ Promote greater presence of women on domestic police forces
Keep Caregiving Economically Rational	■ Equalize standards of living after divorce ■ Set standards of joint ownership of property in marriage ■ Address hiring and pay discrimination ■ Work toward proportional benefits for part-time workers ■ Provide pension benefits for unpaid caregiving ■ Provide paid maternity leave
R2PW	■ Fully implement UNSC and General Assembly resolutions that seek to improve the situation of women ■ Encourage regional IGO commitment to gender equity among member states ■ Monitor and track the situation of women within nations; this may involve gathering new statistics, conducting new research, etc. ■ Rank nations and sanction those with abominable records ■ Inventory best state practices to improve the situation of women ■ Redefine democracy to include whether a nation's women are valued, are secure, and have a voice

change for women in their societies must necessarily depend on the particulars of the history, culture, religion, and attitudes of the nation. It is instructive to consider the range of state initiatives, with an eye to understanding the scope conditions under which each type of initiative has a good chance of success.

INFORMATION STRATEGIES

As clichéd as it may sound, knowledge is powerful, and it can move societies. Too often, the real situation of women is simply invisible, "seen-but-not-seen," deemed natural and not worthy of contemplation or comment. Making visible that which is not seen is a primary strategy used by both state and non-state actors to improve the situation of women.

An important component of this strategy is state documentation of women's condition within the society. Nearly every nation has a statistical bureau, but many do not publish gender-disaggregated statistics. Taking that simple step, along with publishing an annual "state of the women" report, would go far in making visible that which has remained invisible for too long.

The United States goes a step further than this. The annual Country Reports on Human Rights Practices put out by the State Department includes a section that provides a general evaluation of the situation of women in each country. This is an important resource, and serves as a reality check vis-à-vis state reporting of its own society. The State Department also issues country-specific Trafficking in Persons Reports, grading each country on a four-point scale concerning how proactive the country is in protecting its citizens, primarily women and children, from human traffickers. The European Union issues the Harmful Traditional Practices Survey, designed to identify such practices within the EU, survey legislation addressing them, and also identify best practices for ameliorating the effects of these harmful practices.[24] Through an international framework, states can also empower and protect Women's Human Rights Defenders (WHRDs) to investigate and report issues that the state must address to protect women.[25] In practice, however, many states do not support WHRDs in their country, and often oppress them. If states understood the connection between the security of women and national security, they would ensure that WHRDs were protected.

Another important state informational strategy is to educate women about their rights under state law. As we have noted, often there are fairly enlightened laws on the books whose effects never seem to translate into the real lives of women. Part of the problem is that women themselves do not know they are granted these rights; in some countries, high rates of illiteracy among women are part of the problem. But with a modest financial investment, states can rectify the situation. For example, Jordan has recently conducted a campaign to increase basic awareness of legal rights:

> The campaign [in 2006] was launched by the Ministry of Political Development and Parliamentarian Affairs in cooperation with Mizan [an NGO]. "Our goal was to raise awareness about each person's legal rights and obligations," said Rula Haddadin, campaign manager at Mizan, also known as the Law Group for Human Rights. "Since the first days of the campaign, the number of phone calls we've received has increased considerably." In addition to a telephone hotline offering free legal advice, hundreds of billboards, CDs and pocket calendars were distributed in the capital, Amman, and at universities throughout the country aimed at informing citizens of their legal rights as enshrined in the constitution. Newspapers, television and radio spots were also used to spread the message.[26]

States could be even more creative in this endeavor; for example, they could emulate the work of Kristine Pearson and Lifeline Energy, which provides low-cost solar-powered and virtually indestructible radio/MP3 players to women in rural Africa. Radios and boom boxes are usually, in these cultures, the purview of men, as only men typically have the cash to spend on batteries. The provision of these "women's radios" allows women to tap into the larger world around them. One of the most important results, according to Pearson, is that women become cognizant of their legal rights for the first time, by listening in to women's radio programs. Furthermore, Pearson's organization can pre-load the MP3 player with files that not only promote literacy for women but also explain and summarize women's rights, so that every woman who has access to a radio will also have access to the information she needs to understand her legal rights.[27]

But there are further steps to be taken. Marilyn Waring has noted that the economic statistics that drive state policymaking completely omit any accounting of the unpaid labor contributions of women to the economy.[28] It is time for states to develop new measures of gross domestic product or gross domestic well-being that fully take into account the caretaking labor performed by women. When women are invisible in societal accounting, also rendered invisible to policymakers is an understanding of how policies may help or may hurt women. Just as governments perform environmental impact studies before undertaking new development initiatives, so governments should perform female impact studies.

At a minimum, then, states interested in improving the situation of the women in their society must develop the infrastructure to both inform women of their rights and document their real situation as well as their real, though unpaid and often unseen, contributions to the society.[29]

RHETORICAL STRATEGIES

States also have great power to alter societal discourse by altering the terms used to describe heretofore unproblematic practices. Indeed, by altering terms to more resemble those used to describe illegal practices, the state can actually begin to criminalize that which was never considered illegal before. When the government of Sweden began to call prostitution "violence against women," legal abolition of prostitution became possible. Other nations, such as Iceland, Norway, and the United Kingdom, are also examining how a discursive turn can change the legal status of accepted practices. For example, in one UK government pilot program, posters were hung in men's bathrooms in bars.[30] The posters showed the entrance to a brothel and had the line, "Walk in a punter. Walk out a rapist." To begin to label a "john" a "rapist" is the start of something very important in British society. Iceland has recently banned strip clubs and topless waitressing, with the prime minister opining, "I guess the men of Iceland will just have to get used to the idea that women are not for sale."[31]

Prostitution is not the only practice that can be re-termed. One group in Canada is calling for Canada to recognize its state obligations under the Convention Against Torture (CAT) to proactively prevent and punish non-state actor torture within its borders. What is "non-state actor torture"? It is otherwise known as domestic violence.[32] Even without using that term explicitly, the United States has moved firmly in this same direction by making domestic violence a judicial rationale for the granting of asylum, putting state sanction of domestic violence on a par with state sanction of torture.[33] France has moved to outlaw psychological abuse within marriage; while difficult to enforce, the rhetorical turn is most welcome.[34] In Sierra Leone, the Special Court dealing with war crimes in that country has judged that forced marriages are in fact "crimes against humanity," punishable by the ICC.[35] If forced marriages in times of war are crimes against humanity, wouldn't they still be crimes against humanity in times of peace? The court's ruling makes it possible to now raise this question in Sierra Leone society.

Discursive efforts could include state collaboration with media. For example, in Costa Rica, the Ministry of Women, in collaboration with women's NGOs, launched a series of "radio novellas" called *Love's Other Face*. Scriptwriters were hired to write entertaining half-hour chapters that would address issues of domestic violence and refute its normality and its legality.[36] In a sense, satellite television and the Internet have provided a "Radio Free Women" station, where women in nearly every land can see that it is possible for women to be treated as the equals of men. The discursive move is a powerful one that states can use to profound effect. For example, in an experiment run by Rob Jensen and Emily Oster, the provision to rural Indian communities of cable TV shows depicting educated, powerful women characters resulted in a significant decrease in the "aspiration gap" between male and female teenagers, as well as their parents. Just seeing a different and better life for women was sufficient to create new horizons for young women in these communities.[37]

HARVEST LOW-HANGING FRUIT

The government can also send messages to its citizenry through dealing with what we call here "low-hanging policy fruit." By banning a cultural practice that was formerly prevalent but is now comparatively rare, or banning a practice that is in its infancy but does not yet have broad-based societal support, the government can attempt to draw some brighter lines around the security of women.

An example of the former is premarital virginity testing. As this practice has fallen by the wayside in certain countries, some governments, including those of Jordan and Turkey, have taken the initiative to ban the practice outright, knowing there would be minimal backlash. An example of the latter is movement within several Western societies to ban the *niqab* and the burqa in public as inherently invisibilizing of women in the public space of society in a way that distinguishes this dress from the *chador* and *abaya*, as well as to ban sex-selective abortion. Obviously these practices are marginal in Western countries, but to ban something while the practices are still marginal also safeguards against future encroachment on the rights of women in these areas.[38]

Another variant of this strategy is to gradually increase the punishment for crimes against women, making a "lesser" crime into a "greater" crime. So, for example, on July 1, 2009, President Bashar al-Assad {of Syria) abolished Article 548 of the Penal Code, which had waived punishment for a man found to have killed a female family member in a case "provoked" by "illegitimate sex acts," as well as for a husband who killed his wife because of an extramarital affair. The article also lowered penalties if a killing was found to be based on a "suspicious state" concerning a female family member. The article that replaced it still allows for mitigated punishment for "honor killings," but requires a sentence of at least two years.[39] In 2011, President al-Assad increased the punishment to seven years.[40] Now, seven years is hardly acceptable as a punishment for murder, but seven years is a far longer sentence than what was typical less than five years ago, when men would be absolved completely if "honor" were involved. Furthermore, the jump between the sentence of two years and the sentence of seven years under the law occurred in less than three years' time. (Of course, the Assad regime may yet fall; as we write this, the situation is uncertain.)

Governments should be actively engaged in the search for such "low-hanging policy fruit," scrutinizing both new trends and old practices for opportunities to make women's lives more secure.

TAP THE POWER OF STATE PERSONALITIES

In some societies, leaders may play an outsized role in shaping public opinion by sheer force of personality coupled with popularity. Where such leaders have spoken up in behalf of women, the groundwork for societal change can be established. For example, as mentioned in chapter 2, it is hard to overstate the role of Suzanne Mubarak in helping to decrease rates of female circumcision in Egypt. Her tireless campaigning against this practice as harmful to the health of Egyptian women eventually bore fruit, but it took her position and influence to help create the conditions for change. Through her efforts, linked with the efforts of others, female circumcision was catapulted into the public discourse: the Ministry of Religious Affairs has issued a booklet explaining that the practice is not part of Islam; prominent religious leaders have declared the practice *haram* (forbidden in Islam) and harmful; state-run television channels have aired advertisements against the practice; a national hotline was established to answer questions; and television news shows and newspapers have willingly reported on botched operations and the death of young girls undergoing circumcision.

The practice is now, finally, illegal in Egypt. It used to be that 97 percent of all Egyptian women were circumcised, but the figure has been reduced to 66 percent, a stunning decline given that the government has not aggressively enforced the ban.[41] The power of the powerful to steer public opinion can be effectively harnessed to improve the situation of women. We hope this situation is not reversed by the regime change in that nation.

It is also hard to overstate the crucial role played by King Mohammed VI of Morocco in protecting women of his country. A proclaimed descendant of the Prophet Mohammed, the king gave a historic speech on August 20, 1999, in which he stated, "How can society achieve progress, while women, who represent half the nation, see their rights violated and suffer as a result of injustice, violence, and marginalization, notwithstanding the dignity and justice granted them by our glorious religion?"[42] In 2004, the king shepherded an overhaul of family law in Morocco, giving women extraordinary rights compared with their sisters in other Islamic societies. (We detail those changes below.)

The emir of Kuwait, Shaikh Jabir al Ahmad, must also be singled out for special mention. Given the bravery of Kuwaiti women during Iraq's invasion of that country in 1990–1991 (when by and large the women stayed and fought, even in an armed resistance movement, while the men had to flee for their lives), after Kuwait's liberation, the emir began to argue that women could no longer be denied the full rights belonging to Kuwaiti citizens, including suffrage and the right to stand for office. Indeed, as early as 1999, the emir attempted to enact such legislation by decree, only to see his efforts nullified by the Kuwaiti parliament, manned by some of the most conservative (male) politicians in the country. He tried several times and failed each time. Finally in 2003, the emir went so far as to formally request that the Kuwaiti parliament honor him by acceding to his plea on this issue, which plea they rebuffed. The emir appointed two women to the Kuwaiti cabinet in early 2005, even though women still did not have the right to vote.

Finally in May 2005, through an intensive organized bottom-up effort featuring the largest and most inclusive public demonstration in Kuwaiti history, plus the added pressure from the emir, the Kuwaiti parliament granted women their suffrage. Shultziner and Tetreault argue that an important element in the passage of this act—which passage surprised both supporters and opponents—was the material inducements offered to members of parliament for their last-minute support, including increased salaries for government employees and increased pension payments, a price that may have totaled fifty million dollars.[43] When we speak, then, of the importance of state personalities in creating progress for women, we must acknowledge that rhetoric may have to be complemented by material pressure of both the carrot and the stick variety.

Other leaders are also attempting to move in the direction of greater justice and protection for women. Queen Rania of Jordan has called for stiffer sentences for those who perpetrate honor killings. Bashar al-Assad's wife Asmaa is also a force for women in Syria, as is Sheikha Mozah of Qatar and Princess Haya Bint al Hussein of Dubai.[44] King Abdullah of Saudi Arabia set up the Human Rights Commission in 2005, and one of its purposes is to improve the lot of women. The commission recently allowed the divorce of a girl who was wed at age eleven to an eighty-year-old man, and is attempting to set a minimum age of marriage of sixteen for girls in the Saudi kingdom.[45] Abdullah has also appointed the first woman minister in the history of Saudi Arabia, and opened the coeducational King Abdullah University of Science and Technology (KAUST), the first of its kind in the kingdom. Without the support of King Abdullah, such initiatives could scarcely be contemplated.

The culture of rape in Liberia has been condemned by its president, Ellen Johnson-Sirleaf, who was threatened with rape while a prisoner earlier in her life, and she is a forceful advocate for greater protections for women. Conversely, in South Africa, President Jacob Zuma has himself been accused of rape, providing cover to a generalized "rape culture" in that benighted land, which can claim the highest incidence of rapes per capita in the entire world. Bad examples can be as powerful as good examples, unfortunately.

MAKE MATERNAL MORTALITY, ACCESS TO CONTRACEPTION, AND EDUCATION OF GIRLS TOP PRIORITIES FOR STATE ACTION

While we are going to add to this list of what top governmental priorities should be, there are three long-standing priorities that we wish to underscore. We cannot as a species continue to permit sex to mean death for women. When a woman's lifetime chance of dying as a result of conception is one in seven in some areas of sub-Saharan Africa, it is clear that men in that region have no empathy for women when it comes to sex. It falls to the government to provide that empathy.

Prevention of maternal mortality costs pennies per woman, and governments must be held accountable. Assistance from the World Bank (IBRD), the International Monetary Fund, or regional development banks to countries with high maternal mortality rates must be conditional upon effective plans of action to reduce those rates. The international community must treat high maternal mortality rates as it would noncompliance with the Nuclear Non-Proliferation Treaty: it should be a situation of gravest concern to the community of nations, bringing with it a full repertoire of both incentives and punishments at the bilateral and multilateral levels. State action to reduce maternal mortality need not try to uproot maternal health care systems already in place. For example, providing training for traditional birth attendants (TBAs), and providing them with LED lights powered by solar cells as well as inexpensive cell phones, can reduce maternal mortality even where hospitals are not nearby.[46]

Access to contraception is also part of nullifying the equation between sex and death for women, and the world community has enjoyed relative success in helping women obtain the means to control the reproduction of their own bodies. States must continue to subsidize the manufacture or import of contraception, as well as efforts to make it widely available and to provide training in how to use contraception, even to women in remote areas of the country.

Education of girls, as has been noted by many organizations and scholars, is one of the great keys to improving the situation of women. Educated women are better able to control what happens to their bodies, better able to avoid oppression in marriage, better able to safeguard their own health and the health of their children, better able to participate in the deliberations of human society. Many states have introduced innovative incentive systems to prod families to send girls to school. Successful initiatives include scholarships to waive school fees for girls, payments to families who send their girls to school and allow them time to complete their homework, the building of toilet facilities for girls at their schools, provision of sanitary supplies so that girls will not feel they have to miss school during menstruation, construction of schools closer to villages or provision of bicycles to girls so that they are not as vulnerable to attack while traveling to school, the training of female teachers, who are less likely to demand sex from girl students, and so forth. Again, the international community must be prepared to hold nations accountable where the literacy rate of girls is low, and to view such a statistic as tangible harm done to the peacefulness of the interstate system by the nation in question.

ENGAGE FORMAL AND INFORMAL JUDICIAL BODIES AT ALL LEVELS

One of the most effective steps to changing the law of the land is to open the way through judicial rulings. Appeal by judicial bodies to international treaties and covenants to which the nation-state is a party is an important element of such movement. As noted above, the Special Court in Sierra Leone has decided that forced marriage during wartime can be prosecuted as a crime against humanity under the Rome Treaty, and this decision naturally implies that forced marriage in peacetime is also a crime against humanity. The Convention on the Rights of the Child states that minimum age of marriage should be eighteen, which provides grounds for signatory nations to raise their legal age of marriage.

There are several other strategies that the state can use to facilitate improvements in the situation of women through judicial means. One is to disentangle religion from state law. For example, women's activists in Bangladesh pointed out to the courts that there were forty-six fatwas, or religious pronouncements, in one year that superseded or contradicted the judgments of the court. As a result, the state court ruled that no one could issue fatwas that nullified rulings of the court.[47]

Another option is to take "big" questions to as high a judicial level as possible, preferably to the level of the high court of the land. Ugandan activists unsuccessfully petitioned the Constitutional Court to rule bride-price illegal because it made women chattel. However, that failure ironically gives them the opportunity to pursue a ruling by the High Court of Uganda.[48] In Argentina, a coalition of NGOs plus three government agencies filing amicus curiae briefs were successful in persuading the Argentine Supreme Court to extend the right to abortion in the case of rape to all women, not just mentally retarded women, as the then-current law stipulated. The high court drew heavily upon Argentina's accession to both CEDAW and the CRC in making this ruling.[49] Another example, from Nepal, is that of *chaupad*, "a custom in which a woman is kept in a cowshed during and after childbirth. A public interest litigation was filed to eliminate *chaupad*. The Supreme Court has issued a directive order to criminalise such action and has also asked the government to study its implications and launch a massive awareness campaign."[50]

Traditional, less formal judicial systems can also be a force for positive change for women, especially if the government plays a role in encouraging that direction through education of the leaders involved. One educator tells the story of the leader of a Pakistani madrassa, or religious school:

In his village, a young woman was caught talking on her cell phone at 2 a.m. with a boy in another village. The elders felt such action violated their honor code, so the girl was to die and the boy was to lose his nose and ears. . . . This leader said, "This happens all the time, but I felt led, because of our discussion, to go back and confront this on religious grounds." . . . He did, explaining to the elders that nothing in the Quran prohibits a woman from talking with a man. In the end, no one was harmed.[51]

In another case in the Ivory Coast, women presented photographs of their lives, including depictions of domestic violence, to the village chief. The chief raised his arm. "I have heard your message," he said. "I do not want violence of any kind. If such violence goes on in this village, it must stop now." After the show he invited the photographers—who had formed an organization called Anouanze ("Unity")—to join his council of advisors. He invited all village women to attend village meetings. Overnight, cameras in hand, the women of Zatta village, who had never had a voice in public affairs, moved to the center of governance.[52]

Even "judicial systems" within the household itself must be considered a site of persuasion. When China got serious about its abnormal birth sex ratio, the government engaged in many educational outreach efforts. According to several observers, the most effective outreach was to the grandmothers—the mothers of the husbands of the pregnant women. These grandmothers have enormous power within the patrilocal household to force an abortion of a female fetus, and until the government makes them a special focus of education regarding the value of girl children, other educational efforts will have only suboptimal results.

PROHIBIT DEVELOPMENT OF INEQUITABLE FAMILY LAW ENCLAVES

As we noted in chapter 4, our research shows that inequitable family law is tightly correlated with high levels of violence against women. Nations that countenance enclaves of inequitable family law can expect higher rates of violence against women and lower levels of state peacefulness than states that refuse to allow such enclaves. The pressure on Western nations such as Canada, Australia, the UK, and others to permit such enclaves is rising. On the basis of our research findings, we strongly advocate for a complete prohibition of such enclaves, subordinating all households to equitable national family law standards.

Such prohibition demands that practices legal in other countries not be "imported" into a destination country where the practices are illegal. For example, nations such as the Netherlands recognize polygamous marriages if they were entered into within a country where polygamy is legal. This is ironic, because Western nations in general do not condone their citizens' doing things that are illegal in other countries, even if such acts are legal there. So, for example, the United States will prosecute its citizens who are "sex tourists" and have sex with children outside of the United States, even if the practice is not illegal or not prosecuted in that other country. To get the word out, U.S. Immigration and Customs Enforcement has posted prominent signs in places like downtown Phnom Penh, Cambodia, that show a man behind bars with the accompanying statement "Abuse a child in this country, go to jail in yours." If you can be put in prison in a Western country for having sex with underage prostitutes in another country, why would a Western country turn a blind eye to polygamous marriages, even if contracted in another country?

Apparently governments have not yet seen inequitable family law as the serious threat to national security that it is. Such inequity is a hallmark of unmitigated male dominance hierarchies, and societies that embrace such hierarchies, or tolerate them, reap instability, violence, and upheaval. Inequitable family law is not in the first place an issue of religious expression: it is in the first place an issue of gender-based violence and national stability.

Some nations are beginning to understand that proposition. The UK has recently passed the Forced Marriage Act that allows British courts to issue orders of protection for girls whose families are going to send them on "vacation" in their country of origin to become victims of forced marriage. France finally banned polygamy outright in 1993, no matter what the country of origin, and has a fairly successful policy of enforcing "decohabitation," which allows women to move into their own residences with their children.[53]

Muslim communities in these countries are able to adapt, if they are required to do so. For example, in the UK, a civil society group called the Muslim Institute has promoted a new Muslim Marriage Contract, which is completely harmonious with British law but also provides for traditional Muslim elements, such as dower.[54] While the husband keeps his right to initiate divorce (talaq), the wife is also granted an equal right. The husband also waives his right to practice polygamy. The state must insist on this type of adaptation by religious communities if it seeks real security.

MAKE NATIONAL FAMILY LAW EQUITABLE

For those nations with a history of inequitable family law, moving national family law in the direction of greater equity is a crucial move toward greater security. As political scientist Harry Eckstein has put it, "If any aspect of social life can directly affect government, it is the experience with authority that men have in other aspects of life."[55] We believe this applies first and foremost to family law.

As noted above, the nation of Morocco stands as an exemplar in this regard. While Westerners erroneously believe that women's legal rights are incompatible with Islamic law, King Mohammed VI has proven otherwise. The Moudawana, or Family Law, passed in 2004 provides many outstanding examples of how a state can "get" the linkage between the security of women and the security of states. Examples include:

- Legal age of marriage is eighteen for both sexes
- Polygamy is severely constrained, to the point of practical impossibility
- A judge must handle all divorces, even *talaq* divorces in which all that is required is for the husband to say, "I divorce you" three times.
- Children can choose with which parent they wish to live at age fifteen
- Grandchildren from daughters inherit in the same way as grandchildren from sons
- Property is divided equitably after divorce; standard of living for both parties should be similar after divorce
- The duty of a wife to obey her husband is abolished in return for the wife's equal responsibility to support the household
- A divorced wife may retain custody of children even if she remarries

From the point of view of anthropological research, it is the first two items that are the most significant. As we have seen, ensuring that girls are not married at puberty, but several years afterward, and ensuring that polygamy is virtually abolished are two vitally important elements of family law that increase national security. Egypt adds another stipulation, which is also commendable: it forbids marriages between men and women where the age difference is greater than twenty-five years.[56] Also important would be state initiatives to equalize inheritance, especially of land, between male and female heirs, as well as measures to discourage patrilocality, which make brides exceedingly vulnerable to abuse and violence.

We encourage the international community to develop a set of benchmarks in family law, educating and encouraging nations to see equitable family law, and its enforcement in practice, as part of the bedrock of national and international security.

ENACT PRO-WOMEN LEGISLATION

Legislation is a significant means by which the state can advance the situation and security of women. One of the most ambitious and far-reaching recent legislative initiatives is the Philippines' Magna Carta of Women, signed into law in 2009.[57] This Magna Carta is the instrument by which the Filipino government will bring its affairs fully into compliance with CEDAW. In addition to outlawing all forms of violence against women, it requires that each municipality establish a unit focusing on the eradication of such violence.

Other provisions are equally pathbreaking. It commits the government over time to ensuring that high government positions are split fifty-fifty between men and women, and that the media will be required to present nondiscriminatory and nonderogatory portrayals of women. It rectifies remaining vestiges of inequitable family law, such as the priority of the husband's decision making concerning the disposition of household property. Property rights and credit are ensured for women, as well. All in all, the Philippines' Magna Carta of Women is an amazing legislative attack on the lingering inequality faced by Filipino women, and it is remarkable for its comprehensiveness.

Other countries have launched high-visibility legislative campaigns as well, such as Guatemala, with its law against femicide,[58] and Rwanda, with its new Gender-Based Violence Laws.[59] It is noteworthy that still, in 2010, only 89 percent of nations had laws against domestic violence.[60] As we wrote this volume, East Timor, after eight years of existence as an independent nation, finally passed a law against domestic violence. The physical insecurity of women is a critical inequity that must receive priority from the legislative bodies of the state, and then the state must hold its enforcement agencies accountable for the proactive enforcement of the law.

While legislation is sometimes stymied, the open discussion that accompanies the push for measures to improve the conditions of women is a first step. For example, when Egypt amended its divorce laws to make them more equitable for women, there were large street demonstrations against such revision. Eventually, though, the legislation passed. We are seeing the same phenomenon now in Pakistan, where the Council of Islamic Ideology (CII), which advises the government on matters related to religious law, has also called for measures to make divorce law more equitable. "This Council is trying to invent a new sharia," said Mufti Munib-ur-Rehman, a leading conservative cleric who signed a statement with other hardliners criticizing the CII. "They are trying to create anarchy and chaos in the country and if they are not stopped then I fear a movement for enforcement of true Islamic sharia would be launched throughout the country."[61]

Interestingly, while Saudi Arabia inches toward sixteen as the legal age of marriage, Yemen, to the south, is facing stiff opposition in a similar quest, despite horrific cases of young girls dying from intercourse and childbirth after being married as young as age eight to fully adult men. One influential cleric insisted he would gather a million signatures against any legislation that would forbid child marriage. He deemed those supporting a rise in the marriage age as apostates.[62] The weak Yemeni government would rather not upset the micro-level patriarchs whose acquiescence it needs to govern, and it seems likely that the little girls of Yemen will be left with no protection.

CHANGE THE INCENTIVE STRUCTURES

The state has the power to alter the web of incentives and disincentives in which households must operate—and it can do this to the benefit of women. As we have noted previously, some states pay families to send their daughters to school.

Other examples abound. For example, the problem of abnormal birth sex ratios has plagued both China and India. Each state has sought to alter incentive structures for families. In China, a new "Care for Girls" program was launched, which waives school fees for rural girls and guarantees a (small) pension for families that have only daughters. China has also promoted uxorilocal marriages, where a groom marries into his bride's family, supports his in-laws in their old age (something not normally done when an only child, a daughter, goes to live with her husband's parents), and does not pass his surname on to his children. Such families may receive land grants, and the government will build them a house as well.

India has a new pilot program operative in states with the worst sex ratios. If a family has a daughter, they will be paid to keep her with an initial grant of money, and then be paid for various important events, such as vaccinations and school attendance. Then, if the girl reaches the age of eighteen, has graduated from school, and is not yet married, the government will pay several thousand dollars toward her wedding expenses (dowries are technically illegal in India).

Making investment in girls' health and well-being profitable for families is one way in which the state can alter circumstances for the better for women. Furthermore, as we have seen, through proactive enforcement of laws designed to improve the situation of women, the state can ensure that costs rise significantly for those who are tempted to harm women. By both increasing benefits for those who are willing to assist women and girls, and increasing costs for those are not willing, the state can profoundly alter the social context in which its citizens must operate. In effect, the state becomes the alloparent of the girls in the nation.

ENSURE THAT WOMEN ARE VISIBLE AND EQUAL PARTICIPANTS IN ALL DECISION MAKING AND ALL IMPORTANT SOCIETAL ENDEAVORS

One of the most revolutionary changes in human society has been the growing emphasis on including women in the councils of decision making at all levels and in all sectors. In many countries, this has been accomplished through the use of quotas, where a certain percentage of decision-making positions has been reserved for women. These may be found in all branches of government, or they may be at the level of political parties. For example, in France all political parties are required to put forth 50 percent female candidates; whether or not 50 percent of elected candidates are women is up to the electorate.

Sometimes quotas work spectacularly well and sometimes they fail. In some Nordic countries, there is talk of ensuring that there is no less than 40 percent *male* participation in government positions because of the success of quotas. In Rwanda, while the law reserves a third of the parliament's seats for women, Rwandans have recently voted many more women into parliament: the current percentage is 56.25. In other countries, the quota system is laughable — dead women may be placed on the ballot so that men can secretly usurp the slots, or wives may be used as voiceless puppets of the husbands and patrilineal clans that control them. Nevertheless, quotas matter because including women in decision making not only changes attitudes about women and their capabilities; it also changes attitudes about what issues policymakers should address. As Esther Duflo's experiments with Indian panchayats after quotas, or reservations, were implemented show, the longer communities were exposed to seeing women in power in the panchayats, the more accepting they became of women in that role, and the more panchayat policymaking attended to the concerns of women, such as clean water and roads, even after women were no longer in the panchayat.[63] Indeed, the success of the policy at the panchayat level has led Indian lawmakers to contemplate extending the quota system to the state and national governments: the upper house of the national legislature has already approved such legislation.

Ironies abound. While the United States has one of the lowest levels of female representation in the national legislature, the Americans ensured that both of the countries they recently invaded—Afghanistan and Iraq—enshrined quotas for women. Bulgaria now has one of the highest representations in Europe in its executive branch, but the reason for it is that the charismatic male prime minister finds women more pliable to work with than men.[64]

Each society seems to walk the path toward greater female representation in its own idiosyncratic way. So, for example, Saudi Arabia has announced that female lawyers may now appear in court—but only in family court, and only to represent female clients. Egypt, on the other hand, refuses to allow women to serve the Supreme Judicial Council, though they may otherwise be judges. Norway not only has quotas for women in government but also has quotas for women on the boards of publicly traded corporations. Thirty-six percent of the personnel on such boards are women; the highest percentage in the world, and the legislated minimum is 40 percent.[65] Fiji has recently legislated that the minister with the gender portfolio be included as a member of the National Security Council. By government mandate, more than two million women are now involved in the local panchayats of India, bringing water, electricity, and girls' schools to some of the most remote areas of that country.[66]

It is not only at the highest levels that women must be included and visible. When women are visibly making a contribution in public and on the ground, the culture begins to change. One example of this is the Daughters of Iraq unit formed to help combat suicide terrorism in that country. These women—a total of 130 have graduated thus far—are part of the Iraqi security forces, and they are responsible for searching women for explosives. "The women's proudest moment came in March, when thousands of people from across Baghdad, including the country's Shiite prime minister, converged in Adhamiya to celebrate the prophet Muhammad's birthday. The Daughters of Iraq were out in force, patting down women as they approached Abu Hanifa, the city's most revered Sunni mosque. 'A lot of women were happy to see the local women there to protect them,' Dulaimi said. 'They were hugging and kissing us and giving us Pepsis.'"[67] Lamentably, the Daughters of Iraq are an invention of the Americans, and the Iraqi government has no intention of retaining them once the Americans leave. Indeed, when the Iraqi government took control, it stopped paying the women, and many quit to seek paid employment.[68]

There is certainly room for improvement in the visibility and decision making of women. For example, in 2010 the Afghan government, at the prodding of the Americans, held a "peace *jirga*," inviting "moderate" supporters of the Taliban to discuss how they may rejoin the governance structure there as a prelude to the departure of the Americans. Do you believe it would have altered the discussions if fully 50 percent of the Coalition and Afghan government representatives to that *jirga* were women, instead of the paltry 4 percent that were in fact asked to attend? Why didn't the Coalition insist upon that?

KEEP CAREGIVING ECONOMICALLY RATIONAL

Whether fair or not, most of the reproductive work that takes place on earth is performed by women. As we noted in chapter 2, this makes women very economically vulnerable. Abused women may feel they have no choice but to remain in an abusive situation because of the difficulties involved in trying to take care of dependents, whether these be children or the sick or the elderly, while bringing in an income that will support their family. One of the most important roles government can play in the life of women is to promulgate initiatives that help level the uneven economic playing field faced by women, thus diminishing the irrationalities they experience as caregivers.

As we have seen, one important component of this effort is to ensure that both parties have similar standards of living after divorce, or after the death of a husband. When divorce or widowhood can be expected to thrust women and children into poverty, abuse in marriage is perpetuated, a situation that occurs in Western societies just as often as it does in non-Western ones. In some traditional societies, all marital property reverts to the husband's family after divorce or the death of the husband. Several countries, such as Botswana, have rectified such inequities in recent years, especially in light of the AIDS epidemic.

Other helpful government initiatives prohibit discrimination against women in hiring and pay. The Nordic nations have gone furthest in preventing the financial vulnerability of women who have become mothers, by guaranteeing the right of mothers to return to their jobs after a generous paid maternity leave. Other nations may count time spent in caregiving toward government pension allotments. Tax credit schemes may provide a direct infusion of funds to the primary caretaker of dependents. All such measures are praiseworthy, for as social scientist Debbie Taylor has put it,

> The penalties for inequality between women and men are very severe. And they are not borne by women alone. They are borne by the whole world.

Power, tempered by the wisdom and restraint of responsibility, is the foundation of a just society. But with too little responsibility, power turns to tyranny. And with too little power, responsibility becomes exploitation. Yet in every country in the world, power and responsibility have become unbalanced and unhitched, distributed unequally between men and women. . . . The penalties of women's too-great burden of responsibility and their too-small slice of power . . . are hardship, sickness, hunger, even famine. But the penalties of man's disproportionate share of the world's power (without the intimate day-to-day knowledge of the effects of that power, or the responsibility for ensuring that the basic needs of the household are met) are just as great.

Of course, not all men are tyrants or despots and not all women are martyrs to duty and hard work. But masculine and feminine social roles have tilted the majority of men and women in those directions.[69]

It is time, then, for power and responsibility to be married by states. Caregiving must count—really count—in the perspective of national governments.

IMPLEMENT A STATE RESPONSIBILITY TO PROTECT WOMEN (R2PW)

As of 2001, the world began to recognize that states have a Responsibility to Protect (R2P) their citizens, an idea that the UN General Assembly endorsed in 2005. The international community identifies three pillars of R2P:

- States have primary responsibility to protect their populations from genocide, war crimes, ethnic cleansing, and crimes against humanity.
- The international community must commit to provide assistance to States in building capacity to protect their populations from these and assist them both before crises and after crises have broken out.
- It is the responsibility of the international community to take timely and decisive action to prevent and halt atrocities when a State is manifestly failing to protect its populations. The international community has the obligation to intervene at first diplomatically, and as a last result, with force.

It is time to recognize that R2P includes R2PW—a Responsibility to Protect Women. It is time to put the situation of women in the nations of the world as one of the foremost issues facing the international community today. It is time for the UN Security Council and General Assembly to hold nations accountable for how women are treated within their borders. Half of humanity is affected by this issue in the most direct and personal fashion—something that cannot be said about any other international security problem. It is time to make plain the linkage between the security of women and the security of states and the international system. If an R2PW mind-set had been in place, the international community would not have waited until 9/11 to move against the Taliban, for there would have been ample justification to do so years earlier, when women began to be treated like animals under that regime.

The international community is moving in this direction. UNSC Resolutions 1325, 1820, 1888, and 1889 are emblematic, as is the new GEAR (Gender Equality Architecture) and UN Women agency that the United Nations has recently implemented. And yet even GEAR does not require that the United Nations staff include a certain percentage of women. Even UN Security Council members such as the United States do not implement UNSC 1325 in conflicts in which they are involved, such as in Afghanistan and Iraq. UN peacekeeping troops, as we have seen, have been implicated in the sexual and physical abuse of women in areas in which these troops have been deployed. While many have lauded the excellent work that all-female peacekeepers can do in the field, especially in areas with high levels of gender violence, only 2.3 percent of UN peacekeepers and 8.2 percent of UN police are female.[70] There is much work to be done at the international level.

There is also work to be done at the regional IGO level. The EU has been quite proactive in tackling issues of domestic violence and harmful traditional practices concerning women, and ensuring that laws in EU member states harmonize. The Maputo Protocol on the Rights of Women in Africa has been ratified by the majority of states in sub-Saharan Africa, but approximately twenty-six states have yet to ratify it.[71] In 1994 the Organization of American States (OAS) adopted the Inter-American Convention on the Prevention, Punishment, and Eradication of Violence Against Women. Even so, such meetings as the annual Davos World Economic Forum summit where the "big" problems facing humanity are discussed, invite very few women participants (less than 5 percent in 2009)[72] and include almost no mention of problems concerning women on its agenda, sparking a parallel meeting called "Deauville" that includes a better representation of the issues concerning half of humanity.[73]

It is clear that one of the most important first steps the international community must take to put R2PW on the radar of nations is to gather the information necessary to make an informed case for it, and to rank nations according to their level of R2PW. There is simply too much that we haven't bothered to try to know. For example, according to Donald Steinberg, deputy president of the International Crisis Group,

> [I]n pressing for UN action to halt the latest round of violence in eastern DRC in November, a Congolese women's declaration at the Association for Women's Rights in Development could refer only to "thousands of raped women and girls," with no greater specificity. Similarly, an otherwise powerful letter to Secretary-General Ban Ki-moon from the NGO Working Group on Women, Peace and Security could say only that the 66 women treated for rape in Kanyabayonga in North Kivu "represent only a fraction of the crimes of sexual violence being committed throughout the region." [A]dditional authoritative data from the ground are essential in to meeting [sic] the "threshold of credibility" needed to build political will, providing measurement tools to assess new and on-going efforts at prevention, developing specific provisions and programs to maximize our efforts, and ensuring that the critical mass of officials from international organizations, governments and civil society that came together to adopt Resolution 1820 will remain together in the face of shrinking resources that will require tough trade-offs.[74]

We have already noted the need for gender-disaggregated statistics to be produced by national governments; we also need the infrastructure to mandate the phenomena studied by national statistical bureaus. In particular, we need more and better statistics on violence against women, especially violence within the home. Excellent frameworks for the monitoring and collection of such data do exist,[75] but what is missing is the political and international will to implement them. Such frameworks must be multivariate— after all, if you knew only that the representation of women in South Africa's national legislature was one of the highest in the world, would that compensate for not knowing that South Africa has by far the highest rape rate in the world?

Such a multivariate ranking of R2PW not only would serve as a mechanism for action against states that are egregious in their negligence concerning their obligations, but also could help to focus state efforts in areas of particular concern. For example, while most view Sweden as a haven for women, reports indicate that levels of domestic violence in Sweden have spiraled upward in recent years.[76] A detailed and comprehensive analysis of R2PW-relevant measures could be useful in spotting such problems early.

In addition, such an analysis would promote the "impact-on-women" studies that we have advocated should take place before the enactment of any new economic or security policies within a nation. If this indicator system were longitudinal, it could become an extremely useful way to monitor and even forecast likely effects of new policy initiatives on women. This would promote a more holistic approach to policy evaluation than we have now. For example, measures of GDP often exclude women's reproductive unpaid labor, masking policy effects on the rationality of caregiving in society. A new set of measures would remove this opacity concerning women and their labors.

It is imperative to track the discrepancy between a state's international obligations to women, national laws, and the real situation of women on the ground. At the WomanStats Project, we code a multivariate scale of such discrepancy (map 11). The information exists to monitor states' obligations to R2PW, as this map shows.

Academics and researchers have a critical role to play here as well. Inquiry and empirical evidence are at a premium; there needs to be a robust academic research agenda to elucidate the linkage between the security of women and the security of states. At the WomanStats Project, we aim to be part of that contributive effort. But questions remain: are academics in international relations and security studies asking the right questions? For example, is anyone asking whether military intervention improves the security of women? Is anyone asking whether an influx of IMF or bilateral loans changes the situation of women for the better? No one really knows—but this information would provide crucial input for quality policymaking.

Similarly, there are important historical questions that have been neither raised nor answered. When nations make the transition to greater levels of gender equality, which changes have they implemented first? Which other changes then follow? Are there regional or religious variations involved? Can researchers trace the path dependence of nations that have more fully made that transition to greater gender equality? Can nations learn from other nations? For example, what paths did nations like Morocco and Tunisia take to curtail polygamy? Could those be used in other areas of the Islamic world? These types of historical inquiries should not shy away from indicating how nations that currently enjoy relative gender equality could improve their own situation.

With this pertinent knowledge in place, with a tracking and monitoring indicator system, the international community would be poised to do more than ruminate on the problems facing women. The international community would be in a position to apply sanctions—yes, sanctions—to those states that failed in their R2PW.[77]

A FARTHER SHORE

Should the world ever take seriously the concept that the two halves of humanity must be true and equal partners for humankind to flourish, we see a farther shore to which we might aspire to travel. Glimpses of that shore are visible even now.

For example, the 2009 Nobel Women's Initiative Conference issued an extraordinary statement:

> We call upon all states and multilateral institutions to recognize that the democratization process is incomplete, and does not end with elections. No country or society can claim to be democratic when the women who form half its citizens are denied their right to life, to their human rights and entitlements, and to safety and security. Despite this, we women have made extraordinary efforts to democratize the institutions of society that frame our lives and the well-being of all humanity—the family, the community, clan, tribe, ethnic or religious group, political, legal, economic, social and cultural structures, and the media and communications systems. But our search for justice is continually overwhelmed by the violence perpetrated upon us, by the exploitation and colonization of our bodies, our labor, and our lands; by militarization, war and civil conflict; by persistent and increasing poverty; and by environmental degradation. All of these forces affect us, and our children, far more severely and in unique ways. We know that democracy that comes from the heart is not the rule of the majority, but safeguards dissent and difference with equal rights, and fosters a culture of peace. We are in search of democracy that transforms not just our lives, but all society—and we will not be silenced until it is achieved in every part of the world.[78]

Perhaps it is time to redefine the very term "democracy," to insist that its definition include only those states that have made the greatest strides toward gender equality. Perhaps, then, we should make the world safe for this understanding of democracy, reorganizing IGO and alliance commitments according to one's position in the global clash of gender civilizations. Maybe there should be a government list of "state sponsors of gender terror," and that list should prompt sanctions equivalent to those placed on the current "state sponsors of terror" list.

Could we also envision a form of government where every position is staffed by both a man and a woman? Where we would not think of electing only a man or only a woman to be president, but could conceive only of electing a male-female team to be president? Could we envision a society where men and women are co-presidents of human collectives at every level, from the household to the city to the state to the military to the nation and to the international community?

Humankind would finally be as a bird with two good, strong wings. Those wings would take us all where we have never flown before.

6

WINGS OF NATIONAL AND INTERNATIONAL RELATIONS, PART TWO
Effecting Positive Change Through Bottom-Up Approaches

THE WOUNDING OF OUR world's women can seem overwhelming. Even well-intended top-down efforts to provide women with physical security, equity in family law, and opportunities to participate in social and political decision making face many obstacles and may take time to make a difference on the ground. While every top-down approach must be pursued, we cannot simply wait for large organizations and governments to act. Furthermore, top-down efforts will almost certainly be more effective if there is a mirroring effort at the social level. We must further the cause at every level of society, including at the grassroots level, where we can work to protect one woman, and then another, and then another, until more and more women benefit from our efforts. It is reported that Mother Teresa once said, "If I look at the mass, I will never act. If I look at the one, I will."[1]

Bottom-up efforts to improve the status of women are perhaps most needed in countries of the world where government leadership is openly patriarchal and resistant to change. But even governments that proclaim their commitment to improving conditions for women often do not give that commitment the priority it deserves, as they are slow to enact policies and laws that would really make a difference for women. In recent years, some individuals have taken the matter into their own hands and joined their efforts with those of others, creating a groundswell of successful bottom-up work to bring about small changes wherever they can.[2] Women, frequently in concert with men, are starting to make a difference, and their voices are beginning to be heard. While gendered microaggression and structural inequities, as outlined in chapters 1 and 2, appear daunting, the agency of women can never be fully repressed; as we shall see, it finds ever new and creative means of expression.

Over the years as we have studied these issues, we have noticed a wide variety of efforts that appear to have made an important difference for women in many societies around the world. What we would first like to offer is an overview of strategies that we judge to be most commonly associated with successful efforts. Then we will turn to the question of what, more precisely, the pressure points should be. That is, what are the steps involved in real change for women? What do empirical researchers argue should be the skills taught to change a culture of violence and exploitation of women? Last, we ask you to turn your attention inward: how can you further the vision of gender equality by making changes in the way you interact with the women in your life? Many of the examples in this chapter come from Islamic nations, since they exhibit the unique confluence of explicit codification of inequity in family law along with many of the most vibrant and innovative bottom-up initiatives to ameliorate such inequity.

SUCCESSFUL BOTTOM-UP STRATEGIES

BEGIN WITH ONE VOICE, ONE ACT, ONE SMALL STEP

The simplest way to start bringing about changes in the lives of women is to ask for it. In 2009, an eight-year-old girl in Saudi Arabia asked Prince Khaled al-Faisal, the governor of Mecca and one of the most senior members of the Saudi royal family, why it was that only boys could play sports. Prince Khaled replied that he hoped to see sports courts for girls inside girls' schools, a sentiment that he had never before expressed. One small child with one small question brought about the strongest and most high-level endorsement yet for a change in the strict regulations that prohibit physical education classes for girls and female participation in the Olympics.[3]

Nisha Sharma created headlines and a new standard for Indian women when with one decision she sent her groom to prison just moments before their wedding. Nisha had met her groom through a classified ad that her parents placed in a newspaper, a common occurrence in India, where arranged marriages are still highly valued. Munish Dalal, a computer engineer, had impressed the Sharmas, and both families went forward with plans for a marriage. Although dowries were prohibited by law, the age-old tradition has survived in the form of extravagant housewarming gifts for the couple and the groom's family, which the Sharmas provided.

On the day of the lavish wedding with live music, two thousand guests, food, and a dowry of two televisions, two home theater sets, two refrigerators, two air conditioners, and one car, the groom's family demanded an illegal cash payment of $25,000. When Nisha's father said he couldn't pay, the Dalals erupted in anger, and an outbreak ensued between the two families. In the midst of the chaos, Nisha reached for her cell phone and called the police. When the police arrived, they encouraged the families to proceed with the ceremony, but Nisha refused, saying, "If they treated [my father] so badly, they probably would have done the same to me, or worse." In fact, in India it is not uncommon for resentment over small dowries to be connected to suspicious "kitchen fires," which have been responsible for the deaths of several thousand newly married women each year.

Thus, the wedding was embarrassingly canceled, the groom and his mother were arrested, and Nisha became the face of the modern Indian woman. She was hailed for her courageous decision in a situation that often brings shame and mockery upon the bride's family. Shortly after this single decision, similar stories of brave brides and greedy grooms surfaced, with the women following Nisha's example. Six months later she married a computer hardware engineer—*without* a dowry.[4]

Pervinder Kaur arrived in New York as a bride from India to be married to a wealthy man. Instead, vulnerable and knowing very little about America, she was trapped as a prisoner by her new in-laws. They forbade her from making friends outside the family, and her husband beat her and tried to coerce her to turn over money. She had the presence of mind to take a single step and make two phone calls. The first call was to the police, who sent her to the hospital. And the second call was to a support group, Sakhi ("female friend"), that was run by volunteers who help women, one at a time. The women are usually from India, Bangladesh, Pakistan, Nepal, and the Caribbean. Sakhi is part of a growing movement across the country that confronts taboo social issues and hidden abuses in immigrant families. They teach the women about their rights and how to exercise them, help them find safe places to live, provide language assistance and legal advice, and even accompany them to court or interviews with the police. Pervinder recounts the comfort she found in discovering a familiar culture. "They spoke so nicely to me. They talked in my language. Until then, I could not talk about it, what had happened. I always started to cry."[5]

Gang rapes sanctioned by tribal councils as a form of honor revenge are not uncommon in Pakistan, and any self-respecting woman is expected to commit suicide afterward. Instead, Mukhtar Mai, a Pakistani woman from a poor village, prosecuted her rapists and used the compensation money to open schools, provide an ambulance service, and begin a women's aid group. Women and girls stagger into Mukhtar's small remote village with horrendous stories and pleas for sanctuary. Each night a dozen women share Mukhtar's bedroom, and while providing rest, she connects them with the services they need. The cases range from a seven-year-old girl who was raped by a servant of a wealthy family to a thirty-year-old woman who was raped and tortured by eight men for two days. Although under death threats, both victims courageously decided to push forward with the legal aid arranged by Mukhtar.

For another woman, Mukhtar arranged for the prosecution of her assailant and also for three surgeries to repair her nose, which had been cut off, a traditional Pakistani punishment for women. And after the star pupil of the fourth grade in her school was pulled out by her parents to be offered as a child bride to resolve a family conflict, Mukhtar intervened and returned the nine-year-old to school so she could pursue her plans to become a doctor. Mukhtar has been celebrated worldwide for challenging and transcending the violence against women right around her, one woman at a time.[6]

In Afghanistan, the government has been unable to offer all of the needed services for women, including the safe and healthy delivery of babies. The country has the second-highest death rate in the world for women during pregnancy and childbirth—26,000 women die each year. The main causes of death are hemorrhaging and obstructed labor. Most of these deaths could be prevented if trained help was present. Pashtoon Azfar is the head of the Afghan Midwives Association, and since the fall of the Taliban, she has been working night and day to restore the practice of midwifery. She sees this service as a way to save the lives of thousands of women and babies.[7]

Another midwife in Afghanistan, Nasima Kuchi, goes door-to-door teaching women about safe childbirth procedures such as making two knots in the umbilical cord and then using clean string and a clean razor to cut it, not putting lipstick on the belly button of the baby where the umbilical cord has just been cut in hopes of giving the baby redder lips, and not feeding a newborn tea and sugar as a substitute for mother's milk.[8]

In Reina, an Arab town in northern Israel, Israa Zarura has founded a widows' center. It started as a place for widows to gather for breakfast and friendship, but it has slowly evolved and now offers all kinds of services and support to help women get out of the house and become more independent. Israa explains, "Arab society is very traditional, and if a widowed woman decides to go out and work, it is often frowned upon, even if she is doing it to support her family."

One woman who has benefited from the center is Horeya Abo Gohar, whose husband died thirteen years ago, leaving her to raise five children. She explained, "I have learned so much from coming here. It has taken me a long time but I have finally realized that whatever a man does I can do too . . . [T]his center gave me the strength to understand that. In the beginning I thought I would not be able to do anything with my life . . . but last year I found the strength to open my own business as a child minder, and now I take care of other women's children so that they can go out to work."[9]

One of the most stirring cases in recent years illustrating the power of one step is that of Nujood Ali, a ten-year-old Yemeni girl who was married in 2007 at age nine without her consent to a man in his thirties. After her husband forced himself upon her, beat her, and took her out of school, she took the amazing step of hailing a taxi for the first time in her young life. She had heard that judges in courts granted divorces, and she was determined to see a judge. After arriving at the court building, she waited in the hallway, asking to see a judge. The judge was shocked by her story, and he made a momentous decision both for himself and for the country: "I am going to help you."[10] Still another judge took her into his home to protect her, and a female lawyer, Shada Nasser, agreed to represent her; her divorce was granted. Nujood recently won *Glamour* magazine's award for Woman of the Year. She wants to become a lawyer and is helping to raise funds to fight child marriage in Yemen. All of this came from one little girl having the courage to raise her hand to hail a taxi.[11]

In each of these instances, a single individual made one decision—to ask a question, to refuse to give in to social pressure, to reach out for help, or to help others. Such small acts of prosocial behavior significantly affected other women around that individual, and the circumstances in which those women lived started to improve. No act to redress the suffering of women is too small; take one small step wherever you can.

WHEREVER POSSIBLE, ENGAGE OTHERS IN YOUR CAUSE, SPREAD THE WORD, AND ORGANIZE

Having been raped when she was six years old, Betty Makoni understands the devastation that comes from such a traumatizing experience, and she works unceasingly to campaign for protection for young girls in Zimbabwe. The risk for these girls is greater because of the widely held belief that if a man with HIV or AIDS rapes a virgin, he will be cured of his disease. This belief has resulted in tragic cases, including the rape of a day-old baby. As a teacher, Betty began to notice that girls were dropping out of school at an alarming rate, and so she created a space where the girls could talk about the abuses they were experiencing and find solutions. This was the beginning of Betty's Girl Child Network, which grew to more than a hundred GCN clubs by the end of the first year. This organization has now rescued more than 35,000 girls who, according to Betty, would have died. Today GCN has seven hundred girls' clubs and has established three empowerment villages, havens for girls who have been abused. By turning her own tragedy into working for solutions through an extensive network of engagement, Betty has assisted an estimated 700,000 young girls.[12]

Sometimes activists will not even know the extent of support for the cause of women in their own society until they step forward and ask for that support. Promised reforms in Kuwait after the first Gulf War raised hopes that women's suffrage would soon result, but it was only in 2005 that Kuwaiti women were finally allowed to vote. One of the main advocates for change was Dr. Massouma al-Mubarak. After receiving a PhD from the University of Denver, she returned to Kuwait, where she has been a political science professor, a columnist, and a political pundit. In all of these positions her main focus has been to raise awareness among women and men about the status of women in Kuwait. When women did receive the right to vote, they also gained the right to serve in the government, and so in 2005 Mubarak was asked to serve as the minister of planning—the first female ever to serve in a Kuwaiti cabinet.[13] Then, in 2009, she and three other women were elected as the first female members of parliament. In the weeks leading up to the election, Islamists urged Kuwaitis not to vote for women, but all four women were elected in defiance of such calls. The majority of Kuwaitis celebrated the historic election with fireworks and parties, all because Mubarak set out to raise awareness and encourage the participation of women.[14]

With one in every two women in South Asia facing socially supported violence in her daily life, a coalition of more than six hundred organizations from Bangladesh, Sri Lanka, India, Nepal, and Pakistan is working to change attitudes that justify violence against women at the individual, community, and society levels. The "We Can" campaign intends to create a popular movement to do away with social support for violence against women. This campaign is mobilizing five million ordinary men and women—"Change Makers"—to speak up and stop violence against women. Each "Change Maker" in turn is asked to influence ten others, in this way symbolically linking up with the 50 million "missing women" in the region.[15]

"The two messages that are repeatedly communicated are that women are no less valuable than men and that violence against them is unacceptable." It is the position of this movement that deeply entrenched attitudes can be changed only by many people working together. Eighteen-year-old Kavitha of Chowdaripatti village, Nalagonda district, Andhra Pradesh, India, says, "Before becoming part of the campaign, I was accustomed to remaining silent at home and accepting everything I was told. But now I request my father to accommodate my mother's needs and hear her out so that her opinions can also be taken into account. I have been explaining the contents of the campaign communication material to people in the village in the hope that men in other families will do the same as my father. I do not know whether I will succeed but I am trying."

Many other examples of changes in attitudes suggesting that violence is less tolerated have been credited to the campaign. In Nepal, a group of boys who had been enlisted as Change Makers in the We Can campaign and were wearing their We Can T-shirts saw some girls being harassed. The boys rushed to intervene and persuaded the troublemakers not to continue in such behavior. Other boys who had not worn their T-shirts ran home to put them on and returned to the scene. In such small ways, change is beginning, and the organization of individual efforts to bring about change in the acceptability of violence against women increases the power to transform social attitudes.

USE TECHNOLOGY TO AMPLIFY YOUR MESSAGE

One of the more visible accounts of using technology to speak out to thousands and thousands is that of Rania al-Baz, a popular Saudi TV host. During her segments on a show called *The Kingdom This Morning*, she would wear colorful *hijabs* and never cover her face. Her life all changed on one evening in April 2004, when her violent husband pounded her face into a marble floor until he thought she was dead while their five-year-old son watched. As her husband drove to dispose of her body, she started to regain consciousness, so he dropped her off at an emergency room, saying she had been in an accident. She lay in a coma for four days. While she was recovering, her father took photos of her disfigured face, which had thirteen factures.

Knowing that in Saudi Arabia domestic violence was commonly carried out but seldom talked about, Rania decided to go public. Two weeks after the beating, she allowed the photos of her face to be published. News of the attack and of her brave and unprecedented stand spread worldwide.

When asked about her decision, Rania explained, "All my professional life, I had been on television, trying to get people, especially women, to talk about the day-to-day dealings of their lives. And now this has happened in my life—and I am not going to talk about it? Can I tell their stories, but not even tell my own? So I decided that whatever the price, I had to tell the truth. I wanted to be some kind of window into what is actually happening to women in my country. I had no choice but to speak out." And thousands upon thousands heard her.[16]

Waris Dirie, a native of Somalia, is another public figure who chose to speak out about violence against women. When she was five years old, her mother held her down while another woman cut off parts of her genitals with a razor blade and then sewed up what remained, leaving only a small opening for urination.[17] Waris fled Somalia at age thirteen to escape an arranged marriage to an older man and ended up in London. There she grew up to become a world-class supermodel and a James Bond girl. In her professional travels she came to realize that the world had no idea about female genital cutting (FGC) and what was being done to countless girls in the name of promoting chastity. So she threw herself into a campaign to inform people. She wrote an autobiography about her experiences, *Desert Flower*, and later she allowed it to be made into a movie. She also served as a UN special ambassador for the elimination of female genital cutting. In 2002 she established the Waris Dirie Foundation, dedicated to helping everyone in the world recognize that genital cutting is a problem in many countries; to getting religious communities to take a clear stand against the practice; to being sure that every FGC victim who needs help gets it, and to getting governments to pass legislation that will bring perpetrators and their accomplices to justice.[18]

In February 2010, the Waris Dirie Foundation, along with six other NGOs working to eliminate FGC, sponsored a provocative ad campaign with a very attractive blond model covered only by her arms and hands. As the lens pans across the curves and delicate features of her body, the words "beautiful," "wonderful," and "unique" appear on the screen. The advertisement then ends with a concluding and condemning comment: "Just cut out her clitoris, and she'd be perfect."[19]

Television also brings news, talk shows, and educational programs into homes that help to change women's perspectives. In more closed societies, like Saudi Arabia or Iran, these programs are often received via satellite from foreign broadcasting companies, including some Arab-based stations like al-Jazeera out of Qatar and Dubai TV. Two examples of such programs are a 2008 debate between a Saudi cleric and a Saudi women's rights activist on marriage, guardians, driving, and other women's issues,[20] and *The Oprah Winfrey Show*, which did not tackle Islamic-specific issues but certainly introduced new and interesting ideas to women. From its first broadcast in Saudi Arabia in 2004, *Oprah* was an instant hit and became the highest-rated English-language (with Arabic subtitles) program among women age twenty-five and under. According to Katherine Zoepf of the *New York Times*, "Ms. Winfrey provides many young Saudi women with new ways of thinking about the way local taboos affect their lives along with a variety of issues including childhood sexual abuse and coping with marital strife. Above all, Ms Winfrey assures her viewers that no matter how restricted or even abusive their circumstances may be, they can take control in small ways and create lives of value, and she helps them 'find meaning in their . . . existence.'"[21]

Film, too, is challenging ideas in closed societies and is being used as a way to bring about change. A few years ago Tunisian filmmaker Kalthoum Bornaz considered the issue of inheritance rights for women in her movie *Shtar Mahaba* (Half the Love). The story focuses on twins, Selim (male) and Selima (female). When Selima was still young, she learned about Islamic inheritance laws and asked her father if her getting only half of the amount her brother got meant that her father loved her only half as much. When opposition arose against the film, director Bornaz countered that she had made the movie not to challenge inheritance practices but as a way "to discuss the issue of inheritance from a humane and social perspective."[22] Filmmakers in Iran also are beginning to see film as way to bring about change. Female documentary filmmaker Mahnaz Mohammadi explained that "we make films to change the status quo."[23]

One such female filmmaker is Tahmineh Milani, who makes movies about the violation of women's rights and hopes thereby "to create positive changes" in society.[24] A partial list of some of the movies she has created shows her passion for portraying the injustices that women face in modern-day Iran.[25] *Two Women* (1999) focuses on the hurdles, including domestic violence, that two female architectural students encounter in trying to fulfill their dreams. *Vakonesh Panjom* (The Fifth Reaction, 2003) explores the issue of custodial rights through the story of a widow who struggles against her father-in-law to maintain custody of her children and ownership of her home. The more recent *Payback*, released in 2010 after a ban of three years by Iran's Ministry of

Culture and Islamic Guidance, is about four wronged women who meet in prison and vow upon release to pay back the men who caused their unjust imprisonment. To do so, they pose as prostitutes to lure the men to a place where they are bound, given a moral lecture, and then a beating.[26] There are also many other films that explore women's issues.[27] In *Buddha Collapsed Out of Shame* (2007), by Hana Makhmalbaf, a young girl in Afghanistan struggles against the odds to attend a school for girls across the river. In the documentary *Murderer or Murdered?* (2005), Mahvash Sheikholeslam looks at the lives of six women who are on death row for the murder or attempted murder of men who were abusive. And male filmmaker Mehrdad Oskouei created the documentary *The Other Side of Burka* (2004), which looks at the increasing number of women who are committing suicide on the southern Iranian island of Qeshm "because they have no other way out of their marriages."[28]

From the privacy of home, newer forms of technology are also empowering women and letting their voices be heard. Women who have limited access to movie theaters, video stores, or satellite TV stations can now watch those shows and movies on YouTube via their cell phones, and they can also share their thinking about them. As we noted in chapter 5, technology is creating a "Radio Free Women," in a sense. When activist Wajeha Huwaider wanted to vent her frustration at the ban on women being allowed to drive in Saudi Arabia, she made a three-minute video that showed her breaking the ban and driving on a highway. She then posted the video on YouTube in commemoration of the 2008 International Women's Day.[29] Her jaunt was reminiscent of a similar feat in 1990 when dozens of women drove through the streets of Riyadh in protest. The driving campaign also included an online electronic petition for King Abdullah.[30] In 2008 Wajeha posted a video on YouTube in which she called for an end to the ban on women's sports and on Saudi women's participation in the Olympics. The video showed five women covered in long black *abayas* sitting in the middle of a soccer field with their hands and feet taped together.[31]

Social networking sites are also important new ways of getting the word out. In 2006 and under pressure from women activists, Saudi Arabia passed a law stipulating that only women can work in stores that sell women's apparel. The law was meant to remove men from positions in which they interact with women as they sell them bras and panties. As with many other laws relating to women, this law has not been put into practice. The impropriety of such an awkward sales relationship between a salesman and a female customer was duly noted by one Saudi coed, who said, "He's totally checking the girls out! It's just not appropriate, especially here in our culture."[32] In an effort to have the law enforced and to get women working in lingerie shops, college lecturer Reem Assad turned to Facebook, where she created a site titled in Arabic "Women's Undergarments for Women Only." The site, with comments in both Arabic and English, has over 5,700 members, and the law is now being more consistently enforced.[33] Also in Saudi Arabia, MySpace was used by an all-girl rock band. Although they are forbidden from playing in public, they are able to post their music, which can then be downloaded by young Saudis.[34]

Web sites and blogs are other digital tools increasingly used in the Islamic world. In Iran, for example, women mobilized to change laws on marriage, divorce, adultery, and polygyny by organizing the Campaign for One Million Signatures. Because of governmental suppression, it is increasingly difficult to collect signatures through traditional methods of canvassing. This online effort centered on its Web site (www.we-change.org), but the movement has met with strong governmental opposition, including the jailing of several score of its members, prohibiting other members from leaving the country, and the blocking of its Web site more than eighteen times. Still, it has had an impact. One of its founders, Susan Tahmasebi, notes: "We feel we achieved a great deal even though we are faced with security charges. No one is accusing us of talking against Islam. No one is afraid to talk about more rights for women anymore. This is a big achievement."[35]

A mother of three and postgraduate student who is also the anonymous author of Saudiwoman's weblog uses the Web to disseminate her writings, many of which deal with women's issues.[36] In various posts she has condemned the arranged marriage of a sixty-five-year-old man to an eleven-year-old girl and attacked the Saudi gender apartheid that is found in all sectors of society, including women's sections in government ministries that are housed inside buildings and accessed through back doors. In several posts she calls for change in the driving laws. While this blog is perhaps limited in its influence, the number of positive comments on it shows that technology facilitates the discussion on women's issues and that they are of interest to many.

Silence Speaks is an international digital storytelling initiative offering a safe environment for telling stories that too often remain unspoken. Participants from all over the world share and bear witness to tales of struggle and courage, resulting in short digital videos. These first-person stories aim to challenge media legacies by ensuring that workshop participants, not producers, have primary control over what is shared and how events and people are portrayed. The guiding vision is to listen deeply, facilitate reflection and transformation, and encourage involvement in collective action to support justice. Since 1999, Silence Speaks has led more than thirty-five intensive media production workshops across the United States and in South Africa, Brazil, Australia, and Uganda specifically to assist survivors and witnesses of gender-based violence in sharing their stories. The participants talk with courage and honesty about how domestic violence, childhood sexual abuse, and sexual assault have affected their lives.[37] Technology can help us see what has gone unseen, and in this way it opens the space for a reconsideration of the situation of women in society.

NEVER GIVE UP, KEEP UP THE PRESSURE, PRESS ON, STAND READY

Tenacity is a virtue when you are trying to change conditions on the ground for women. This is reflected in the history of women's rights in the West. It is instructive to remember that Switzerland did not give women the right to vote until 1971. Princeton University did not admit women until 1969; Johns Hopkins in 1970; Columbia in 1983. In the year we pen this volume (2010), the U.S. Navy has for the first time announced that women officers may serve aboard submarines. Thus, when we think of the long road ahead in countries where women still do not have the right to vote, or where there are no laws against domestic violence, we must remember how tenacious our own foremothers had to be in pursuing these causes.

Consider the decades-long effort to allow women to even play sports in Iran. Following the 1979 revolution, athletic opportunities for women were severely curtailed, with most sports being banned. For years it looked as though women might never be able to play golf, ski, or play soccer again. Part of the problem was that it was difficult to play a number of sports in a billowing chador or cumbersome coat. Then things began to change—slowly. Perseverance was required. Dress codes eased up a bit and women were allowed to wear smaller headscarves and body-hugging tunics. In addition, the official sports federation started to urge women to play certain sports, in part because Iran was once again interested in participating in international sporting events for women. This change was instigated in the early 1990s by Faezeh Hashemi, daughter of the country's president at the time, Ali Akbar Hashemi Rafsanjani. These gradual changes, over a period of twenty years, have now made it possible for women to take up the sport of golf again, and they are doing so in increasing numbers.[38]

Sometimes the best way to pursue change might be to seriously and continuously prepare yourself for the day when opportunity will knock. Who would have thought that one day women would be designing mosques or that they would be able to worship in an inviting space? In Turkey, with its long tradition of magnificent mosque architecture, a woman interior designer has shaken things up with a new mosque, whose interior she designed with "women in mind." The *mihrab*, indicating the direction of prayer, is bright turquoise and in the shape of a seashell, and the *mimbar* (pulpit) is made of acrylic rather than of the traditional wood or stone. Perhaps most importantly, unlike most mosques where women are segregated into poorly lit, partitioned-off back sections and balconies, this mosque positions the women's section in a well-lit open balcony with a nice view of the beautiful central chandelier.[39] For many years to come, women will be psychologically uplifted and better able to worship in such an inspiring setting, never before available to them. Fortunately, one woman prepared herself well long before she was given an opportunity to use her training in such a beneficial way for women.

Several scholars have noted that the most impressive progress for women has occurred when women stood ready and organized to press for their demands during times of unforeseen upheaval. As noted in chapter 5, when the emir of Kuwait was able to bring pressure again on parliament in 2005 to extend suffrage to women, the parliament was considering a partial suffrage in municipal elections only. Sensing that the moment was now or never, women's groups reached out to other groups in society and organized the largest demonstration in Kuwaiti history, creating the momentum for the emir to push through full and complete suffrage for women in a whirlwind of events. If women had not been ready when the moment came, they might never have achieved their goal.[40]

Civil or interstate war, or irregular regime transitions, can also provide opportunities for women, if women are ready to seize them. At these times of upheaval, if women are organized and tenaciously push their cause, remarkable progress can be achieved. We can see this dynamic in Rwanda, where organized women's groups stood ready to press for gains in the wake of the genocide of 1994 and the subsequent reconstruction of the government. Rwanda now boasts the highest percentage of women legislators of any country in the world—more than half of the legislators in the country are women.

We also see this in Liberia, where women's groups played an important role in forcing a peace settlement and helped elect Ellen Johnson-Sirleaf as the first postwar president of that nation. Alternatively, when women are not organized, they may find their position eroded by the sweep of events. At the time of this writing, for example, the overthrow of Hosni Mubarak in Egypt has occasioned the creation of an extraordinary constitutional committee that will oversee the legal reform necessary to hold new elections. Ominously, there is not one woman on that committee, despite the fact that there are many able women jurists in Egypt, and the quota for women in the national legislature was summarily eliminated. Women must always be ready to seize such moments, lest they find when the dust finally settles that women's concerns are being overlooked or even newly threatened.

While such revolutionary moments can provide rapid progress (or regress) for women, oftentimes change for women comes more slowly, over the course of several generations. Tenacity can mean riding the tiger of upheaval and revolution, but tenacity can also mean putting one foot in front of the other every day, every month, every year, every decade until change endures. For example, change has slowly been creeping forward among the Masai in Kenya. Although the Masai are deemed the most traditional of Kenya's forty-two tribes, more and more Masai girls have been attending school, often to avoid being given early in marriage by their fathers. Of the 650 girls at Priscilla Nangurai's school, three-quarters are Masai. While more parents have become obliging about school for their daughters, Priscilla, who denies accusations that she is out to destroy Masai culture, recognizes the deep-seated beliefs of the community. Parents feel that when a girl goes to school she gets spoiled because she gets to a point where she is equal to the men, and she is not supposed to be equal to them or to make her own decisions.

Since the school was founded in 1959 by Protestant missionaries and for the eighteen years Priscilla has been there, it has acquired a reputation for taking in students with troubled backgrounds, from sexual assault to domestic violence. The recent history of the school reveals some compromises made with the culture in order to stay open. The school has erected a fence and imposed family visitation limits to safeguard the girls from being pulled out; and while its policies are far from supporting genital cutting, the school encourages the girls to schedule such a procedure around the holidays to maximize healing time and limit their time away from school. Such compromises have kept the school from becoming what it is fully intended to be, but they have also allowed it to survive. Because it has tenaciously survived, real change can occur over time. In fact, a saying has emerged that captures a growing acceptance of change: "Even the Masai are wearing underwear now." The father of one student, Christine Shuaka, suddenly announced after school one day that she was to be married. He dropped talk of marriage, however, when he was able to see that she was doing well in school and has said that it is very important for her to be educated.[41]

When change for women does not come because it is impeded by culture or religion, some women have chosen to protest, resist, or challenge the system. One of the more poignant accounts of standing up for what is in the best interest of women and the future of their country comes from a girls' school in Afghanistan. We mentioned the story of Shamsia Husseini and her sister in chapter 2. As they were walking to school, some men who objected to education for girls sprayed them with acid. Scars, jagged and discolored, now spread across Shamsia's eyelids and most of her left cheek. These days, her vision goes blurry, making it hard for her to read. Although the attack was meant to terrorize the girls into staying home, it appears to have completely failed. Nearly all of the wounded girls returned to the Mirwais School, including Shamsia, whose face was so badly burned that she had to be sent abroad for treatment. Perhaps even more remarkable, nearly every other female student in this deeply conservative community returned as well—about 1,300 in all. Only a couple of dozen girls regularly miss school now; three of them are girls who were injured in the attack.[42] Never give up.

THERE ARE ALWAYS CULTURALLY SENSITIVE WAYS TO IMPROVE CONDITIONS FOR WOMEN; REDEFINE HONOR AS PROMOTING PROGRESS FOR WOMEN

Some of the most effective efforts in facilitating women's progress and furthering peace require that the agents of change build upon the cultural and religious roots of those with whom they are working—even in cases where one is working with one's own fellow citizens. Whether we speak of the West, the East, or any other region of the world, culture is a powerful force and must be respected. When this approach is used, improvements for women are viewed as being compatible with local values, and when at least some values are shared, some predictable conflicts can be avoided and progress thus expedited. Consider the story of Isnino Shuriye, who was revered throughout northeastern Kenya as an expert female genital cutter. She started out as a young apprentice who held down the legs of girls while her mother performed the procedure; she grew to hold great prestige among her people and earned a substantial income from her skill. However, after a quarter-century of performing the traditional procedure on thousands of girls, she is now an active opponent of it. "I was full of pride," said Isnino. "I felt like I was doing the right thing in the eyes of God. I was preparing them for marriage by sealing their vaginas."

For Isnino, the change began when local members of the grassroots organization Womankind Kenya approached her hut seeking her influential voice in the community. She chased them off her property every time they came until they arrived with religious leaders. As a devout Muslim, Isnino finally listened. These imams were convinced that the tradition of female circumcision was not only harmful but a sin, inconsistent with the teachings of Islam. By their framing the practice of female circumcision as inappropriate within her own religious views, Isnino began to see that the practice should cease. Furthermore, she was told that she would have to compensate the girls she disfigured with eighty camels for each girl. Unable to meet this impossible demand, Isnino sobbed and pleaded. It was explained to her by the religious authorities whom she respected that the only other way she could be forgiven was to seek forgiveness from each girl she had cut. She began visiting the homes of the girls, many of whom were now women. In tears she explained her change of heart and sought their forgiveness, gaining pardon from most. Even though she lost the prestige that she had enjoyed and was even publicly denounced in some mosques, she has continued speaking out against genital cutting.[43]

We see, then, that religious authorities play a crucial role in helping a culture remove impunity from those who hurt and exploit women. For example, in the United States, the case of Juanita Bynum, a black female evangelist who accused her husband, also a black evangelist, of beating and choking her during their five-year marriage, was a watershed event. Bynum's choice to go public with this accusation in 2007 created a firestorm. Domestic violence had been routinely swept under the rug in this culture in the United States, and Bynum was forcing the faith community to take a stand against what had previously been viewed as normal behavior. Since one of the functions of religion is to help its adherents distinguish between good and evil acts, the Bynum case became a teaching opportunity for this religious tradition. Pastors were enjoined to do more than urge reconciliation or increased prayer; they were enjoined to help victims and openly denounce domestic violence from the pulpit.[44]

In Turkey, women have sought greater rights to participate within the organizational structure of Islam. Turkey's religious institutions, to their credit, have taken these requests seriously and have acted to effect progress. They have appointed hundreds of women as preachers (*vaizes*) and as deputies to muftis with the task of monitoring the work of imams in local mosques, particularly as it relates to women. Zuleyha Seker, one of eighteen *vaizes* in Istanbul, explained that she does not give sermons or lead prayers; her main duty is to teach religion classes for women. She said, "In the past, [women] believed anything told to them by their older brother, father, or teacher. But as they are becoming more educated, they are coming up with more questions. We need new answers for new questions." Seker holds a degree in theology and with these new opportunities to teach women, she and others are in unique positions to strengthen women from within the Islamic structure.[45]

Sometimes traditions can be reinterpreted in a way that allows progress for women. Rather than pitting culture in a zero sum game against the rights of women, activists look for a win-win reinterpretation of a cultural practice. For example, though dowry is illegal in India, it is still widely practiced. However, some elite families have asserted that the money they spend on a high-quality college education (and even postgraduate degrees) for their daughters is in fact the dowry they provide to the groom's family. In this case, rather than denying the practice of dowry, they are reinterpreting dowry itself to value educational investment in women.

Whenever better practices for women can be seen as compatible with already accepted theological and cultural foundations, people should not be asked to give up their roots but rather to build upon them. This approach validates core concepts of the self-image and at the same time helps individuals transcend misconceptions with newer, more equitable ways to view women. In a way, roots are necessary for wings.

The work of Kwame Anthony Appiah is noteworthy in this regard. Appiah suggests that invoking the deep honor/shame emotions and simultaneously redefining what honor means is what leads to the swiftest, surest change for the better. In his book *The Honor Code: How Moral Revolutions Happen*, Appiah recounts how Confucian scholar Kang Youwei, through interaction with foreigners, came to feel ashamed of the practice of foot-binding for women. Appiah writes, "In 1898, Kang sent a memorandum to the emperor. 'All countries have international relations, and they compare their political institutions with one another,' he began, 'so that if one commits the slightest error, the others ridicule and look down upon it.' And he added, 'There is nothing which makes us objects of ridicule so much as foot-binding.'"[46] This feeling of shame was one of the crucial turning points in the elimination of that disfiguring and painful practice.

Shultziner and Tetreault note that this same phenomenon occurred as Kuwait moved toward suffrage for women in this century. They quote Mohammad al-Sager, head of the Foreign Affairs Committee of Kuwait, who gave a speech before the Kuwaiti parliament in May 2005 in which he stated,

> We should also talk about the embarrassment that the Kuwaiti delegations feel when they participate in the international parliamentarian conferences, and how they are often bombarded with questions of how Kuwait is denying the identities of some of its citizens. How come Kuwait is not granting women their political rights, which is considered a basic human rights issue? Those who say we respect and revere women as mothers, wives, sisters, and daughters but advocate for them to stay at home should know that such statements are unacceptable because the civilized world would not accept such a point of view.[47]

Honor is a powerful concept, and shame is a potent motivator. We have seen honor work to the detriment of women, but it is also important to consider the ways in which those who care for women could possibly harness the power of honor and shame to serve a better cause by redefining male honor as championing progress for women.

BE CREATIVE, TRY SOMETHING UNUSUAL

Creativity is often a critical key to success. Sometimes the most efficacious way forward is an indirect route. In Saudi Arabia, for example, a group of women came up with an idea to create a women-only hotel, the Luthan Hotel and Spa in Riyadh. Its management and staff, including engineers, IT technicians, and bellgirls, are all women, as are its guests. In a country where jobs for women are limited due to restrictions on male and female intermingling, the hotel has offered employment to women with all kinds of skills. In fact, men are hired only as needed as electricians or plumbers. The hotel is preferred by foreign women travelers, for once they are inside its doors they can remove the required headscarves and long black *abayas* and let their hair down in rooms with pink and purple decor.[48]

In Amman, Jordan, the mobility of women has been given a boost by the installation of new flat sidewalks lined with park benches. According to the urban planners who designed them, the sidewalks were viewed as powerful tools of social planning, tearing down walls between rich and poor, helping a city bereft of an identity to develop a sense of place and ownership. While perhaps not initially intended as such, the new pedestrian pathways and benches have also provided an acceptable way for women to get out and about. Twenty-year-old Reem al-Hambali explained, "If you're a girl and you're just hanging out on a regular street or sitting on a sidewalk, it's considered inappropriate. Everyone will look at you and ask, 'Why is this girl sitting there?' But here it's okay. We can sit here and it's normal."[49]

Sheema Kerma of Pakistan has used theater as a creative way to teach people about women's rights. She resisted great pressure in order to revive theater and dance when everything was banned during General Zia ul-Haq's regime. She did so because she believes that art is one of the most powerful ways to communicate with others and present them with new ideas. Sheema founded Tehrik-e-Niswan (Women's Movement) and has staged plays that consider such forbidden topics as domestic violence, rape, child molestation, and education for girls. Her work is often met with opposition and threats. A few years ago, Sheema's troupe planned to perform a play about girls' education in a large slum in Karachi. The men of the community insisted that they screen the play before any women were allowed to see it. Given the message of the show, the men chose to not allow it. "The decision should have made me sad," Sheema says. "But it only reinforced that this medium is so powerful that people are scared of it. Those men thought the play would inspire or incite women to think for themselves—and that's what we want." In spite of all of her creative efforts, Sheema admits that there is growing resistance to the arts. She laments, "For years, I've been performing in all corners of Pakistan, and no one has shut us down. But the mullahs [clerics] in the crowd are growing in number. I don't know if theater can defeat the fashion of fundamentalism."[50]

While Ann Jones was a volunteer with the International Rescue Committee, she went from country to country on the committee's Gender-Based Violence Unit with a project titled "A Global Crescendo: Women's Voices from Conflict Zones." This project was designed to document all aspects of women's daily lives, including widespread sexual exploitation and wife beating, in order to help them talk together about their problems and create their own agenda for change. The women were given digital cameras and worked in groups of two or three. They were asked to use the cameras to take pictures of their problems and blessings. Once a week for four or five weeks these teams gathered to look at their photos and talk about why they took photographs of the things they did.

The content of the photographs varied widely, some showing men beating women in the house and the street, some showing men throwing women to the ground or wielding sticks to punish women or force them to do things they hadn't the will or strength to do. Others were of abandoned women, often pregnant, with their children, and one was of a woman working knee-deep in a pit of red palm oil while her husband stood by to pocket the proceeds from her sales. In addition, many of the pictures showed women working in fields, forests, and plantations; women harvesting, selling, fetching wood, and carrying water—all bearing witness that violence against women is not just wife beating or sexual servitude. For countless women, it is the relentless forced hard labor of daily life that they must endure just because they are women.

Each project culminates in a photo show. Each photographer selects her most important images and speaks about why she took her photos and what they show about what's right or wrong with the community. In the village of Zatta in Ivory Coast, one woman displayed a photograph of a woman's bruised and bleeding leg, which was only part of her battered body. The woman's husband had beaten her and would have killed her if he had recognized her in the photo. At that moment, it is reported, the chief raised his arm and decreed that the violence women faced in the village must stop. As noted previously, he then invited women to join his council of advisors and all women to attend village meetings. Although this change in this village was a success for the project, in other places the outcome has not been as positive.[51] Nevertheless, the creative use of photographs to help initiate discussions with men and women about issues that are critical to women has begun, which is a success in itself.

We have saved our favorite example of creativity for the last. It is the case of Moudhi, a school headmistress in Riyadh, Saudi Arabia.[52] Refusing to accept the ban on females driving in that country, Moudhi first began her protest by driving herself. When the police stopped her and insisted that she have a driver, she hired a driver—to sit in the back of her car! When the police said that was still unsatisfactory, she began to ride a bicycle in the city streets. Told that even riding a bicycle was not appropriate for women, she took to riding a donkey—a practice documented in the Koran as being the usual mode of transportation for the wives of the Prophet Mohammed. Checkmate, Islamic style: the police were forced to retreat by this impeccable religious logic. Moudhi is now reportedly pressing for "donkey parking" at office build-ings and shops!

INVOLVE MEN IN YOUR INITIATIVES

Men still hold the lion's share of structural power and voice within human societies. Sometimes one's efforts can be much more successful if men are involved with the initiative. It may be that men in patriarchal societies listen only to other eminent men, and what they say will be men's primary source of encouragement to treat women more equitably and humanely.

In the fall of 2009 history was made when for the first time a Palestinian female soccer team competed on the international level by playing a team from Jordan. For team manager Rukayya Takrori, the game was more than just a game. She explained, "In our culture Palestinian women work side by side with the men in the fields and factories. They fight together, demonstrate together. Sometimes she takes the place of the man because he is in jail or is in the mountains, hiding." She then concluded: "Palestinian women can do everything—even football."

The women's team was the brainchild of a man—Jibril Rajoub, the presi-dent of the Palestinian Football Association and the former chief of a feared security organization in the West Bank. In that position of importance, he encouraged the hiring of women in all departments, something that he boasts "erased forever the idea of ladies being only secretaries." When he took over the command of the football association in 2008, he created a women's soccer league. In their first game, the women played before ten thousand cheering West Bank fans, one-quarter of them men. Most of the women played bare-headed, but one Palestinian team member and a few from the Jordanian team wore *hijabs* while playing. Without a man like Rajoub throwing his support and creativity behind the team, we cannot imagine how such an event would ever have happened.[53]

When men change, they can describe the process of change for other men in a way that women cannot. Women for Women International launched its Men's Leadership Program in one province of the Democratic Republic of Congo where there was pervasive gender-based violence and deeply en-trenched barriers regarding gender roles and authority. Educating influential community members has been successful in creating more women's rights advocates among Congolese men. One man describes the program as open-ing his eyes and giving him a new life. He had previously considered his wife to be his property, but his new perspective compelled him to put his property in her name so she would inherit it.

Another man, Kayembe Tshibangu, has continued to spread his new perspective to another fifty-eight families. Before his participation, he believed that his wife was his slave because he had paid the dowry at the time of their marriage, which he supposed gave him the authority to treat her as he wished. He admitted, "I was a complete tyrant in my home . . . because I did not know any alternative way of living." After his involvement in the program, things completely changed. Tshibangu took on a new life, claiming that "my family members and I are now friends, comrades. We talk and laugh together, and there is peace in the home. . . . My wife has become my friend. I now listen to her and take her advice." Afterward, he, joined by his wife and children, traveled from house to house to teach his friends about his new ways. Although they were shocked and surprised, they eagerly listened and were touched, thus forwarding the work with the support of men.[54]

In Syria, a man is the founder and head of the Syrian Women Observatory. Bassam al-Kadi founded the organization in 2005 "with the aim of raising awareness about violence and discrimination against women, children and the disabled." Since then this organization participated in the Say No to Violence Against Women campaign organized by the United Nations Development Fund for Women in 2008; it lobbied for a change to Syrian laws that provided for only a very light sentence for honor killings; and it also fought against a proposed fundamentalist law that was intended to curtail rights for women (which was dropped after a hard-fought campaign).

In his ongoing campaign against honor killings, Bassam had this to say: "The killing of women because they are women is a worldwide phenomenon. The problem with us is not that we kill [women], while others do not, the problem is that we reward the killer by saying that he was defending his honor and therefore of good character."

While these campaigns have been impressive, Bassam feels that the greatest impact has been made in the changes that have been achieved in the way the country's media cover women's and children's issues: "Before the Observatory was founded, you couldn't find more than three articles about honour killings in the Syrian media. Since we launched our campaign, more than 1,000 articles and programmes about honour killings have been aired on local TV channels, radio stations and published in print and online publications." His fundamental position is that women should not be violated because it is simply their right as human beings and as Syrian citizens not to be.

When asked why a man would take on the cause of women's rights, Bassam explained, "Trying to stop violence and discrimination against women is generally defined as defending women's rights. But I believe that by doing so I am also defending men's rights. Women are the *prima facie* victims of violence and discrimination, but men are also victims. When you violate women's rights, restrict their development and treat them as second-class citizens, you create an unstable marital relationship and an unbalanced family. This takes its toll not only on women, but on husbands, children and the whole of society."[55]

The global aid agency Oxfam Great Britain, along with the Lebanese women's rights organization, KAFA, has released the first-ever pan-Arab training guide on practical ways to engage men and boys in the fight to end violence against women. The title of this guide is "Women and Men . . . Hand in Hand Against Violence." Oxfam GB and KAFA have been jointly running a pilot initiative in the Bekaa Valley region of Lebanon and hope to replicate the successful project in other Arab countries. Ghida Anani, KAFA program coordinator of the joint project, said: "Men are part of the problem, but they are also part of the solution. We are against violence, not men. But men in the Arab world almost always dominate the public and private spheres so working with them is strategically critical. If we want to begin making real change in ending violence against women it is simply nonsensical to leave men and boys out of the equation whether it's in Lebanon, Iraq, Egypt, Yemen or anywhere in the world for that matter." In its physical, psychological, and sexual forms, violence against women can be found in the household, the community, and public institutions. Furthermore, it has serious economic, social, and health implications for the whole family, including men and boys. Ghida Anani added: "Poverty increases violence, and in turn, violence increases poverty as abused women are often unable to help support the family. It undermines and destroys women's dignity, confidence, and self-respect, often preventing them from seeking out and taking advantage of opportunities that could better their lives and that of their families. While it is important that women learn about their own rights and how to receive help if they are abused, it is at least equally important that the mindset that allows for men to commit acts of violence begins to change. Because once that changes, the abuse itself will decline."[56]

In summary, the seven strategies that have been presented above have proven to be effective ways to undertake bottom-up changes that would benefit women by decreasing the wounds they receive, healing the wounds they have, and increasing their physical security, their equity in the family and under family law, and their participation in social and political decision making. While these strategies provide guidelines for how to structure bottom-up efforts for effective results, we have not yet described what the most critical areas are that need to be addressed in order for violence against women to be reduced. We turn now to that discussion.

THE THREE CRITICAL STEPS TOWARD CHANGE

Often well-meaning individuals who want to help heal the wounds of women do not know *what* it is that they should do, even if they recognize the aforementioned principles of *how* they should proceed. Although it might appear that any effort that could improve conditions for women would be of value to pursue, researchers have identified steps of change that must be addressed. If we are ignorant of these steps, our efforts to produce meaningful change will not be as effective. Evidence has shown us that focusing on particular areas will bring about change that is more likely to endure than focusing on others. After our examination of hundreds and hundreds of antiviolence programs across the world, with a few specifically designed to decrease gender violence, three specific areas have emerged that must be addressed if the wrongs against women are to be curtailed.[57]

These three critical areas are (1) preventing violence by making violence dysfunctional through creating laws, enforcing them, and modifying the social power of traditions; (2) providing new patterns of thinking and acting that are more likely to keep gender conflicts from arising and resolve those conflicts that do occur; and (3) helping all people to internalize gender-equity principles that are the basis of peaceful interaction with the other sex.

PREVENT VIOLENCE AGAINST WOMEN THROUGH THE USE OF EXTERNAL CONTROLS THAT ENSURE CONSEQUENCES

Efforts that directly prevent violence against women create an atmosphere in which aggression and violence are unlikely because laws and social norms that inhibit cruelty to women and girls are enforced to the detriment of perpetrators. Here is where we see the "pincer" movement described in chapter 5 in action: without top-down efforts to create laws that can be enforced, bottom-up change will be far less likely. Social sanctions and collective behavior can also be powerful tools in punishing violent behavior and thus inhibiting future aggression. Because violence is perpetuated only when it is viewed by the perpetrator as functional or effective in providing what it is that the perpetrator wants, systematically denying the reward or sought-after result will soon extinguish the behavior. It is important, however, that gender violence *never* be allowed to be functional. Even if violence is only occasionally functional, the tendency to be violent will be strengthened, because at each occurrence the perpetrator will gamble that this time will be the time when the desired reward will be forthcoming. It should be remembered that this is only the first step in improving conditions for women. Violence prevention simply helps men and women coexist without overt aggression by repressing violent and antisocial behaviors; it does not teach higher-order social skills that directly help develop peaceful relations between men and women, but it is a necessary step.

Because of the critical role that punishment plays in preventing violence, and the role that laws play in defining what behavior is to be acceptable and what behavior is to be punished, it is very important to keep track of proposed laws and the opinions of those who both oppose and support them. This process is especially important when both sides of the issue see their opinions as being in concert with the teachings of the broader culture. As we mentioned in chapter 2, in March 2009 Afghan legislators quietly passed a law that allows a husband to demand intercourse with his wife every four days. The law, which applies only to the Shi'a of Afghanistan, also determines when and why a wife can go out of her home alone. Appalled at Afghanistan's backsliding, more than a hundred protesters in Kabul called for the law to be repealed, saying it did nothing but legalize marital rape. They were challenged by more than eight hundred counter-protesters who vilified their opponents as agents of the West and not true to Islam. In an effort to defuse the issue, Afghan president Karzai—under intense Western pressure—suspended enforcement and remanded the law to the Justice Department for review. It would have been better if bottom-up forces in Afghan society had had in place a mechanism to monitor the development of such government initiatives, so that pressure, even if that pressure was foreign, could have been applied before the debate became public, since the public debate encouraged open demonstration of the lamentable view that protecting women was somehow un-Islamic.

Even when laws are passed, the challenges associated with implementing and enforcing them are enormous and require scrutiny and vigilance by bottom-up forces. Years after passing the much-hailed 2004 Moudawana (Family Code), which we outlined in chapter 5, Morocco is still struggling with enforcement of the code. One part of the code established eighteen as the minimum age for marriage, but in 2008 more than 31,000 girls under the minimum age were permitted to marry. The code allows judges the right to grant exceptions to the rule, and that they do! Moroccan organizations that worked to get the Moudawana passed are now working to see that it is enforced. Samira Boufaracha, from the association Together for Women's Development, lamented, "Almost every request is granted, which just encourages families to continue this practice, even though when the Moudawana first came in, we thought things would change." Tradition seems to be the main hurdle. One sociologist explained, "Mindsets are much harder to change than laws. Parents living in the midst of poverty and illiteracy continue to believe that girls must be married off as soon as possible. They can't imagine a future outside marriage."[58] Bottom-up groups must develop the infrastructure to monitor the enforcement of laws and also present data on the non-enforcement of law to the general public as well as to the government. As we have mentioned previously, shadow CEDAW reports created by indigenous civil society groups are another excellent venue for publicizing enforcement problems.

Publicizing vivid stories about the punishment of those who harm women is also an important tool that can be used by civil society groups, the media, and the government in concert. Egypt has sexual harassment laws on the books, but it has been only recently that women have stood up and demanded that these laws be enforced. The harassment case of Noha Rushdi Saleh, a documentary filmmaker, is an excellent illustration of this. In 2008, as is common on the streets of Egyptian cities, a driver reached out and fondled her breasts as she was walking past his truck. She protested and the driver tried to drive away, but Noha jumped on the truck; soon it was surrounded by neighbors who volunteered to beat the man and send him on his way. Noha rejected the vigilante approach and decided to press charges. When she went to the police, they tried to talk her out of it, but her father stood by her and told her to file the complaint. In what has become a landmark case, the driver was convicted and sentenced to three years of hard labor.[59]

In a country where, according to one survey, 83 percent of Egyptian women (the number is much higher for foreign women—98 percent) have been sexually harassed and where 97 percent of those indicated they did not report the crime, the case of Noha has inspired real change.[60] As a result of these and other cases, more and more women are choosing to forgo shame and silence and are seeking instead to have laws enforced, thereby allowing the violence against them to be punished. If consistent punishment could be administered in such cases and simultaneously publicized, sexual harassment would greatly decrease. As long as men think they can get away with it, they will continue to do it. A culture of male impunity must be replaced by a culture of strict male accountability.

Even when a behavior is not illegal, strategic publicizing of shocking events can change the political and social context, allowing new legislation to be passed criminalizing what was previously acceptable in society. In May 2009, after three formal attempts, an eight-year-old girl was finally granted a divorce from her fifty-year-old husband in Saudi Arabia.[61] The case reopened the debate about the propriety and legality of allowing young girls to marry. In response to the trial, Saudi columnist Amal al-Zahid called for the outlawing of the "trafficking of child brides—a most reactionary practice that takes us back to the days of concubines [and] slave girls." In a similar and more recent case in the same country, a twelve-year-old girl filed for a divorce from an eighty-year-old man—her father's cousin, whom she had been forced to marry a year earlier.[62] The government-run Human Rights Commission is providing a lawyer for the girl and activists are hoping that this case might result in establishing a minimum legal age for marriage. The government is clearly using the publicity surrounding these cases to press for reform. Once again, we see the pincer of top-down and bottom-up efforts working to produce a positive result. Saudi Arabia is now moving rapidly toward setting age sixteen as the minimum marriage age for girls.

Survivors who are willing to publicly recover from abuse and go on to live normal, happy lives provide another avenue to stymie the functionality of violence. As we mentioned earlier in the chapter, Mukhtar Mai was gangraped by order of a village council as punishment for her brother's alleged illicit relations with a woman from a rival clan. Rather than commit suicide, as many rape victims are expected to do, brave Mukhtar decided to stand up against her attackers in court where the charge against her brother was found to be a cover-up for a different sex crime committed by other clan members. As an additional sign of bravery, Mukhtar then agreed to become the second wife of the policeman who was assigned to guard her when she pressed charges against the rapists. Once again, she shattered the taboos that generally relegate rape survivors to suicide or to a life with no hope of ever marrying. Through her use of legal and social processes to keep her rapists from covering up the real crime and also her determination against all odds to reclaim a normal, happy life, she has become "a symbol of hope for voiceless and oppressed women" in Pakistan.[63]

When laws and the enforcement of laws along with attempts to redefine social mores do not work in eliminating the harsh treatment of women, other extreme measures must be considered to prevent violence against women. The most important thing is that the violence must be stopped. Such was the situation for a group of women in Kenya. Judging by appearances, the village of Umoja looks no different from any another village. But a closer look will reveal a very distinctive characteristic: within the mud huts, walking down the dirt roads, and working throughout the village there are only women. This makes Umoja quite a novelty, especially in the midst of the patriarchal milieu in Africa. Founded more than a decade ago to provide a home to roughly three dozen women, the village is the result of the growing acts of sexual violence committed by British soldiers who trained in the area. Unfortunately, after the rapes, husbands would retaliate against their *wives* and not the soldiers for bringing dishonor and the possibility of STDs. Many of Umoja's inhabitants were chased away by their husbands and barely escaped with their lives, but others left on their own. Together they have created a home in unity, the theme and name of the village.

Rebecca Lolosoli, the leader of the village, remarked upon the extraordinary change that Umoja inspires in the women. "They're healthier and happier. They dress well. They used to have to beg. Now, they're the ones giving out food to others." Also, with greater financial autonomy afforded by making and selling their trademark intricate bead necklaces, the women have chosen to send their children to school. On occasion, their success has also sparked indignation from their husbands, followed by demands that they return. The self-sufficient women refuse and are backed by local authorities should things turn violent. Both the women and the men have learned that women do not need to remain mistreated under the rule of their husbands. Umoja gives them a liberating alternative: they can leave. The important thing is that the violence is stopped, even if that means that normal (which in this case also means "abusive") family relations are disrupted.[64]

RESOLVE GENDER CONFLICTS BY PROVIDING MEN AND WOMEN WITH PRE-SCRIPTED WAYS OF THINKING AND ACTING

Women and men need to learn how to think about each other and how to speak to each other appropriately in order to avoid conflicts as much as possible and to resolve those conflicts that do occur in everyday life before they escalate into episodes of violence. All people have in their minds basic ideas about how they should behave, which they have learned in the context of growing up in families from various traditions and cultures. As children express themselves within family life, their patterns of behavior are shaped by the consequences of their actions, experienced primarily through the reactions of others. Behavior that is successful in getting individuals the rewards they want will be repeated, while behavior that is not effective in obtaining the desired results will be less likely to appear again. In cultures where amicable male-female relationships have never been seen or reinforced, young people do not learn how to interact in mutually supportive ways with the other sex. They do not know how to avoid the possibility of gender conflict, and if such conflict occurs, they have no idea of how to resolve it without violence. Asking men and women to live together with respect and equity in such societies may be asking them to behave in ways that are utterly foreign to them. They simply do not know how to go about it.

Therefore, the next step in the fight against gender violence and exploitation is to provide scripts of interaction when they are absent in society. Researchers have found that new patterns of behavior can be created through the use of such scripts. These can prescribe what to say in the middle of tense moments or how to break down dysfunctional gender stereotypes and create new, healthy, respectful ones. Techniques used by the advertising industry to great effect, such as songs and jingles, can sometimes be used to help women and men remember what to do in given circumstances. Once memorized, they become guidelines of what to say in similar situations. Individuals can also create gender-appropriate behavior, and these examples can be used to posit new definitions of what it means to be a girl or a boy, a woman or a man. People can be encouraged to develop definitions that might portray men as considerate of their wives and daughters and dedicated to the development of their talents and abilities. Furthermore, it would be a great deterrent to violence against women if male stereotypes included the idea that men's self-esteem and eminence derive from positive, peaceful behavior toward women. The societal measure of a man, rather than the degree of domination and control over the women in his life, should be how well he appreciates them and to what extent he helps them become healthy and educated participants in all aspects of life.

Alexander B. Morrison, a religious authority with whom we are familiar, had the calling to travel and interact with members of his church in other lands. He found ways to inculcate a new definition of manhood through example. At a dinner attended by the local ecclesiastical authorities and their wives in West Africa, for instance, he stood and proposed a toast to his wife, recounting in great detail all of the things he admired about her and reciting the many contributions she had made to him and to the whole family. He then invited the other leaders present to stand and give similar toasts to their own wives. Though their toasts were not necessarily eloquent, the men complied with the request. Several of the women took Morrison aside afterward and told him that they had never heard such words of appreciation from their husbands before, even though these were good and religious men. The women were grateful to Morrison for modeling this behavior for their husbands. In another example, at a church meeting held outdoors in the same area, the men took seats inside a tent that had been erected for the purpose, while the women and children sat outside in the sun. Morrison announced that the church meeting would not proceed until wives and children were seated with their husbands. Changing the definition of what it means to be a "man" is a key focus for the efforts of men dedicated to gender equality. Sometimes eminent men can provide an example that will be persuasive to other men, in a way that women cannot.

Women, too, must learn new language about what it means to be a woman. They might learn to talk about themselves in terms of their strengths and how important it is for them to gain an education — important for themselves, their husbands, and their children. They might begin to talk about how the future of their nation depends on whether women are able to stand shoulder to shoulder with the men of their society. They might begin to speak of themselves as women who will not bow to social pressure, who will speak up for themselves and other women, and who will not settle for inappropriate and violent behavior by men. They may label themselves survivors, rather than victims, and seek to erase the shame that would silence them. Such new scripts expressed in songs, chants, stories, or catchy slogans help people to begin to think about themselves in more equitable ways, which in turn is foundational in efforts to resolve conflicts and defuse potentially violent situations.

Women in India have come up with just such a slogan: "No Toilet, No Bride." They are requiring that grooms provide toilets or they will not marry them. Consider the impact of these four little words. The lack of sanitation is inconvenient and contributes to the spread of diseases such as diarrhea, typhoid, and malaria. "Women suffer the most, since there are prying eyes everywhere," said Ashok Gera, a doctor who works in a one-room clinic. "It's humiliating, harrowing, and extremely unhealthy. I see so many young women who have prolonged urinary tract infections and kidney and liver problems because they don't have a safe place to go."

Previous attempts to bring toilets to poor Indian villages mostly failed. A 2001 project sponsored by the World Bank never took off because many people used the latrines as storage facilities or took them apart to build lean-tos. But linking toilets to courtship—"No Toilet, No Bride"—has been the most successful effort so far. Walls in many villages are painted with the slogan, and popular soap operas have featured dramatic plots involving the campaign. "The 'No Toilet, No Bride' program is a bloodless coup," said Bindeshwar Pathak, founder of Sulabh International, a social service organization and winner of the 2009 Stockholm Water Prize for developing inexpensive, eco-friendly toilets. "When I started, it was a cultural taboo to even talk about toilets. Now it's changing. My mother used to wake up at four a.m. to find someplace to go quietly. My wife wakes up at seven a.m. and can go safely in her home."

This mini-script that started with the toilets has resulted in other advantages as well. Pathak runs a school and job-training center for women who once cleaned up human waste by hand. They are known as untouchables, the lowest caste in India's social order. As more toilets come to India, women are less likely to have to do such jobs. "I want so much for them to have skills and dignity," Pathak said. These four little words, "No Toilet, No Bride," are also helping women to see themselves as having value, and to see that they are valuable enough that they deserve a toilet before they marry. Their potential husbands also begin to see the women as having more value, as someone for whom they may have to obtain the required toilet. The jingle also gives a woman something to say if a young suitor does not provide her with a toilet—she has a socially approved script to follow, and society will justify her decision to refuse the marriage.[65]

Drama has always been a pivot point for massive social change, and some television programs have been helpful to both women and men by demonstrating new ways for them to interact. The powerful influence of television is noted by Iranian feminist Syma Sayah, who states: "Satellite has shown an alternative way of being. Women see that it is possible to be treated equally with men."[66] One of the more noted shows that models new gender interaction behavior is the Turkish soap opera *Noor*. After being dubbed into colloquial Syrian Arabic, this show became an instant hit in the Arab world. Dubbed foreign soap operas are nothing new to the region, but what is new is a soap opera about Muslims living in an Islamic country. The draw for its mostly female audience is that it portrays an attractive, somewhat observant Muslim couple (Noor and Mohannad) who love and support each other and who treat each other equally and respectfully. The show is probably the most popular series ever to be shown on Arab TV. Its grand finale in 2008 attracted 85 million viewers—51 million of whom were women over the age of fifteen, which is more than half the total number of women in the Arab world.[67] Because of its popularity with women and because it often contradicts long-held traditions, the show has been opposed by religious clerics in Saudi Arabia. Nevertheless, it is having a discernible impact. A young housewife from Amman, Jordan, explained that she has told her husband that he should learn from Mohannad and follow the way "he treats her, how he loves her, how he cares about her."[68] This new type of couple interaction provides guidelines for behavior and scripts for dialogue that viewers can integrate into their own marriages, as chivalric texts did during the Middle Ages in Europe.

Another approach is to take an existing cultural script and change it to include an equitable vision for women. An example of this approach is found in Somalia, which is ruled by five main clans, with several important subclans. In 1992, when Somalia was still racked with intertribal conflict, Asha Hagi Elmi founded Save Somali Women and Children (SSWC), with the goal of promoting equal rights for women in politics. It was the first organization of its kind to include members from all of Somalia's five main clans, thus making it a new kind of structure. Hagi and SSWC worked hard to get women included in the rebuilding of Somalia. In 1997, when a peace conference was announced in Arta, Djibouti, Hagi lobbied both the UN and U.S. president Clinton to ensure that women be allowed to attend *as the Sixth Clan of Somalia*. Within the language of clan structure, Asha Hagi Elmi argued that since women were excluded from the governance of the five major clans, they therefore constituted a sixth clan of their own. Her efforts to re-script an existing cultural script paid off, and she and other women from the SSWC were invited. This new Sixth Clan restructured traditional thought and impressed the president of Djibouti so much that he allowed Hagi and a hundred other women to attend the Arta peace conference. In 2000, delegates from the Sixth Clan participated in the drafting and approval of the Transitional National Charter. These women were able to secure twenty-five seats (10 percent of the total) for Sixth Clan representatives in the national assembly. Of that momentous accomplishment to secure a place for women in government, Hagi said, "For the first time ever in Somali history, Somali women were given their quota. I call that a total revolution." A few years later the proportion of women in the parliament was increased to 12 percent and Hagi was elected as one of its members.[69] None of this would have happened if Hagi had not been able to write a new political script that included a new Sixth Clan representing more than half of the people of Somalia—the women.

Patterns for behaving in a more respectful and healing manner can also be instantiated in new rituals that can be adopted by the society. Even more tragic than African girls being abducted to fight in rebel forces is that when they are able to return to their communities, they are rejected. It is a very long and difficult process for them, inasmuch as they do not receive the same assistance boys receive to help them become reintegrated into the society. Furthermore, girls who have violated cultural gender norms through aggressive behavior and being raped experience enormous shame and guilt. Families and communities, unprepared or unwilling to accept them, often harass, threaten, and sexually or physically abuse them, leaving them with little hope that they will be able to work or marry.

One effective way to heal and reconnect the girls to their communities in northern Uganda and Sierra Leone has been the use of new, community-created rituals. These prescribed rituals, coupled with religious prayers, songs, and dancing, symbolically sever the past from a future of reconciliation and forgiveness, a process that involves the aid of ancestors, wards off evil influences, and facilitates social reintegration. The rituals are varied, and some call for costly materials. For example, the reunion of one girl named Ann was marked by her stepping on an egg before entering the community, the sacrifice of a goat, and the community assembling to celebrate. Then, at the church, the members fasted, gave thanks to God, and allowed Ann to return to schooling. Even after long separations and manifold offenses, the instrument of these rituals has proven to be a highly effective scripted intervention in forgiving and forgetting, allowing for full reconciliation for these women, who otherwise would not receive it in the same way as their male counterparts do.[70]

Rituals have also been used as substitutes for more harmful practices. In Kenya some groups have created new rites of passage for girls that take the place of female circumcision in pronouncing a girl to have crossed into womanhood. Another possibility is to use rituals to celebrate in a woman's life what was formerly not recognized as an occasion for celebration, thereby adding value to the everyday lives of women and girls. In several Western societies, for example, families are now celebrating the first menstruation of their daughters with a scripted celebration and blessingway. Rituals hold great power through the meaning they create for us, and it is incumbent upon the members of society to develop rituals that honor, and do not harm, women.

Likewise, Iris Bohnet and others have used new insights from behavioral economics and neuroscience to develop the concept of "gender nudges."[71] The classic example of a gender nudge is the way professional orchestras moved from auditions that took place in front of a curtain to auditions that took place behind a curtain. When the evaluators could not see the sex of the musician auditioning, the percentage of women who gained orchestra seats was dramatically increased. Bohnet suggests there may be other ways to overcome our inherent stereotypes concerning gender. For example, she and her colleagues found that when job candidates were evaluated sequentially, one by one, interviewers were more likely to base their decisions on the sex of the candidates. However, when male and female candidates were evaluated simultaneously, the past performance of the candidates became more important than their sex to the evaluators. New scripts, even for such mundane matters as hiring job candidates, may be all the "nudge" that is needed to improve gender equity.

TEACH PRINCIPLES OF GENDER EQUITY THAT CAN BE INTERNALIZED, LIBERATING MEN AND WOMEN TO INTERACT PEACEFULLY

Suppressing violence and defusing conflicts will not by themselves guarantee that peaceful gender interactions will appear. Specific programs are needed that focus directly on teaching gender equality, including the development of specific skill sets that men and women need in order to treat each other as equals. Both men and women have to learn to value themselves and the other sex enough to want the fullest possible development and participation for both. Because peace is much more than the mere absence of violence, it requires that basic human rights principles be understood and internalized and also that a range of prosocial behaviors be developed that are capable of not only equally bettering the lives of both men and women, but also creating unity between them.

It is also important that the principles of equality and behavior that are consistent with those principles be taught to children. If male and female children are taught to apologize when they are wrong, to share their food and other resources with their siblings regardless of sex, and to value all life, both male and female, constructive gender interactions will begin to appear. It is important to remember that peaceful relationships will not be created by just one thoughtful act; what is required will be continued explaining and reinforcing behavior that models equality among men and women. Eventually more peaceful behavior will begin to appear and will permeate social and political structures.[72]

As one parent discovered, gender equality can be taught:

> We do not live in a complete bubble, but the outside world is somewhat limited because we do not watch TV. But that is not the only place where templates are given to our children. There have been two shockers for us in the last few months. Savannah, our middle child, mentioned that she would like to be a doctor (of course that changes several times a day between dancer, artist, teacher, mom, doctor etc). Conner, her older brother, abruptly told that she could not be a doctor. My wife and I made very clear that he was wrong and he even knew female doctors and that he had no right to try and limit his sister's dreams. On another occasion, Savannah was talking about girls in the army. Conner told her that girls could not be in the military because they were not strong enough. This time Savannah stood up to him and told him girls were strong! We watched them banter back and forth a little and then more gently this time told Conner that Savannah was correct, girls could be in the military. This was a little puzzling still to him, but he accepted it.
>
> We weren't sure he had "gotten it," but then saw this teaching pay off at the bus stop later on. At the bus stop near our house, the elementary school boys have always enforced the rule that boys get on the bus first, and girls are last. On this particular day, we noticed that Conner was first in line, with his sister second. The other boys were trying to push her out of the way. Conner then intervened and insisted that Savannah, even though she was a girl, should not have to give up her place in line—and he held his ground as the other boys tried to get past him. That is when we knew that what we were teaching in the home was not falling on deaf ears, and that we had an obligation to teach our children what was right concerning how to treat the other sex.[73]

A change of perspective is not only for the young; it is also for the fully mature. In Japan, after a law was passed in 2003 giving a wife who files for divorce the right to claim up to half her husband's company pension, men began to examine their marriages, and many decided they did not like what they had become. After decades of husbands' working long days, drinking through the night, and then staggering home to their brokenhearted wives, some husbands have banded together to join the National Chauvinistic Husbands Association, a misnomer that is clarified once one realizes that the association is for husbands who feel they need help in giving greater respect and priority to their wives and children. This organization of businessmen has grown to more than four thousand; Shuichi Amano, the association's founder, credits this to the fact that "to be divorced is the equivalent of being declared dead—because we can't take care of ourselves."

The perilous state of Shuichi's marriage dawned on him several years ago when his wife asserted that she was "99 percent" sure she would divorce him. He, like many other members of the association that he founded, have now turned their attention to strengthening their marriages by helping around the house, listening to their wives, and, for the bravest, giving thanks, apology, or an expression of love. For another member, Yoshimichi Itahashi, the law has helped focus his mind. His wife said that before, it was as though "he didn't exist in the family," and she gave an example: "Up until my 60th birthday, he had not given me anything at all. But on my 60th, he sent me 60 flowers." With slow moves to make amends for the past, their evolving relationship has followed the same pattern of changing behaviors and attitudes as that of many members. Yoshimichi explained that there is more at stake than just their pensions, saying, "Japan is a peaceful country, but the household is at war."[74] The purpose of this example is to illustrate that it may take a law to draw attention to the issue, but the key is that men are trying to learn the principles that will help them behave in thoughtful ways, ways that demonstrate their appreciation for their wives, ways that will bring peace home.

Education for women is a key to internalization of gender equality on the part of both women and men. Throughout the world, more and more people are coming to realize that educating women is valuable and an important part of a better future for everyone. Many of these converts are men. On a recent visit to Sana, Yemen, journalist Thomas Friedman was walking through the streets with a Yemeni friend when they passed a group of four bearded men with traditional daggers in their belts who were busy discussing a poster that urged fathers and mothers to send their daughters to school. When Friedman asked what the men thought about the message of the poster, one man replied that he was "ready to give up part of a meal each day so that my girls can learn to read." He even admitted to having just retaped the poster to the stone wall so that others could see it.[75]

In his best-selling book, *Three Cups of Tea*, Greg Mortenson tells the story of Haji Ali, the village chief of Korphe in northern Pakistan, who sought Mortenson's help in building a school for the children of his village. When the school was almost completed, Haji Mehdi, a neighboring village chief who through intimidation and threats controlled the economy of the valley, came to Korphe to log his protest against the school and especially the school-ing of girls—which he said was forbidden by Allah. When Haji Ali defended the school, Mehdi demanded that a price—twelve of the best rams from the village—be paid to ensure that the school would remain. Without hesitation, Haji Ali called for the rams, paid the bribe, and sent his neighbor and his henchmen on their way. Of that moment Mortenson writes: "Haji Ali had just handed over half the wealth of the village to that crook, but he was smil-ing like he had just won the lottery." Ali then assured the villagers that even though they had lost the rams, and even though Haji Mehdi would have food for that day, the children of Korphe would have 'education forever.'"[76]

When gender equality has been internalized, even searing introspection and great sacrifice in its pursuit become deeply meaningful. When the heart has changed, it takes no effort to change one's actions; they spring forth from us without necessity of coercion. True, lasting, powerful change comes only with the internalization of a healthy understanding of who women really are, and why they are worth changing for.

WHAT CAN YOU PERSONALLY DO TO REDUCE VIOLENCE AGAINST WOMEN AND FURTHER PEACE?

You have the opportunity to join the most important movement of the twenty-first century—the movement to reduce violence against women and in that way to help establish household, local, national, and even international peace. In addition to joining the existing organized efforts that are under way in every nation today, as this chapter has detailed, internalization of gender equity must start with a moral inspection of our own everyday lives. The following benchmarks might be helpful to you in this important endeavor.

REFUSE TO PARTICIPATE IN ANY ACTIVITY THAT MIGHT TRAIN YOU TO PERPETUATE GENDER VIOLENCE

For Xhosa women in South Africa, marriage may involve physical and psy-chological abuse. Many wondered how such norms were perpetuated. Knowing that the young men were given orientation sessions by the older men before they were married, the women wondered what the young men were being taught. In an interview given in 2006, one female informant reported the following incident:

> This one time I was hiding behind the *kraal*, because that's where they give them all the rules and stuff, like on how to live like a man, and I was just hiding and I was listening to what they were telling them. They were telling them, "From now on you are a man. You never ever listen to a woman. Whatever you say goes in the house. You are the one who makes the rules. A woman doesn't tell you what to do. You are the man; you can have as many women as you want." And they were telling them all these things, and I was saying to myself, *Oh my word, so that's why they become so ignorant in everything they do!*[77]

Although the settings may be different, perhaps locker rooms for athletes or good-ol'-boy clubs for executives, every society's cultural traditions have ways of telling young men and young women what is socially acceptable for them to do. Any instructions you may be giving or receiving that are contrary to the value of gender equality must be critically examined and discarded if necessary. Rise up in such situations, open your mouth, and say that while men and women are not the same, diversity is no rationale for hierarchy between them. Say to all within the sound of your voice that men and women are to be treated with equal respect and value. Do not laugh at jokes that poke fun at or objectify the other sex. Do not join in with harassment of the other sex, even if that harassment is considered "just having a little fun." If you see someone being harassed, step in and make your views on such behavior known. Do not buy into advertising that demeans or exploits the other sex. You should never ask a member of the opposite sex to do something that you would not be willing to do.

NEVER EXERT UNDUE POWER OR INFLUENCE OVER A MEMBER OF THE OPPOSITE SEX IN YOUR RELATIONSHIPS

To be a credible part of the movement toward gender equality, it is important that you examine your own personal relationships with members of the other sex. If you are talking the talk, as noted above, are you also walking the walk? Whether you are selecting something you might want to do together on an evening out or considering acts of physical intimacy, the decision as to where and how far you go with a member of the other sex must be mutually decided upon. No intimidation or manipulation should ever be used to get your way, by either gender. This includes not only physical coercion but also psychological coercion. No woman should ever have to feel she "owes" anyone anything if that person is nice to her. No person, male or female, should feel used in a relationship.

A rising problem in the United States is the effect of pornography on respectful gender relationships. We have seen evidence that girls are repeatedly lied to and manipulated into relationships, even marriage, by young men who have secret addictions to pornography. The insidious impact of this addiction begins to be apparent when the new husband or boyfriend starts to criticize and then ridicule the woman's body. The verbal attacks are usually more than demeaning—they are psychologically abusive and destroy the self-confidence of the young woman, blaming her for the man's own problems and asking her to participate in degrading sexual activities. As the true nature of the young man's addiction to pornography becomes clear, the damage to the shattered young woman may be irreversible. Such instances of relationship fraud are becoming common fare in many countries throughout the world. If a young man who claims to love a young woman can put her through such torture, is it any wonder that he becomes capable of condoning collective violence against women or even other groups?

It is not only in relationships with intimate others that our allegiance to gender equality, or our betrayal of it, may be seen. How do we treat our mothers, our sisters, our daughters, our female colleagues? Do we actually hear what the women in our lives speak to us about? Do we dismiss their authority to speak on any specific topic because they are women? Do we think of them only as instrumentalities to fulfill our needs, or do we view them as whole human beings with independent wills and perspectives and needs of their own? Do we feel that no decision would be a sound one without asking for their views? Or do we believe that men have the final say on important decisions regardless of the position of women? Do we put women in impossible double binds, such as encouraging them to speak, but then considering them bossy if they do speak? Or believing that a woman can be nice or competent at what she does, but not both? Do we address accomplished women by their first names but address accomplished men by their titles?

One of our male students recounted an anecdote that has stayed with us. He was attending a reunion of people, men and women, who had worked together some years earlier. The reunion was held in the lovely home of the man who had been their leader during that time. After dinner, the men went to the living room to talk, and the women went into the kitchen to do the dishes. At first, our student sat down in the living room, and then it occurred to him that this was one of the small and simple things, accepted as natural and unremarkable, that was part of the foundation of gender inequity that we had been discussing in class. Without making a fuss, he quietly got up and went into the kitchen to help the women with the dishes. No, the other men did not join him. But he had performed that personal moral inventory and taken a stand, however minor it might have seemed, for he knew that without all of the myriad minor inequities and gendered microaggressions, the major inequities could not stand.

Women themselves may harbor beliefs and practices that perpetuate a cycle of misery for all women. Do we as women cheer the successes of other women or seek to tear down "the competition"? Do we protect younger women, or believe that it is only just that they should face the same abuse we have faced in our lives? Do we as women always find ourselves apologizing when things do not go well, even though nothing is actually our fault? Do we apologize even for voicing our own opinion publicly? Do we always feel we are deficient, no matter how experienced and competent we actually are? Do we speak when given the opportunity, or do we pass up those opportunities? Are we willing to sacrifice what is right in our quest to maintain a relationship with the ones we love? Are we willing to sacrifice who we are to maintain a relationship with the ones we love? Are we willing to put up with abuse, and even turn a blind eye to the abuse of others, to maintain a relationship with the ones we love? Are we willing to sweep gender violence and exploitation under the rug and remain silent even when to do so is itself a form of gender violence against our own sex?

One young man of our acquaintance laments the mechanics of relational submission that seem to rob women of their self-respect. He recounts:

Last month, I became engaged in an interesting experience: a couple sat down to lunch in my apartment. The young man forgot his sandwich and made the statement, "Woman, get my sandwich for me." At this point I had a decision to make as I saw her begin to get up and proceed to get his sandwich, to either ignore the situation or to speak up in behalf of this young lady. In my normal manner, I chose the latter of the options. I stated that she did not need to get his sandwich for him and that he was perfectly capable of retrieving what he himself forgot. I then proceeded to give them this explanation:

The use of the term "woman" was the point of the contention. In biological terms, the young man had correctly stated the sex of the young lady. However, by stating "woman" to the young lady, the young man wanted to parade his dominance in the relationship to all those present and especially to the young lady. He wanted to let her know that he was the dominant character in the relationship, thus his needs and wants came before hers. To many his behavior should be a clear warning sign of a relationship with future problems. It should never be necessary to show dominance in this type of relationship due to the simple fact that both needs and wants of both the man and woman are equal in importance and must be satisfied through cooperation and sacrifice. The use of dominating labels and titles between a man and woman in a relationship does nothing but degrade trust and cooperation.

The effects of such behavior are clearly shown by the young woman's reactions. First, she began to complete the task order by the young man, showing submission to his will. Secondly, and the more shocking of reactions to my mind, was the lack of support or voice from her when I corrected the young man. She sat there quietly, almost embarrassed that another had to step in [with] an act of prevention. During my explanation she laughed and giggled with him so as to show that she did not want to upset him by agreeing with me. The young woman showed clear signs of submission and lack of will. Sadly, many of the people who will read this know other women who are suffering in a submissive relationship. The question I pose is why women submit to this or choose to be in these types of relationships? As a young man, other men tell me to go to the gym and gain muscle because women love to feel safe and protected by a strong man, but yet many of these men feel the need to use this power not to protect but instead to dominate the woman in the relationship. I feel strongly that this is wrong and unhealthy, and I support the understanding that a relationship is a partnership of understanding and love towards one another's needs and wants to create harmony and trust, not domination. But the question remains, why do women submit?[78]

Clearly, enacting male domination and permitting male domination both need critical examination; as much introspection is needed by women as by men in order to erase the bad old ways of gender inequality.

BELIEVE THAT YOU ARE NOT ONLY CAPABLE OF
DECREASING VIOLENCE AGAINST WOMEN BUT
PERSONALLY RESPONSIBLE FOR DOING SO

As we have seen, efforts to outlaw child marriages and to establish a minimum age of marriage in Saudi Arabia have yet to be successful. To rectify the problem, one doctor has deemed it his personal responsibility to use nontraditional means to postpone marriage through the intentional delay of legally required blood tests. Dr. Hani Harsani explains: "Two sisters came to us accompanied by their parents to undergo pre-marital blood analyses. The first one was five, and the other 11 years old. When we asked the mother why they wanted to do the tests, she told us that she wanted to marry the girls to cousins to preserve the family's property rights. . . . We cannot technically impede a marriage with a girl of this age. However, we can delay the process (by refusing to carry out the tests)."[79] It may not be Dr. Harsani's legal obligation to stand up for these girls, but he has made it his personal obligation.

We are reminded of the poignant story told by one of our friends. He was on his high school's basketball team, and one year they were so successful that they won a state championship. The team went out to celebrate, and a young woman went with them. Our friend decided at the last minute that he didn't feel right about things, and he decided not to go. The next day it was revealed the girl had been gang-raped by members of the team, who had then been arrested. Our friend commented to his father, "Aren't you glad I didn't go?" To which his father replied, "No, I wish you had gone. If you had been there, you would not have let that girl be raped and her life destroyed, and your friends would not now be in jail." That father had a healthy understanding of the agency of even one person to turn others away from gender violence. We all must feel the same sense of obligation in our daily interactions with others: no bystanders allowed!

ENVISION WHAT THE WORLD COULD
BE LIKE IF YOU WERE SUCCESSFUL

Removing obstacles to women's progress and making it possible for their talents to flourish will have major, positive effects on human societies. A vision of what such a world would look like should motivate all of us to unceasingly seek to accomplish those goals. If, for example, every woman was free from physical abuse, she could step out of the shadow of fear and offer her best contributions to her children, her family, and her nation. If every woman was in a relationship where there was no fear, but rather deep appreciation for her views and all of her contributions to the marriage and to the family, both men and women would flourish in the emotional security of true partnership. If the law reflected the same appreciation for female life and concerns as it does for male, the entire society would be based on equity and fairness, and a single standard of integrity would be applicable to all. Investing in women in fundamental ways, such as seeing that girls were educated to a level equal to that of boys, would ensure that nations were more likely to be prosperous, to be healthy, to be stable, and to be meaningfully democratic. If women were to make up a substantial percentage of corporate boards, their aversion to risky investments and corruption would likely diminish the number of banking failures and strengthen the global economy. If women were also consulted in decision making at all levels, the decisions would lead to better consequences overall, because they would have been made on the basis of the thoughtfulness of all the people, not just half of the people.

Imagine a world with double the intellectual and creative talent available to help solve unprecedented global problems such as escalating violence, economic crises, and global warming. Such problems demand that every available ounce of mind power and life experience be fully utilized in finding solutions. Women have the potential to play a key role in helping this world reach its next level of development, not by taking over the world but by standing shoulder to shoulder as equal partners with the men of their societies.

Removing obstacles to women's progress will also eliminate the detrimental effects on children now being raised by distressed mothers who are subjected to all kinds of injustices. Can you imagine what removing the suffering of these mothers would do to maximize the capabilities of their children—all the world's children? Fully functioning children would likely double again the creative forces available to alleviate crises in the world as well as eliminate some of the problems caused by troubled youth. The world has never witnessed the effects on generations of children who have been raised by self-actualized mothers. If your own mother had been free from the stresses of being female in a world grossly inequitable to females, how would your life be different? And would your peers' lives be different as well?

Finally, those societies that have greater levels of gender equality will be less likely to resort to conflict and warfare to secure their national interests. If the systemic insecurity of half of the world's population is reduced, the insecurity of the nations of the world will also be significantly diminished.

The security of women would in time reduce conflict in the international system, and literally become the basis of greater security for the nations of the world. Our research confirms the assertion of Secretary of State Hillary Clinton that "the subjugation of women is a direct threat to the security of the United States."[80] Indeed, it is a direct threat to the security of every nation in the international system. The systemic insecurity of women undercuts the security of all in a real and measurable way. The pressing questions facing us at this juncture of human history are, Will we choose to see that linkage, and what will we choose to do about it?

There is not a zero-sum game being played between men and women in which if women are elevated, then men are debased. We were meant to win together. As the two halves of humanity forge a truly equal partnership at all levels of society, female contributions will not only be valued equally with men's but will be honored as the necessary counterpart to men's thinking without distorting that which is unique to each. Neither will think to operate without the other—not the man without the woman nor the woman without the man—in all human societies throughout the world. The synergy that would emerge from such partnership would generate an unprecedented human wisdom that would propel the accomplishments of the human race and more than double again the human potential not only to solve the problems of the world but to prepare the world for true peace, a peace that extends from the home to the community to the nation and to the international system.

7

TAKING WING

> *The world of humanity is possessed of two wings: the male and the female. So long as these two wings are not equivalent in strength, the bird will not fly. Until womankind reaches the same degree as man, until she enjoys the same arena of activity, extraordinary attainment for humanity will not be realized; humanity cannot wing its way to heights of real attainment. When the two wings . . . become equivalent in strength, enjoying the same prerogatives, the flight of man will be exceedingly lofty and extraordinary.*[1]

THERE IS SOMETHING spectacular about watching a bird take flight: a flock of flamingos awkwardly rising from the water; a single kingfisher leaving its perch on an overhanging branch to drop down into the water to spear a fish; a robin returning with food to her nest of hungry babies. More often than not it is in the security and protection of trees that birds seek refuge and from which birds take flight.

That image of birds and the trees that harbor them echoes the theme of roots and wings that we have developed over the course of this book. Roots, no matter the depth or direction of growth, are crucial for the survival of the tree. When they are neglected, abused, or cut off, the tree suffers and perhaps even dies. Throughout history, the perspectives of women have likewise been ignored, their labor exploited and their rights curtailed. The outcome is a world out of balance; a world less secure, less humane, and less wise than it otherwise would be.

Likewise, when a bird's wing has been injured or broken through violence, the bird will not be able to fly. If the women have never had the opportunity to experience a true "peacetime" in their lives, the lives of not only women but also men and children will be crippled and unable to reach their full potential. Without healing for women, the world of states will continue to be unstable and insecure. Are we willing to let it all continue? Who would really benefit from such a continuation? We argue that the answer is no one: no one, male or female, old or young, benefits from the wounding of women.

We are encouraged by those people and institutions that are already working for change, many of whom have been highlighted in the two previous chapters. We are also encouraged by shifts in U.S. foreign policy as highlighted by Secretary of State Hillary Clinton in a December 2010 address to the TEDWomen Conference in Washington, D.C. In that talk she explained that the United States had "made empowering women and girls as a cornerstone of [its] foreign policy because women's equality is not just a moral issue, it's not just a humanitarian issue, it is not just a fairness issue, it is a security issue." It is something that is "in the vital interest of the United States of America." She went on to state: "Give women equal rights, and entire nations are more stable and secure. Deny women equal rights and the instability of nations is almost certain. . . . The subjugation of women is, therefore, a threat to the common security of our world and to the national security of our country." [2] Clinton gets it. She sees the roots. She knows that improving the status of woman and girls will have a direct and positive impact on world security. Indeed, this approach to foreign policy is beginning to be termed "the Hillary Doctrine."[3]

But it's also true that not everyone in the U.S. foreign policy bureaucracy gets it. When we were completing this book, the *Washington Post* interviewed a senior official concerning what the Obama administration was doing to ensure that Afghan women would not find themselves in the same situation they were in in 2001. "Gender issues are going to have to take a back seat to other priorities," said the senior official, who spoke about internal policy deliberations on the condition of anonymity. "There's no way we can be successful if we maintain every special interest and pet project. All those pet rocks in our rucksack were taking us down."[4] Yes, you heard the man right—Afghan women are pet rocks, weighing down our rucksack.

Despite overwhelming evidence such as that provided in this volume— that protecting the rights of women and supporting them toward the goal of economic independence is critical to United States and, indeed, global security, made-in-the-USA chauvinism continues to trump the sound, hardheaded common sense expressed by Secretary Clinton. Indeed, we would argue that there is a deep-seated American bureaucratic misogyny that parallels what we see in Afghan society and that has been a constant stumbling block to improving conditions for women in Afghanistan.

This "speak softly and carry no stick whatsoever" approach of the administration to issues of women does not apply only to the case of Afghanistan. Consider the Arab Spring. At the time when we were writing this book, the constitutional reform committee created in Egypt had no women members; the draft of the revisions to the constitution indicated that only a man can stand for president in Egypt; the interim cabinet contained no women at all; and the quota for women in parliament was summarily eliminated. That this should be the case is unsurprising: men see men as the only other "real" players in the game of politics. When power issues become serious, attention to women's voices disappears while the men cut the cards among themselves and for themselves. Women's activists decided to demonstrate publicly to re- mind the men that they were there and wanted a place at the table, but only a few hundred women showed up—to face a crowd of anti-women protesters shouting slogans like "Men are men and women are women and that will never change and go home, that's where you belong,"[5] The *Christian Science Monitor* reported, "'Go home, go wash clothes,' yelled some of the men. 'You are not married; go find a husband.' Others said, 'This is against Islam.' To the men demonstrating with the women, they yelled, 'Shame on you!' Sud- denly, the men decided the women had been there long enough. Yelling, they rushed aggressively upon the protest, pushing violently through the rows of women. The women scattered. Eyewitnesses said they saw three women being chased by the crowd. A surge of men followed them, and Army officers fired shots into the air to make the men retreat."[6]

Yes, this is the same Tahrir Square in which women and men stood side by side to gain their freedom just a few weeks before this spectacle. The *Monitor* quoted one Egyptian woman taking part in the march as saying, "'They can't just send us home after the revolution.'" Well, that is the issue, isn't it? Can "they"? And what would the United States and the international community be prepared to do to prevent that from happening?

As we discussed in chapter 5, now is the time for the international com- munity—and the United States—to develop an R2PW action plan for situa- tions such as what we see in Afghanistan and Egypt today. Instead of dropping women like irrelevant "pet rocks," we need to be thinking creatively about how the world can avoid regressing in the areas of women's rights. It is abso- lutely true that only Afghan women, Egyptian women, Tunisian women, and Yemeni women can protect their own rights. That is true for the women of every nation, even the United States. But they have always needed partners, public support, and material assistance.

The first step is to understand in the fullest sense possible that the security of states is in fact linked to the security of women—and that that is not the idealist position but the realist position. Those who adhere to the tenets of realpolitik, or any of realism's modern variants, should realize that this philo-sophical position commits them to seeing the evidence placed in abundance before their eyes. What happens with women affects the security, stability, prosperity, bellicosity, corruption, health, regime type, and (yes) power of the state. Accepting that evidence should be a hallmark of the realist approach to foreign policy. It is one of the few intersections between idealism and realism in foreign policy, and it should be acknowledged as such. The international community is moving in the direction of such acknowledgment. During the February 1, 2011, launch of UN Women, the new entity that is tasked with ensuring that the concerns and perspectives of women are represented in all UN deliberations and programs, the first director, Michelle Bachelet, stated:

> It is no longer acceptable to live in a world where young girls are taken out of school and forced into early marriage, where women's employment op-portunities are limited, and where the threat of gender-based violence is a daily reality—at home, in the street, at school and at work. The neglect of women's rights means the social and economic potential of half the popula-tion is underused. In order to tap this potential, we must open up spaces for women in political leadership, in science and technology, as trade and peace negotiators, and as heads of corporations.
>
> As the Secretary-General said, supporting faster progress for women is not only morally right; it makes good political and economic sense. This holds true whether we are talking about countries or companies. The World Economic Forum, which tracks performance on gender equality measures in 134 countries, reports a clear correlation between progress in gender and GDP per capita. And a recent study found that Fortune 500 companies with the highest number of women on their boards were 53-percent more profit-able than those with the fewest women board members. Where women have access to secondary education, good jobs, land and other assets, na-tional growth and stability are enhanced, and we see lower maternal mor-tality, improved child nutrition, greater food security and less risk of HIV and AIDS.
>
> This is not an issue confined to any one group of countries or societies. It is a universal issue. We must convince all political actors—including ministers of finance and trade as well as health and education—that we are not only talking about rights, we are talking about social vitality, political stability, and economic growth.[7]

Our own empirical research buttresses Bachelet's assertions. We have found in conventional aggregate empirical testing that the best predictor of a state's peacefulness is not its level of wealth, or its level of democracy, or whether it is Islamic or not. The very best predictor of a state's peacefulness is its level of violence against women. Even democracies with poor physical security for women are less peaceful than democracies with good physical security for women. The greater the inequity in family law concerning women, the less stable and the less peaceful the nation. And the less willing a country is to enforce laws protecting women within its own borders, the less likely it is to comply with international treaty obligations. These empirical findings, we believe, are only the tip of the iceberg. As we develop our database and make it more comprehensive and longitudinal in nature, we believe we will not only confirm these initial findings but expand them as well.

And ours are not the only findings that underscore the link between the security of women and the security of states. As we more fully outlined in chapter 4, scholars have found that the larger the gap between men and women in the society, the more likely a nation is to be involved in intra- and interstate conflict, to be the aggressor, to use force first in a conflict, and to resort to higher levels of violence in a conflict. And, of course, if one turns to issues of national health, economic growth, corruption, and social welfare, the best predictors are those that incorporate measures of the situation of women. The days when one could claim that the situation of women had nothing to do with matters of national or international security are, frankly, over. The empirical results to the contrary are just too numerous and too robust.

Acknowledgment of this reality, then, is the first, foundational step. The second step is for the international community to devote the resources necessary to develop a meaningful set of indicators on the situation of women that can be monitored and tracked over time. Regress for women can happen suddenly, it can happen surreptitiously, and it can happen under the radar of the large media outlets. For example, though it is illegal in Russia to require women to wear a headscarf, Chechnya has begun to force such a dress code on women. Women are prohibited from going to school or working for the government if they do not wear the headscarf. Men on the streets, egged on by Chechnya's provincial leader, have taken to shooting women with paintball guns if they are not wearing headscarves.[8] The Kremlin has not uttered one word of protest about these activities. If a monitoring system were in place, this issue would now be on the to-do lists of not only UN Women, not only the CEDAW Commission, but also the Human Rights Council, the General Assembly, and the Security Council, which would be pressuring Russia about this unseemly lapse in the oversight of its provinces. Why would the UN Security Council bother about Chechen women being paintballed into wearing headscarves? Because the UN Security Council would have realized that security is a seamless garment. When it begins to unravel for women, it begins to unravel for all.

There are many fine databases that monitor the situation of women around the world (including our own, the WomanStats Database). It is time for the United Nations to aspire to the same standards. We suggest at a minimum that the three wounds we have discussed in this volume be closely monitored: the physical security of women, the level of inequity in family law and its practice on the ground, and the degree of participation by women in decision-making councils in their society at all levels. While no doubt this monitoring system would be overseen by UN Women, it is important that its findings be reported in a timely and regular manner to the major deliberative bodies of the United Nations—the General Assembly and the Security Council. This would be in keeping with the perspective that women's issues are not just women's issues but issues of the greatest importance in achieving national and international security.

The third major element in changing our world through an international commitment to R2PW is to develop a set of rewards and sanctions, a web of incentives and disincentives, under which nations in the international system will operate. The creation of these policy options is not simply a job for the United Nations but is also a task that each nation's foreign policy bureaucracy must tackle. How are both the world community and the nations of the world to react when another nation is neglecting its R2PW? In chapter 5, we submitted that this should be treated as any other breach of a major treaty, such as a breach of the Nuclear Non-Proliferation Treaty. A wide array of diplomatic and economic instruments should be deployed, just as it would be if the treaty in question were the NPT.

Take, for example, the problem of the ominous developments in Egypt, or the U.S. exit from Afghanistan, and what these events portend for women there. What could the United States government be doing? What could be done? Some public pronouncements supporting women activists and their positions in Egypt, Tunisia, Yemen, and other countries, accompanied by insistent reference to the issue through diplomatic channels, would be welcome. At the Women of Courage awards ceremony in March 2011, Secretary of State Hillary Clinton said she speaks about this issue when she is in contact with Egyptian officials: "Because it would be a shame, with all of the extraordinary change that's going on in Egypt if women were somehow not given their opportunity to be part of bringing about the new Egypt. . . . I think it's important that we always raise it, because we think it will be a better outcome. We don't want to see Egypt, or Tunisia, or any place eliminate half the population when they think about the future. That would make no sense at all."[9] Apparently her concerns have not caused the Egyptians, at least, to include any women in their transitional government: perhaps even when one is U.S. Secretary of State, some still believe a woman's voice can be ignored. We need male American officials at the highest level, including the president of the United States, to speak out both publicly and privately on this issue.

In Afghanistan, we need to be thinking in concrete terms about how to ensure a softer landing for Afghan women when American forces leave. Specific measures would include setting up the following legal and practical infrastructure before we leave: an asylum policy for Afghan women who face the threat of femicide; a scholarship program to take the best and brightest female Afghan students into U.S. universities; assurance that women are well represented in the peace *jirga* talks with the "moderate" Taliban; pursuing indictments in the International Criminal Court (ICC) against top Taliban leaders who have ordered femicide; complete funding for a Radio Free Women of Afghanistan station; establishing mosque-based female education, which locations would be less likely to be attacked; insisting to the Afghan government that women's shelters should not be taken over by the government; and finally, continuing to tie aid to Afghanistan to specific and measurable improvements in the situation of women in that land—including assisting them with the kinds of projects that protect female inheritance and land rights.

We are not helpless, either as individual nations or as the international community, when faced with a poor or worsening situation for women in the countries of the world. First, we need to nip retrogression in the bud through strong and united support of those in the affected country who oppose such retrogression; next, we need to assist women in countries where baseline conditions need improvement. *We can do this.*

Nearly a century ago, nations fought a war to end all wars. While noble in intent, that effort was a failure. Perhaps the world is now ready for another effort to ensure world peace. We are recommending one important and strategic front where that battle should be waged—in healing the wounds that women received in the house of those who should have been their friends. Sex and world peace, then: recognizing and acting upon the knowledge that there will never be peace for our nations unless there is peace between the sexes.

If you want to start today, you don't have to be president of the United States or secretary-general of the United Nations. Individual, bottom-up efforts are an equally important component of protecting and providing for women at risk, especially when the various societal structures seem unwilling or unable to help. As we discussed in chapter 6, sometimes all it takes is one voice, one act, one small step to bring about change. From there we need to spread the word and enlist the help of others—men included. Just as social media helped to bring about moves toward democracy in Tunisia and Egypt, these and other technologies are already proving useful in furthering the rights of women and opening up dialogue, particularly in those countries where women have limited public voice. We are encouraged by the creative and brave efforts of many throughout the world who have already made a difference. Look to them for ideas and inspiration. When change is slow in coming, don't give up. Tenacity is the mother of progress.

For many who read this book, the violence and discrimination against women that we have quantified, mapped, and described may seem to be something pertinent to some other country or continent. That is no excuse not to act. If you just look, you will find ways to help women in your own home and community as well in those in distant countries where the treatment of women is outwardly much more disturbing. Combating date rape and lower pay for women in the United States is as worthy of our efforts as speaking out against forced veiling and acid attacks in Afghanistan. As we speak out, as we act, as we teach others, and as we begin to internalize a new perspective on women, we will begin to see changes. We will begin to see women treated as equals, we will begin to see more women involved in decision making and peacemaking, we will begin to see a greater desire among the nations of world to live in peace—and we will see a greater understanding of how to do so.

We reiterate that we are not suggesting that sex is the only root of societal and inter-societal conflict, nor are we suggesting that the dynamic runs only from sex to national security and not in a reciprocal direction. We are also not suggesting that positive change for women will immediately result in a peaceful world. What we are suggesting, and attempting to show empirically, is that we can no longer speak of achieving national and international security without speaking, in the same breath, about the security of women.

On the basis of the research we have laid out in this volume, we believe the primary challenge facing the twenty-first century is to eliminate violence against women and remove the barriers to the development of their strength and creativity and voice. Establishing gender equality in interpersonal relationships, in homes, in the workplace, and in decision-making bodies at all levels will change states and their behaviors, and in turn will bring prosperity and peace to the world. The three wounds—the physical insecurity of women, inequity in family law, and lack of parity in the councils of human decision making—must be attended to with all vigilance and care at levels both high and humble.

A bird with one broken wing will never soar. We know that; our species has experienced it for millennia, and paid for that sure knowledge with rivers of blood and mountains of needless suffering. The nations of the world must try a different path, a path that we have every reason to believe will lead to greater well-being, prosperity, security, and peace for the entire international system—the path of equality between men and women.

We cannot fail . . . it's time for the bird to finally take wing.

APPENDIX A

OPERATIONALIZATIONS FOR DATA ANALYSIS IN CHAPTER 4

To test the hypotheses listed in chapter 4, each variable must be operationalized.

- Physical Security of Women, operationalized as the Physical Security of Women (PSOW) scale. This five-point ordinal scale attempts to capture the degree of physical threat experienced by women generally within the society. The scale focuses in particular on the level of violence against women, including the prevalence of domestic violence, rape, marital rape, and murder of women in the nation. These subcomponents are examined in terms of custom, practice, law, and statistics related to these four forms of violence against women. This index is coded as MULTIVAR-SCALE-1 in the WomanStats Database; coded July 2007; coding scheme outlined in the codebook found at http://womanstats.org/CodebookCurrent.htm#psow.
- Physical Security of Women Index Including Son Preference (PSOWSP) scale. Using the ordinal PSOW score as a baseline, this variant includes the degree to which son preference is present within a society, and to what degree such a preference is enacted in society by offspring sex selection. That is, not only is the physical security of existing women important, but it is certainly a matter of physical security for women if the births of female fetuses are selectively precluded. The variable ISSA-SCALE-1 in the WomanStats Database is thus used to supplement the PSOW scale point for each nation; coded February 2007; coding scheme found in codebook listed above.
- Physical Security of Women Minus Marital Rape (PSOWMMR) scale. Because PSOW as normally scaled includes an examination of marital rape, which is also a variable examined by the Inequity in Family Law scale, we engaged in a recoding of the 2009 PSOW that eliminated marital rape as a con-

sideration in determination of PSOW level. In this way, IFL and the recoded PSOW have no overlapping variables at all. The acronym for this variable is PSOWMMR, for Physical Security of Women Minus Marital Rape.

- The Global Peace Index (GPI) is coded by the Economist Intelligence Unit (EIU). The EIU notes: "Most people understand the absence of violence as an indicator of peace. This definition also allows for the measuring of peacefulness within, as well as between, nations. The GPI ranks Independent countries by their 'absence of violence' using metrics that combine both internal and external factors" (www.visionofhumanity.org/about). The EIU uses twenty-four indicators (since 2010, twenty-three indicators) to compose its state scores, which can be found at www.visionofhumanity.org; rounded ordinal scores for 2007 (www.visionofhumanity.org/gpi-data/#/2007/scor/), with scores ranging from 1 to 5, were used in our analysis.

- States of Concern to the International Community (SOCIC). As noted above, while this scale overlaps GPI in conceptualization, its operationalized form contains information lacking in the GPI—specifically, the degree to which the nation deviates from security-related international treaties and covenants. Thus, noncompliance with several important treaties, such as the NPT, is included in this index. This ordinal scale is elucidated in Valerie M. Hudson and Carl H. Brinton, "Women's Tears and International Fears: Is Discrepant Enforcement of National Laws Protecting Women and Girls Related to Discrepant Enactment of International Norms by Nation-States? (paper presented at the annual meeting of the American Political Science Association, Chicago, August 29–September 1, 2007. scale coded July 2007; http://womanstats.org/APSA07HudsonBrinton.pdf; data available at http://vmrhudson.org/socic.html.

- Relations with Neighboring Countries (RN). This five-point ordinal measure, coded by the Economist Intelligence Unit, seeks to capture how strained or how peaceful interstate relations are between nations with contiguous borders. In our analysis, we use the 2007 scores; www.visionofhumanity.org/gpi-data/#/2007/rela/.

- Level of Organized Intrastate Conflict. This dependent variable is taken from the Economist Intelligence Unit's variable Level of Organised Conflict (Internal). According to the Web site, it is a "Qualitative assessment of the intensity of conflicts within the country. Ranked 1–5 (very low–very high) by EIU analysts. 2008 Data." www.visionofhumanity.org/gpi-data/#/2008/inco/.

- Level of Democracy. Coded by Freedom House as a trichotomy (free, partly free, not free). Although there are several good sources for a scaling of democracy, including the Polity IV data, the Freedom House measures are often used in international relations scholarship; they offer a methodological advantage in this particular analytic effort in that polytomous logistic regression results can be affected by a serious mismatch in number of scale points between independent and dependent variables. Our dependent variables are all five-point scales; Freedom House is a three-point scale, and Polity IV is a twenty-one-point scale. We used the Freedom House data coded 2007; www .freedomhouse.org/template.cfm?page=1.

- Level of Wealth, operationalized as GDP per capita. Although GDP per capita is a crude measure, it is often used in empirical analysis for its broad indication of level of national wealth and economic development. In our analysis, we use GDP per capita as coded by CIA World Factbook, 2007, countries identified by quintile; https://www.cia.gov/library/publications/the-world-factbook/index.html.

- Prevalence of Islamic Civilization. This scale indicates the degree to which adherence to the Islamic religion is prevalent within the nation. This dichotomous variable is coded by S. Matthew Stearmer and Chad F. Emmett in "The Great Divide: Revealing Differences in the Islamic World Regarding the Status of Women and Its Impact on International Peace" (paper presented at the annual meeting of the American Political Science Association, Chicago, August 29–September 1, 2007. http://womanstats.org/StearmerEmmettAPSA 07.pdf.

- Inequity in Family Law/Practice (IFL) scale. This scale was developed by Rose McDermott and was coded in 2007 (Rose McDermott, "MULTIVAR-SCALE-3," http://womanstats.org/CodebookCurrent.htm#inequity, 2007). The index utilizes the information provided by the WomanStats Database, the largest and most comprehensive database concerning the status of women in the world, coding for more than 320 variables in 175 countries (http://woman stats.org). McDermott chose to examine law and practice concerning age of marriage, polygyny, consent in marriage, abortion, divorce, whether marital rape is recognized as a crime, and inheritance law and practices. McDermott scales these variables along a five-point ordinal scale, ranging from 0 to 4, with the 0 scale point representing equitable family law/practice and 4 representing highly inequitable family law/practice. McDermott has placed the definitions of her scale points online (McDermott,2007), so we will not repeat those here; http://womanstats.org/CodebookCurrent.htm#inequity.

- Prevalence of Polygyny Scale. McDermott, originally coded in 2007 and then recoded according to new scale points in 2009 (McDermott 2009).

McDermott used the WomanStats Database for her data, and used all PW variables to do her scaling. Her scaling for PW-SCALE-1 is available at http://womanstats.org/CodebookCurrent.htm#PW.

■ Huntington's Classification of Civilizations. While Huntington's classification is sometimes ambiguous, we used the discussion in his book on the subject; Samuel P. Huntington, *The Clash of Civilizations and the Remaking of World Order* (New York: Simon and Schuster, 1996). Where we honestly could not determine which civilization a country should be in, we marked that country as "missing." This occurred with some of Huntington's "cleft" countries, such as Nigeria, though not with others, such as France. It also occurred when Huntington himself either was silent on a country or declared it a "lone" country (such as Israel). For purposes of this analysis, we merged "Western," "Orthodox," and "Latin" cultures together, as well as "Sinic" and "Buddhist" cultures. Thus, there were five civilizational categories used: Christian (Western/Orthodox/Latin), Muslim, Hindu, Sinic-Buddhist, and sub-Saharan African.

■ Discrepancy Between State Law and National Practice Concerning Women. This multivariate scale, taken from the WomanStats Database, examines to what extent the state is enforcing laws that protect women—or even has such laws at all. It is a measure of how much the states cares about the situation of women. Coded in 2007, it has three subcomponents: laws concerning physical and bodily security for women, laws concerning the education of women, and laws concerning women and the family. The full-scale operationalization can be found at http://womanstats.org/CodebookCurrent .htm#discrepancy.

APPENDIX B

DATA ANALYSIS RESULTS FOR CHAPTER 4

TABLE B.1 Chi-Square Results: Physical Security of Women (PSOW, PSOWSP) and Measures of State Security (GPI, SOCIC, RN)

VARIABLES	CHI-SQUARE (LIKELIHOOD RATIO)	DF	SIGNIFICANCE $P<$
PSOW and GPI	41.212	12	.0001
$N = 105$	(47.077)		
PSOWSP and GPI	36.623	12	.0001
$N = 105$	(44.162)		
PSOW and SOCIC	88.122	12	.0001
$N = 140$	(88.050)		
PSOWSP and SOCIC	78.136	12	.0001
$N = 140$	(84.320)		
PSOW and RN	45.884	12	.0001
$N = 106$	(46.438)		
PSOWSP and RN	44.029	12	.0001
$N = 106$	(44.697)		

Note: PSOW = Physical Security of Women; PSOWSP = Physical Security of Women and Son Preference; GPI = Global Peace Index; SOCIC = States of Concern to the International Community; RN = Relations with Neighbors

TABLE B.2 Cox and Snell Pseudo-R-Squareds for Bivariate Polytomous Logistic Regression: Measures of Physical Security of Women, Control Variables, and Three Dependent Variables of State Security

VARIABLES	PSEUDO-R-SQUARED VALUE[a]
GPI on PSOW, $N = 105$	.299
GPI on Democracy, $N = 105$	.203
GPI on Wealth, $N = 105$	Fails parallel line test; measure unreliable
GPI on Islamic Civilization, $N = 105$	.084
SOCIC on PSOW, $N = 140$	.426
SOCIC on Democracy, $N = 141$	.412
SOCIC on Wealth, $N = 141$	.313
SOCIC on Islamic Civilization, $N = 141$	.106
RN on PSOWSP (PSOW fails parallel line test), $N = 106$	.309
RN on Democracy, $N = 106$	.246
RN on Wealth, $N = 106$	Fails parallel line test; measure unreliable[b]
RN on Islamic Civilization, $N = 106$	.103

Note: PSOW = Physical Security of Women; PSOWSP = Physical Security of Women and Son Preference; GPI = Global Peace Index; SOCIC = States of Concern to the International Community; RN = Relations with Neighbors; Democracy = Level of Democracy, Wealth = Level of Wealth, Islamic Civilization = Prevalence of Islamic Civilization

[a]All model-fitting measures are significant at the 0.001 level.

[b]Another measure, Enduring Rivalries (ER), coded by Paul Diehl and Gary Goertz, *War and Peace in International Rivalry* (Ann Arbor: University of Michigan Press, 2000), correlates significantly with Relations with Neighbors. The Cox and Snell pseudo-R-squared for ER on GDP per capita Quintile is .036, and the model-fitting measures are not statistically significant. This may give us some insight into the relationship between wealth and relations with neighbors.

TABLE B.3 Multivariate Polytomous Logistic Regression of GPI (Global Peace Index) on Four Independent Variables Parameter Estimates

	ESTIMATE	STD. ERROR	WALD	DF	SIG.	95% CONFIDENCE INTERVAL LOWER BOUND	95% CONFIDENCE INTERVAL UPPER BOUND
Threshold [GPI = 1]							
Most Peaceful	−5.488	1.068	26.409	1	.000	−7.582	−3.395
[GPI = 2]	−1.958	.892	4.811	1	.028	−3.707	−.208
[GPI = 3]	.828	.869	.907	1	.341	−.875	2.530
[GPI = 4]	2.890	1.077	7.200	1	.007	.779	5.001
Location [PSOW = 1]							
Most Secure	−2.499	1.059	5.570	1	.018	−4.574	−.424
[PSOW = 2]	−1.570	.774	4.113	1	.043	−3.087	−.053
[PSOW = 3]	−.446	.586	.579	1	.447	−1.595	.703
[PSOW = 4]	0[a]	.	.	0	.	.	.
[Democracy = 1] Free	−.973	.652	2.224	1	.136	−2.252	.306
[Democracy = 2]	−.693	.610	1.288	1	.256	−1.889	.504
[Democracy = 3]	0[a]	.	.	0	.	.	.
[Wealth = 1] Wealthiest	−2.067	.949	4.745	1	.029	−3.926	−.207
[Wealth = 2]	−.844	.860	.962	1	.327	−2.530	.842
[Wealth = 3]	.469	.828	.320	1	.571	−1.154	2.092
[Wealth = 4]	.523	.880	.353	1	.553	−1.202	2.247
[Wealth = 5]	0[a]	.	.	0	.	.	.
[Islamic = 0] Non−Islamic	−.140	.647	.047	1	.828	−1.409	1.128
[Islamic = 1]	0[a]	.	.	0	.	.	.

Link function: Logit.

Note: GPI = Global Peace Index; PSOW = Physical Security of Women; Democracy = Level of Democracy; Wealth = Level of Wealth; Islamic = Prevalence of Islamic Civilization

[a]This parameter is set to zero because it is redundant.

TABLE B.4 Cross-tabulation of Democracies Dichotomized According to High-Low PSOW (Physical Security of Women) and GPI* (Global Peace Index)

			GPI ROUNDED		
			IF DEMOCRACY, 0 = GOOD PSOW (0,1); 1 = POOR PSOW (2,3,4)		
			0	1	TOTAL
GPI	1	Count	4	7	11
		% within GPI	36.4	63.6	100.0
		% within If democracy, 0 = Good PSOW (0,1); 1 = Poor PSOW (2,3,4)	50.0	15.2	20.4
		% of Total	7.4	13.0	20.4
	2	Count	4	22	26
		% within GPI	15.4	84.6	100.0
		% within If democracy, 0 = Good PSOW (0,1); 1 = Poor PSOW (2,3,4)	50.0	47.8	48.1
		% of Total	7.4	40.7	48.1
	3	Count	0	15	15
		% within GPI	0	100.0	100.0
		% within If democracy, 0 = Good PSOW (0,1); 1 = Poor PSOW (2,3,4)	0	32.6	27.8
		% of Total	0	27.8	27.8
	4	Count	0	1	1
		% within GPI	0	100.0	100.0
		% within If democracy, 0 = Good PSOW (0,1); 1 = Poor PSOW (2,3,4)	0	2.2	1.9
		% of Total	0	1.9	1.9
	5	Count	0	1	1
		% within GPI	0	100.0	100.0
		% within If democracy, 0 = Good PSOW (0,1); 1 = Poor PSOW (2,3,4)	0	2.2	1.9
		% of Total	0	1.9	1.9
	Total	Count	8	46	54
		% within GPI	14.8	85.2	100.0
		% within If democracy, 0 = Good PSOW (0,1); 1 = Poor PSOW (2,3,4)	100.0	100.0	100.0
		% of Total	14.8	85.2	100.0

TABLE B.4 (*continued*)

SYMMETRIC MEASURES

		VALUE	ASYMP. STD. ERROR[a]	APPROX. T[b]	APPROX. SIG.
Ordinal by Ordinal	Kendall's tau-b	.332	.092	2.721	.007
	Kendall's tau-c	.269	.099	2.721	.007
	Gamma	.778	.127	2.721	.007
	Spearman Correlation	.354	.098	2.727	.009[c]
Interval by Interval	Pearson's R	.334	.094	2.552	.014[c]
N of Valid Cases		54			

Note: GPI = Global Peace Index; PSOW = Physical Security of Women
[a]Not assuming the null hypothesis
[b]Using the asymptotic standard error assuming the null hypothesis
[c]Based on normal approximation

TABLE B.5 Ordinal by Ordinal Measures of Association (same as above, but using SOCIC (State of Concern to the International Community) as dependent variable)

SYMMETRIC MEASURES

		VALUE	ASYMP. STD. ERROR[a]	APPROX. T[b]	APPROX. SIG.
Ordinal by Ordinal	Kendall's tau-b	.417	.079	3.760	.000
	Kendall's tau-c	.357	.095	3.760	.000
	Gamma	.917	.085	3.760	.000
	Spearman Correlation	.441	.083	3.842	.000[c]
Interval by Interval	Pearson's R	.375	.067	3.161	.002[c]
N of Valid Cases		63			

[a]Not assuming the null hypothesis
[b]Using the asymptotic standard error assuming the null hypothesis
[c]Based on normal approximation

TABLE B.6 Ordinal by Ordinal Measures of Association (same as above, but using RN (Relations with Neighboring Countries) as dependent variable)

		VALUE	ASYMP. STD. ERROR[a]	APPROX. T[b]	APPROX. SIG.
SYMMETRIC MEASURES					
Ordinal by Ordinal	Kendall's tau-b	.396	.070	3.397	.001
	Kendall's tau-c	.307	.090	3.397	.001
	Gamma	1.000	.000	3.397	.001
	Spearman Correlation	.414	.073	3.275	.002[c]
Interval by Interval	Pearson's R	.361	.065	2.793	.007[c]
N of Valid Cases		54			

[a]Not assuming the null hypothesis
[b]Using the asymptotic standard error assuming the null hypothesis
[c]Based on normal approximation

TABLE B.7 Cross-tabulation of Polygyny with GPI (Global Peace Index)

			GPI ROUNDED[a]					
			POLYGYNY 2007, 0–4 RANGE					
			0	**1**	**2**	**3**	**4**	**TOTAL**
GPI	1	Count	10	1	0	0	0	11
		% within GPI	90.9	9.1	0	0	0	100.0
		% within Polygyny 2007, 0-4 range	16.9	12.5	0	0	0	10.5
		% of Total	9.5	1.0	0	0	0	10.5
	2	Count	25	1	9	4	2	41
		% within GPI	61.0	2.4	22.0	9.8	4.9	100.0
		% within Polygyny 2007, 0-4 range	42.4	12.5	42.9	40.0	28.6	39.0
		% of Total	23.8	1.0	8.6	3.8	1.9	39.0
	3	Count	20	3	9	5	4	41
		% within GPI	48.8	7.3	22.0	12.2	9.8	100.0
		% within Polygyny 2007, 0-4 range	33.9	37.5	42.9	50.0	57.1	39.0
		% of Total	19.0	2.9	8.6	4.8	3.8	39.0
	4	Count	4	2	2	1	1	10
		% within GPI	40.0	20.0	20.0	10.0	10.0	100.0
		% within Polygyny 2007, 0-4 range	6.8	25.0	9.5	10.0	14.3	9.5
		% of Total	3.8	1.9	1.9	1.0	1.0	9.5
	5	Count	0	1	1	0	0	2
		% within GPI	0	50.0	50.0	0	0	100.0
		% within Polygyny 2007, 0–4 range	0	12.5	4.8	0	0	1.9
		% of Total	0	1.0	1.0	0	0	1.9
Total		Count	59	8	21	10	7	105
		% within GPI	56.2	7.6	20.0	9.5	6.7	100.0
		% within Polygyny 2007, 0-4 range	100.0	100.0	100.0	100.0	100.0	100.0
		% of Total	56.2	7.6	20.0	9.5	6.7	100.0

TABLE B.7 (*continued*)

SYMMETRIC MEASURES

		VALUE	ASYMP. STD. ERROR[a]	APPROX. T[b]	APPROX. SIG.
Ordinal by Ordinal	Kendall's tau-b	.218	.073	2.969	.003
	Kendall's tau-c	.177	.060	2.969	.003
	Gamma	.333	.108	2.969	.003
	Spearman Correlation	.255	.085	2.682	.009[c]
Interval by Interval	Pearson's R	.235	.077	2.449	.016[d]
N of Valid Cases		105			

[a]GPI Rounded, 2007; (Raw Range = Rounded Value) 1.0–1.49 = 1; 1.5–1.99 = 2; 2.0–2.49 = 3; 2.5–3 = 4
[b]Not assuming the null hypothesis
[c]Using the asymptotic standard error assuming the null hypothesis
[d]Based on normal approximation

TABLE B.8 Polygyny's Association with SOCIC (States of Concern to the International Community)

SYMMETRIC MEASURES

		VALUE	ASYMP. STD. ERROR[a]	APPROX. T[b]	APPROX. SIG.
Ordinal by Ordinal	Kendall's tau-b	.261	.063	4.190	.000
	Kendall's tau-c	.236	.056	4.190	.000
	Gamma	.352	.084	4.190	.000
	Spearman Correlation	.322	.075	4.009	.000[c]
Interval by Interval	Pearson's R	.269	.074	3.289	.001[c]
N of Valid Cases		141			

[a]Not assuming the null hypothesis
[b]Using the asymptotic standard error assuming the null hypothesis
[c]Based on normal approximation

TABLE B.9 Polygyny's Association with RN (Relations with Neighboring Countries)

SYMMETRIC MEASURES

		VALUE	ASYMP. STD. ERROR[a]	APPROX. T[b]	APPROX. SIG.
Ordinal by Ordinal	Kendall's tau-b	.284	.070	4.038	.000
	Kendall's tau-c	.232	.057	4.038	.000
	Gamma	.419	.100	4.038	.000
	Spearman Correlation	.336	.083	3.641	.000[c]
Interval by Interval	Pearson's R	.272	.078	2.881	.005[c]
N of Valid Cases		106			

[a]Not assuming the null hypothesis
[b]Using the asymptotic standard error assuming the null hypothesis
[c]Based on normal approximation

TABLE B.10 Polygyny's Association with Level of Organized Conflict (Internal)

SYMMETRIC MEASURES

		VALUE	ASYMP. STD. ERROR[a]	APPROX. T[b]	APPROX. SIG.
Ordinal by Ordinal	Kendall's tau-b	.333	.067	4.844	.000
	Kendall's tau-c	.289	.060	4.844	.000
	Gamma	.461	.087	4.844	.000
	Spearman Correlation	.392	.078	4.704	.000[c]
Interval by Interval	Pearson's R	.406	.076	4.905	.000[c]
N of Valid Cases		124			

[a]Not assuming the null hypothesis
[b]Using the asymptotic standard error assuming the null hypothesis
[c]Based on normal approximation

TABLE B.11 Pearson's R; IFL (Inequity in Family Law/Practice) and PSOW Minus Marital Rape (Physical Security of Women)

IFL AND	PEARSON'S R[a]	GAMMA[a]	SIGNIFICANCE OF EACH ($P \leq X$)
PSOW Minus Marital Rape ($N = 141$)	.630	.744	.0001

[a]Asymptotic Standard Error, .048 and .051, respectively, for Pearson's R and Gamma

TABLE B.12 Bivariate Cox and Snell Pseudo-R-Squareds PSOW Minus Marital Rape (Physical Security of Women); IFL (Inequity in Family Law/Practice), Level of Democracy, Level of Wealth, Presence of Islamic Civilization

VARIABLES (N)	PSEUDO-R-SQUARED VALUE[a]
PSOWMMR on IFL ($N = 141$)	.402
PSOWMMR on Democracy ($N = 141$)	.386
PSOWMMR on Wealth ($N = 141$)	.353
PSOWMMR on Islam ($N = 141$)	.227

[a]All model-fitting measures are significant at the .001 level

TABLE B.13 Bivariate Cox and Snell Pseudo-R-Suareds, GPI (Global Peace Index) on IFL (Inequity in Family Law/Practice), Level of Democracy, Level of Wealth, Prevalence of Islamic Civilization

VARIABLES (N)	PSEUDO-R-SQUARED VALUE[a]
GPI on IFL ($N = 105$)	.339
GPI on Democracy ($N = 105$)	.203
GPI on Wealth ($N = 105$)	Fails test of parallel lines; measure unreliable
GPI on Islam ($N = 105$)	.084

[a]All model fitting measures are significant at the .001 level

TABLE B.14 Multivariate Polytomous Regression: GPI on IFL, Democracy, Wealth, Islamic Civilization

PARAMETER ESTIMATES

| | | ESTIMATE | STD. ERROR | WALD | DF | SIG. | 95% CONFIDENCE INTERVAL | |
							LOWER BOUND	UPPER BOUND
Threshold	[GPI = 1] Most Peaceful	-6.890	1.269	29.468	1	.000	-9.378	-4.402
	[GPI = 2]	-3.102	1.075	8.324	1	.004	-5.210	-.995
	[GPI = 3]	-.245	1.006	.059	1	.808	-2.217	1.728
	[GPI = 4]	1.932	1.176	2.700	1	.100	-.373	4.236
Location	[IFL = 0] Most Equitable	-3.713	1.195	9.660	1	.002	-6.054	-1.371
	[IFL = 1]	-1.626	.953	2.911	1	.088	-3.494	.242
	[IFL = 2]	-1.082	.905	1.431	1	.232	-2.856	.691
	[IFL = 3]	-1.823	.878	4.316	1	.038	-3.543	-.103
	[IFL = 4]	0[a]	.	.	0	.	.	.
	[Democracy = 2]	-.626	.620	1.021	1	.312	-1.841	.588
	[Democracy = 3]	0[a]	.	.	0	.	.	.
	[Wealth = 1] Wealthiest	-2.067	1.042	3.935	1	.047	-4.109	-.025
	[Wealth = 2]	-1.024	.988	1.074	1	.300	-2.961	.913
	[Wealth = 3]	.300	.985	.093	1	.761	-1.631	2.232
	[Wealth = 4]	.895	.924	.938	1	.333	-.916	2.706
	[Wealth = 5]	0[a]	.	.	0	.	.	.
	[Islamic = 0] Non–Islamic	-.774	.574	1.819	1	.177	-1.898	.351
	[Islamic = 1]	0[a]	.	.	0	.	.	.

Link function: Logit.

Note: IFL = Inequity in Family Law/Practice; GPI = Global Peace Index; Democracy = Level of Democracy; Wealth = Level of Wealth; Islamic = Prevalence of Islamic Civilization

[a]This parameter is set to zero because it is redundant.

TABLE B.15 Association of Discrepancy Between National Law and Practice Concerning Women with SOCIC (States of Concern to the International Community)

			SYMMETRIC MEASURES		
		VALUE	ASYMP. STD. ERROR[a]	APPROX. T[b]	APPROX. SIG.
Ordinal by Ordinal	Kendall's tau-b	.438	.060	7.000	.000
	Kendall's tau-c	.417	.060	7.000	.000
	Gamma	.557	.071	7.000	.000
	Spearman Correlation	.522	.067	7.209	.000[c]
Interval by Interval	Pearson's R	.528	.060	7.338	.000[c]
N of Valid Cases		141			

[a]Not assuming the null hypothesis
[b]Using the asymptotic standard error assuming the null hypothesis
[c]Based on normal approximation

NOTES

1. ROOTS OF NATIONAL AND INTERNATIONAL RELATIONS

1. A small minority of people are neither biologically male nor biologically female; they are intersex. Other individuals may be transsexual. In these cases, the perception of sex, rather than sex itself, may determine the societal treatment of such people. In some cultures it is possible to change gender even if sex is unchanged; for example, in Albania an ancient code allows women in certain circumstances to proclaim themselves to be men and to live as men, even though their sex remains acknowledged as female.

2. Jan Jindy Pettman, *Worlding Women: A Feminist International Politics* (New York: Routledge, 1996).

3. "Christian Man Who Got 39 Lashes and One Year in Jail Is Free," *Arabic News*, August 6, 1997, www.arabicnews.com/ansub/Daily/Day/970806/1997080619 .html, accessed May 18, 2010.

4. To access these variables, go to http://womanstats.org. The WomanStats Database codes for more than 320 variables concerning the situation of women in 175 countries. Access is free.

5. V. Spike Peterson, "Security and Sovereign States: What Is at Stake in Taking Feminism Seriously?" in V. Spike Peterson, ed., *Gendered States: Feminist (Re)Visions of International Relations Theory*, 31–64 (Boulder, CO: Lynne Rienner Publishers, 1992).

6. "Purdah" refers to the practice of sequestering women in private quarters and generally not allowing their entry into public space. "Infibulation" refers to a form of female genital cutting that involves sewing the stumped ends of cut labia together to form a seal with a tiny hole over the vaginal opening.

7. Valerie M. Hudson and Andrea M. Den Boer, *Bare Branches: The Security Implications of Asia's Surplus Male Population* (Cambridge, MA: MIT Press, 2004).

8. In some cultures, there may be additional elements to family honor besides the chastity of female relatives, but chastity is an almost universal element and often the primary element of the concept of "honor" cross-nationally.

9. Rhea Wessel, "Interview with Serap Cileli," *World Politics Review*, February 1, 2007, www.worldpoliticsreview.com/blog/blog.aspx?id=516, accessed May 18, 2010.

10. Khalid Tanveer, "Pakistani Man Discusses 'Honor' Killings," *USA Today*, December 28, 2005, www.usatoday.com/news/world/2005-12-28-pakistan-honor-killings_x.htm, accessed May 18, 2010.

11. Elisabeth Bumiller, "Deny Rape or Be Hated: Kosovo Victims' Choice," *New York Times*, June 22, 1999, www.nytimes.com/1999/06/22/world/crisis-in-the-balkans-crimes-deny-rape-or-be-hated-kosovo-victims-choice.html?scp=1& sq=deny%20rape%20or%20be%20hated%20kosovo&st=cse, accessed May 18, 2010.

12. Though we pause to note that several countries, such as Qatar, practice almost universal consanguineous marriage.

13. PBS, "China from the Inside: Women of the Country," transcript, www.pbs .org/kqed/chinainside/pdf/pbschina-ep2.pdf, accessed May 18, 2010.

14. Ibid.

15. Brinton's Law is named after Carl Brinton, one of our student coders, who discovered that when a law was passed in a South American nation mandating maternity leave and other benefits for mothers if the number of women in the company was at least nineteen, what ensued was that a rash of companies fired all but eighteen of their women employees. We use the term "Brinton's Law" to refer to the consistently observed regularity that even initiatives taken to correct an obvious gender inequity often wind up being used to hurt women, and that even cultural practices that seem at first glance to be completely opposite to one another (bride-price versus dowry, for example), and therefore assumably opposite in their effects on women, will both be found to hurt women. A wonderful example of Brinton's Law appears in Nicholas Kristof and Sheryl WuDunn's Half the Sky. They tell of an incident in which a development entity had helped poor village women create businesses processing food crops; the minute those businesses began turning substantial profit, the men from the village took over the businesses and ousted the women (Nicholas D. Kristof and Sheryl WuDunn, *Half the Sky: Turning Oppression Into Opportunity for Women Worldwide* (New York: Alfred A. Knopf, 2009).

16. Hudson and Den Boer, *Bare Branches*.

17. UN Division for the Advancement of Women, "Violence Against Women: Good Practices in Combating and Eliminating Violence Against Women," 2005, 12, www.un.org/womenwatch/daw/egm/vaw-gp-2005/docs/experts/kishwar .dowry.pdf, accessed May 18, 2010.

18. CNN, "Child Rape Survivor Saves 'Virgin Myth' Victims," June 5, 2009, www .cnn.com/2009/LIVING/06/04/cnnheroes.betty.makoni/index.html, accessed May 18, 2010.

19. Kristof and WuDunn, *Half the Sky*.

20. Marilyn Waring, *Counting for Nothing: What Men Value and What Women Are Worth*, 2nd ed. (Toronto: University of Toronto Press, 2004).

21. UNECA, "A Background Paper on Engendering Budgetary Policies and Processes," 2001, www.uneca.org/acgd/Publications/en_0112_latigo.pdf, accessed May 18, 2010.

22. See, for example, http://salary.com, accessed May 18, 2010.

23. FAO, "Food Needs and Population," World Food Summit, 1996, www.fao.org/ docrep/x0262e/x0262e23.htm, accessed May 18, 2010.

24. Claudia von Werlhof, "Women's Work: The Blind Spot in the Critique of Political Economy," in Maria Mies, ed., *Women: The Last Colony*, 13–26 (Atlantic Highlands, NJ: Zed Books, 1988).

25. Ann Crittenden, *The Price of Motherhood* (New York: Henry Holt, 2001).

2. WHAT IS THERE TO SEE, AND WHY AREN'T WE SEEING IT?

1. John Ward Anderson and Molly Moore, "Third World Women: A Lifetime of Oppression," *International Herald Tribune*, February 15, 1993.

2. For a video of Suzanne Mubarak explaining her position on female genital cutting and others issues, see www.youtube.com/watch?v=S1oOgySZNvM, accessed May 18, 2010.

3. Maggie O'Kane, "The Mistake of Being Muslim," *Guardian Weekly*, March 28, 1993, 9.

4. As recounted in Stephen Lewis, "Nairobi Press Conference on Ending Sexual Violence in the Eastern Region of the DRC," September 13, 2007, http://216.95.229.16/news_item.cfm?news=1988&year=2007, accessed May 18, 2010.

5. Anna Quindlen, "Victim and Valkyrie," *New York Times*, March 16, 1994, www .nytimes.com/1994/03/16/opinion/public-private-victim-and-valkyrie.html?sc p=2&sq=quindlen%20victim%20valkyrie%201994&st=cse, accessed May 18, 2010.

6. Dexter Filkins, "Afghan Girls, Scarred by Acid, Defy Terror, Embracing School," *New York Times*, January 13, 2009, www.nytimes.com/2009/01/14/wo rld/asia/14kandahar.html?scp=4&sq=acid%20attacks&st=cse, accessed May 18, 2010.

7. Pam Belluck, "Women's Killers Are Very Often Their Partners, Study Finds," *New York Times*, March 31, 1997, www.nytimes.com/specials/women/warchive/ 970331_1651.html, accessed May 18, 2010.

8. U.S. Department of Justice, "Female Victims of Violent Crime," December 1996, www.ojp.usdoj.gov/bjs/pub/ascii/fvvc.txt, accessed May 18, 2010.

9. Eva Lundgren, Gun Heimer, Jenny Westerstrand, and Anne-Marie Kallio-koski, "Captured Queen: Men's Violence Against Women in 'Equal' Sweden: a Prevalence Study," Uppsala University, 2001, www.unece.org/stats/gender/vaw/surveys/Sweden/publication.pdf, accessed May 18, 2010.

10. UNIFEM, "Women in Afghanistan to Mark International Women's Day with Public Prayer for Peace and Justice," March 6, 2009, www.unifem.org/news_events/story_detail.php?StoryID=844, accessed May 18, 2010.

11. Phaedra Starling, "Schrodinger's Rapist," October 8, 2009, http://kateharding.net/2009/10/08/guest-blogger-starling-schrodinger's-rapist-or-a-guy's-guide-to-approaching-strange-women-without-being-maced/, accessed May 18, 2010.

12. Kevin Sullivan, "A Mother's Final Look at Life: In Impoverished Sierra Leone, Childbirth Carries Deadly Odds," *Washington Post*, October 12, 2008, www.washingtonpost.com/wp-dyn/content/article/2008/10/11/AR2008101102165.html, accessed May 18, 2010.

13. World Health Organization, "Risking Death to Give Life," 2005, www.who.int/whr/2005/chapter4/en/index1.html, accessed May 18, 2010.

14. Human Security Report Project, "Mini-Atlas of Human Security," Vancouver, British Columbia, 2008.

15. Sullivan, "A Mother's Final Look."

16. All quotations from Women for Women International, "Ending Violence Against Women in Eastern Congo," Winter 2007, 20–22, www.womenforwomen.org/news-women-for-women/files/MensLeadershipFullReport_002.pdf, accessed June 1, 2010.

17. Seth Faison, "Women's Meeting Agrees on Right to Say No to Sex," *New York Times*, September 11, 1995, www.nytimes.com/1995/09/11/world/women-s-meeting-agrees-on-right-to-say-no-to-sex.html?scp=1&sq=seth%20faison%20right%20to%20say%20no%20to%20sex&st=cse, accessed May 18, 2010.

18. Catherine Maternowska, "Truck Stop Girls," *New York Times Magazine*, August 18, 2009, www.nytimes.com/2009/08/23/magazine/23lives-t.html?emc=eta1, accessed May 18, 2010.

19. Carolyn Hannan and Ingvar Andersson, "Gender Perspectives on Ecological Sanitation" (paper prepared for the 97th annual meeting of the Association of American Geographers, New York, February 27–March 3, 2001).

20. World Bank, *Gender and Poverty in India* (Washington, DC: World Bank, 1991).

21. World Vision, "Female He Created Them," *World Vision Today*, Spring 1998, 2.

22. Valerie M. Hudson and Andrea M. Den Boer, *Bare Branches: The Security Implications of Asia's Surplus Male Population* (Cambridge, MA: MIT Press, 2004).

23. Christopher Guilmoto, "Sex Ratio Imbalance in Asia: Trends, Consequences, and Policy Responses," UNFPA, 2007, www.unfpa.org/gender/docs/studies/summaries/regional_analysis.pdf, accessed November 1, 2007.

24. A wonderful overview of this topic is Freda Banda's "Project on a Mechanism to Address Laws That Discriminate Against Women," Office of the High Commissioner for Human Rights, March 6, 2008, www.ohchr.org/Documents/Publications/laws_that_discriminate_against_women.pdf, accessed May 18, 2010.

25. "Om Gad," in Nayra Atiya, *Khul Khaal: Five Egyptian Women Tell Their Stories*, 14–15 (Syracuse, NY: Syracuse University Press, 1982).

26. Mohammed Jamjoom, "Age 12 Girl—Child Bride of Forced Marriage—Dies in Painful Childbirth, Infant Also Perishes," CNN, September 14, 2009, http://edition.cnn.com/2009/HEALTH/09/14/yemen.childbirth.death/index.html?iref=mpstoryview, accessed May 31, 2010.

27. Martha Nussbaum, *Sex and Social Justice* (Oxford: Oxford University Press, 2000).

28. Aditi Bhaduri, "Muslims in India Design New Marriage Contract," *Womens ENews*, August 4, 2008, www.womensenews.org/story/the-world/080804/muslims-india-design-new-marriage-contract, accessed May 18, 2010.

29. Ann Crittenden, *The Price of Motherhood* (New York: Henry Holt, 2001).

30. Mehranguiz Kar and Homa Hoodfar, "Women and Personal Status Law in Iran," *Middle East Report*, no. 198 (January–March 1996): 36–38.

31. Stephanie Sinclair and Barry Bearak, "The Bride Price," *New York Times Magazine*, July 9, 2006, www.nytimes.com/2006/07/09/magazine/09BRI.html, accessed May 18, 2010.

32. Farah Stockman, "Women Pay a Price in War on Afghan Drug Trade," *Boston Globe*, September 28, 2005, www.boston.com/news/world/middleeast/articles/2005/09/28/women_pay_a_price_in_war_on_afghan_drug_trade/, accessed May 18, 2010.

33. Elizabeth Rubin, "Women's Work," *New York Times Magazine*, October 9, 2005, www.nytimes.com/2005/10/09/magazine/09afghan.html?pagewanted=1, accessed May 18, 2010.

34. Tabibul Islam, "Bangladesh: Rape Victims Married Off to Rapists," IPSNews, June 16, 2003, http://ipsnews.net/interna.asp?idnews=18765, accessed May 18, 2010.

35. Calvin Sims, "Justice in Peru: Victim Gets Rapist for a Husband," *New York Times*, March 12, 1997, www.nytimes.com/1997/03/12/world/justice-in-peru-victim-gets-rapist-for-a-husband.html, accessed May 18, 2010.

36. Craig Smith, "Abduction, Often Violent, a Kyrgyz Wedding Rite," *New York Times*, April 30, 2005, www.nytimes.com/2005/04/30/international/asia/30brides.html, accessed May 18, 2010.

37. UNFPA, "Bride Kidnapping," 2006, www.unfpa.org/16days/documents/pl_bridenapping_factsheet.doc, accessed May 18, 2010.

38. "Legal Experts Recommend Canada Legalize Polygamy," *Vancouver Sun*, January 13, 2006, www.canada.com/vancouversun/news/story.html?id=e20244cb-63b2–47f9–893e-390453fa5067&k=24668, accessed February 2, 2011. In November 2011, the Constitutional Court of Canada upheld Canada's ban on polygamy.

39. Nicholas Bala, "Canada: Not Cut Out for Polygamy," *Globe and Mail*, January 18, 2006, www.wluml.org/node/2677, accessed May 18, 2010.

40. UNDP, "Swaziland Human Development Report: HIV and AIDS and Culture," 2008, http://hdr.undp.org/en/reports/nationalreports/africa/swaziland/Swaziland_NHDR_2008.pdf, accessed May 18, 2010.

41. Seth Mydans, "In Pakistan, Rape Victims Are the 'Criminals,'" *New York Times*, May 17, 2002, www.nytimes.com/2002/05/17/international/asia/17RAPE.html?scp=1&sq=Mydans%202002%20Pakistan%20rape&st=cse, accessed May 18, 2010.

42. Abira Ashfaq, "Reform in Pakistan: Real Change, or a Band-Aid?" *PeaceWork*, issue 372 (February 2007), www.peaceworkmagazine.org/reform-pakistan-real-change-or-band-aid, accessed May 18, 2010.

43. "Syria Stiffens Punishment for Honour Killings," January 11, 2011, http://gulfnews.com/news/region/syria/syria-stiffens-punishment-for-honour-killing-1.744322, accessed February 9, 2011. Just two years previously, the government had raised the punishment to a minimum of two years; see "Syria Amends Honor Killing Law," BBC, July 2, 2009, http://news.bbc.co.uk/2/hi/middle_east/8130639.stm, accessed May 18, 2010.

44. James Brooke, "Brazil Tries to Curb Crimes Against Women," *New York Times*, November 17, 1991, www.nytimes.com/1991/11/17/world/brazil-tries-to-curb-crimes-against-women.html?scp=1&sq=james%20brooke%20Brazil%20curb%20crimes%20against%20women&st=cse, accessed May 18, 2010.

45. CNN, "In Texas, Man Gets 4 Months for Killing Wife, 15 Years for Wounding Man," January 6, 2005; www.cnn.com/2005/LAW/01/06/jealous.husband.ap/index.html, accessed February 17, 2005.

46. U.S. State Department, "Country Report on Human Rights: Rwanda," 2007, www.state.gov/g/drl/rls/hrrpt/2007/100499.htm, accessed March 14, 2008.

47. Julia Preston, "US May Be Open to Asylum for Spouse Abuse," *New York Times*, October 29, 2009, www.nytimes.com/2009/10/30/us/30asylum.html, accessed May 18, 2010.

48. USAID, "Land Tenure, Property Rights, and HIV/AIDS," 2008, www.ardinc.com/upload/photos/LAND_TENURE_AND_PROPERTY_RIGHTS_AND_HIV.pdf, accessed May 18, 2010.

49. Interview by Valerie Hudson with staff of the Cultural Development Center for Rural Women, Beijing, China, March 2009.

50. Rosemary Okello-Orlale, "The Debate on Women's Property Rights Takes Centre Stage in the Kenyan Media," *Women in Media and News*, June 26, 2008, www.wimnonline.org/WIMNsVoicesBlog/2008/06/26/the-debate-on-

women's-property-rights-takes-centre-stage-in-the-kenyan-media/, accessed May 18, 2010.

51. UNIFEM, "Women's Land and Property Rights," n.d., www.unifem.org/gender_issues/women_poverty_economics/land_property_rights.php, accessed May 18, 2010.

52. Certain female rulers, such as Queen Elizabeth I, were accorded male status and thus were not perceived as undermining the template.

53. Female leaders may be accorded male status as stand-ins for famous male relatives; here we think of Benazir Bhutto, Corazon Aquino, Violetta Chamorro, and others.

54. www.freerepublic.com/focus/news/811070/posts, accessed May 18, 2010.

55. www.freerepublic.com/focus/news/810823/posts, accessed May 18, 2010.

56. Washington Memorial Chapel, Valley Forge, Pennsylvania, http://209.200.101.38/?t=c&cid=13, accessed May 18, 2010. There is (finally) a movement in the United States to create a national monument dedicated to women who died as a result of pregnancy and childbirth; http://mothersmonument.org.

57. Quoted in Urvashi Butalia, "Mother India," *OneWorld*, March 7, 2001, www.oneworld.org/issue277/mother.htm, accessed May 18, 2010.

58. Arthur Gilbert and James Cole, "Revolutionary Theory and Gender Theory: The Iranian Case" (paper presented at the annual meeting of the International Studies Association, Chicago, February 21–25, 2005).

59. Harriet M. Johnston-Wood, "Letter to the Editor," *New York Times*, March 17, 1910, http://query.nytimes.com/mem/archive-free/pdf?res=9D0DE0DA1430E2 33A25752C2A9659C946196D6CF, accessed May 18, 2010.

60. Carol Cohn, "Wars, Wimps, and Women: Talking Gender and Thinking War," in Miriam Cooke and Angela Woollacott, eds., *Gendering War Talk* (Princeton, NJ: Princeton University Press, 1993), 227.

61. Inter-Parliamentary Union, "Women in National Parliaments," www.ipu.org/wmn-e/world.htm, accessed September 30, 2009.

62. Global Database of Quotas for Women, www.quotaproject.org/country.cfm, accessed May 18, 2010.

63. D. Kaufmann, "Challenges in the Next Stage of Corruption," in *New Perspectives in Combating Corruption* (Washington, D.C: Transparency International and the World Bank, 1998).

64. World Bank, "Engendering Development: Through Gender Equality in Rights, Resources, and Voice," *World Bank Policy Research Report* (Washington, DC: Oxford University Press, 2001).

65. Inter-Parliamentary Union, "Politics: Women's Insight," 2000, www.ipu.org/iss-e/women.htm, accessed December 26, 2007.

66. Ann Crittenden, *If You've Raised Kids, You Can Manage Anything: Leadership Begins at Home* (New York: Gotham, 2004), 76–77.

67. Ibid., 188.

68. Ibid., 234.

69. Ester Boserup, *Women's Role in Economic Development* (London: Allen and Unwin, 1970).

70. World Bank, "Engendering Development."

71. John Hoddinott and Lawrence Haddad, "Does Female Income Share Influence Household Expenditure Patterns?" *Oxford Bulletin of Economics and Statistics* 57, no. 1 (2001): 77–97.

72. Duncan Thomas, "Intrahousehold Resource Allocation: An Inferential Approach," *Journal of Human Resources* 25 (1990): 635–664; Duncan Thomas, D. Contreras, and Elizabeth Frankenberg, *Child Health and the Distribution of Household Resources at Marriage* (Los Angeles: RAND and UCLA, 1997).

73. Stephan Klasen, *Does Gender Inequality Reduce Growth and Development? Evidence from Crosscountry Regressions*, 1999, http://siteresources.worldbank .org/INTGENDER/Resources/wp7.pdf, Washington: World Bank, accessed May 18, 2010.

74. United Nations, "Statistics and Indicators on Men and Women," http://unstats .un.org/unsd/demographic/products/indwm, accessed May 18, 2010.

75. World Bank, *Engendering Development*.

76. Berta Esteve-Volart , "Sex Discrimination and Growth" (IMF working paper WP/00/84, Washington, DC: International Monetary Fund, African Department, 2000).

77. Shireen J. Jejeebhoy, *Women's Education, Autonomy, and Reproductive Behavior: Experience from Developing Countries* (Oxford: Clarendon Press, 1995); T. Paul Schultz, "Investments in the Schooling and Health of Women and Men: Quantities and Returns," *Journal of Human Resources* 28, no. 4 (1993): 694–725.

78. Albino Barrera, "The Role of Maternal Schooling and Its Interaction with Public Health Programs in Child Health Production," *Journal of Development Economics* 32 (1990): 69–91.

79. Lisa Smith and Lawrence Haddad, "Overcoming Child Malnutrition in Developing Countries," *2020 Vision Briefs*, no. 64 (Washington, DC: Food Policy Research Institute, 2000), http://ideas.repec.org/p/fpr/2020dp/30.html, accessed December 26, 2007.

80. J. M. Coates and J. A. Herbert, "Endogenous Steroids and Financial Risk Taking on a London Trading Floor," *PNAS* 105, no. 16: 6167–6172, April 22, 2008, www.pnas.org/content/105/16/6167.full, accessed May 18, 2010.

81. Judith Dobrzynski, "Maybe the Meltdown's a Guy Thing," *New York Times*, November 15, 2008, www.nytimes.com/2008/11/16/weekinreview/16dobrzynski. html?ei=5070&emc=eta1, accessed May 18, 2010.

82. Some of the paragraphs that follow this sentence are adapted with permission from Valerie M. Hudson, "Good Riddance: Why Macho Had to Go," *Foreign Policy* (July/August 2009), www.foreignpolicy.com/articles/2009/06/19/good_riddance, accessed May 31, 2010.

83. Quoted in Michael Lewis, "Wall Street on the Tundra," *Vanity Fair*, April 2009, www.vanityfair.com/politics/features/2009/04/iceland200904, accessed May 18, 2010.

84. Brad Barber and Terrence Odean, "Boys Will Be Boys: Gender, Overconfidence, and Common Stock Investment," *Quarterly Journal of Investment* (February 2001): 261–291, http://faculty.haas.berkeley.edu/odean/papers/gender/BoysWillBeBoys.pdf, accessed May 18, 2010; Angela Lyons, Urvi Neelakantan, and Erik Scherpf, "Gender and Marital Differences in Wealth and Investment Decisions" (Networks Financial Institute Working Paper No. 2008-WP-02, 2008), http://papers.ssrn.com/sol3/papers.cfm?abstract_id=1109103, accessed May 18, 2010.

85. Chris Karpowitz and Tali Mendenberg, "Groups and Deliberations," *Swiss Political Science Review* 13, no. 4 (2007): 645–663; Chris Karpowitz and Tali Mendenberg, "Groups, Norms, and Gender: Initial Results from the Deliberative Justice Experiment" (paper presented at Southern California Political Psychology Workshop, University of California-Irvine, May 16, 2009).

86. Karpowitz and Mendenberg, "Groups, Norms, and Gender."

87. Marilyn Waring, *Counting for Nothing: What Men Value and What Women Are Worth*, 2nd ed. (Toronto: University of Toronto Press, 2004), 13.

88. UNDP, *The Human Development Report* (Oxford: Oxford University Press, 1995).

89. Salary.com, 9th Annual Mom Salary Survey, 2009, www.marketwire.com/press-release/SalaryCom-NASDAQ-SLRY-984585.html; Jennifer Steinhauer, "The Economic Unit Called Supermom," *New York Times*, May 8, 2005, 14, www.nytimes.com/2005/05/08/weekinreview/08stein.html?scp=1&sq=Steinhauer%202005%20supermom&st=cse, accessed May 18, 2010.

90. Crittenden, *The Price of Motherhood*.

91. Ibid.

92. Waring, *Counting for Nothing*, 3.

93. Nancy Folbre, *The Invisible Heart* (New York: New Press, 2001).

94. Waring, *Counting for Nothing*, 21, 10, 23, 65.

95. Harris Collingwood, "The Sink or Swim Economy," *New York Times Magazine*, June 8, 2003, www.nytimes.com/2003/06/08/magazine/the-sink-or-swim-economy.html?scp=2&sq=wet%20dreams%20economists&st=cse&pagewanted=4, accessed May 18, 2010.

96. Joan S. Williams, *Unbending Gender: Why Family and Work Conflict and What to Do About It* (Oxford: Oxford University Press, 2001).

97. Matthew Connelly, *Fatal Misconceptions* (Cambridge, MA: Harvard University Press, 2008), 297, 160, 375.

98. Dilraj S. Sokhi, Michael D. Hunter, Iain D. Wilkinson, and Peter W. Woodruff, "Male and Female Voices Activate Distinct Regions in the Male Brain," *Neuroimage* 27, no. 3 (2005): 572–578.

99. Karpowitz and Mendenberg, "Groups, Norms, and Gender."

100. Nicholas Kristof, "When Women Rule," *New York Times*, February 10, 2008, www.nytimes.com/2008/02/10/opinion/10kristof.html, accessed May 18, 2010.

3. WHEN WE DO SEE THE GLOBAL PICTURE, WE ARE MOVED TO ASK HOW THIS HAPPENED

We are grateful to the *Journal of Peace Research* for permission to include in this chapter sections of Mary Caprioli, Valerie M. Hudson, Rose McDermott, Bonnie Ballif-Spanvill, Chad F. Emmett, and S. Matthew Stearmer, "The WomanStats Database: Advancing an Empirical Research Agenda," *Journal of Peace Research* 46, no. 6 (2009): 839–851. We also thank *International Security* for permission to include sections of our article Valerie M. Hudson, Mary Caprioli, Bonnie Ballif-Spanvill, Rose McDermott, and Chad F. Emmett, "The Heart of the Matter: The Security of Women and the Security of States," *International Security* 33, no. 3 (2008/2009): 7–45.

1. Mary Caprioli, "Primed for Violence: The Role of Gender Inequality in Predicting Internal Conflict," *International Studies Quarterly* 49, no. 2 (2005): 161–178.

2. This book goes to press as the Arab Spring is under way, so we cannot foresee how regime change in these countries will affect laws and practices concerning women. There are some positive signs, such as the interim Tunisian regime requiring that parties interweave female and male candidates in a 1-1-1 system on their lists. But there are some negative signs, such as the quota for women in the Egyptian legislature having been dropped. Only time will tell whether the Arab Spring was a springtime for Arab women also.

3. Thanks to Lindsey Hulet for her valuable help in creating the scales and writing the narrative for this section. Also thanks to Maren Reynolds for assisting.

4. Freedom House, "Women's Rights in the Middle East and North Africa–Saudi Arabia," 2005, http://freedomhouse.org/template.cfm?page=383&report=56, accessed May 31, 2010.

5. Emory University School of Law, "Islamic Family Law," 2002, www.law.emory.edu/ifl, accessed May 31, 2010.

6. United Nations Development Programme, "Arab Human Development Report 2005," http://hdr.undp.org/en/reports/regionalreports/arabstates/RBAS_ahdr2005_EN.pdf, accessed May 31, 2010.

7. Bradley Thayer, *Darwin and International Relations: On the Evolutionary Origins of War and Ethnic Conflict* (Lexington: University Press of Kentucky, 2004), 8–9.

8. Richard Dawkins, *The Selfish Gene* (Oxford: Oxford University Press, 1989), 331.

9. Theodore D. Kemper, *Social Structure and Testosterone* (New Brunswick, NJ: Rutgers University Press, 1990), 138.

10. Richard D. Alexander, "Evolution and Culture," in Napoleon A. Chagnon and William Irons, eds., *Evolutionary Biology and Human Social Behavior: An Anthropological Perspective* (North Scituate, MA: Duxbury, 1979), 59–78, quote from 77.

11. Richard Wrangham and Dale Peterson, *Demonic Males: Apes and the Origins of Human Violence* (New York: Houghton Mifflin, 1996), 24–25.

12. Ibid., 231.

13. Barbara Smuts, "Male Aggression Against Women: An Evolutionary Perspective," *Human Nature* 3, no. 1 (1992): 1–44; Barbara Smuts, "The Evolutionary Origins of Patriarchy," *Human Nature* 6, no. 1 (1995): 1–32.

14. Smuts, "Evolutionary Origins of Patriarchy," p. 1.

15. When one turns to evolutionary theory's account of male-female relations formative evolutionary environment (FEE) of tens of thousands of years, one quickly finds two apparently contradictory viewpoints in the theoretical literature. One major school of thought, exemplified by the work of Wrangham and Peterson (*Demonic Males*), suggests that the FEE produced a generalized social system of male dominance hierarchies, encoding a deep hierarchical relationship between men and women whose long duration surely and profoundly shaped natural selection. However, another school of thought, exemplified by the work of Leacock (Eleanor Leacock, "Interpreting the Origins of Sexual Inequality: Conceptual and Historical Problems," *Dialectical Anthropology* 7 [1983]: 263–284), suggests that in the hunter-gatherer societies representative of the FEE, there was no generalized male dominance over females, and thus human beings and the collectives they form have not been subject to more than ten millennia of male dominance. Both schools concur that once agriculture and animal husbandry became mainstays of human food systems, approximately 10,000 years ago, generalized male dominance did arise globally across human societies. Maria Mies, "Social Origins of the Sexual Division of Labor," in Maria Mies, Veronika Bennholdt-Thomsen, and Claudia Von Werlhof, eds., *Women: The Last Colony*, 67–95 (London: Zed Books, 1988).

16. R. L. Trivers, "Parental Investment and Sexual Selection," in B. Campbell, ed., *Sexual Selection and the Descent of Man, 1871–1971*, 136–179 (Chicago: Aldine, 1972). See also John Archer, "Does Sexual Selection Explain Sex Differences in Aggression?" *Behavioral and Brain Sciences* 32, nos. 3/4 (2009): 249–311.

17. Archer, "Sexual Selection," 250.

18. Smuts, "Evolutionary Origins of Patriarchy."

19. Patricia Adair Gowaty, "Sexual Dialectics, Sexual Selection, and Variation in Reproductive Behavior," in Patricia Adair Gowaty, ed., *Feminism and Evolutionary Biology: Boundaries, Intersections, and Frontiers*, 351–384, quote from 378 (New York: Chapman and Hall, 1997).

20. Patricia Adair Gowaty, "Sexual Natures: How Feminism Changed Evolutionary Biology," *Signs: Journal of Women in Culture and Society* 28, no. 3 (2003): 901–921.

21. Sue V. Rosser, "Possible Implications of Feminist Theories for the Study of Evolution," in Patricia Adair Gowaty, ed., *Feminism and Evolutionary Biology: Boundaries, Intersections, and Frontiers*, 21–41, quote from 32 (New York: Chapman and Hall, 1997).

22. Patricia Adair Gowaty, "Evolutionary Biology and Feminism," *Human Nature* 3 (1992): 217–249, quote from 219.

23. Smuts, "Male Aggression Against Women," 30.

24. Ibid.

25. Anne Campbell, "Sex Differences in Direct Aggression: What Are the Psychological Mediators?" *Aggression and Violent Behavior* 11, no. 3 (2006): 237–264.

26. Smuts, "Male Aggression Against Women," 8. Very different social systems can emerge where female networks are in place. Rebecca Hannagan supports the theory of the cooperative female, arguing that women made a significant contribution toward the development of cooperative groups in hunter-gatherer societies ("Gendered Political Behavior: A Darwinian Feminist Approach," *Sex Roles* 59 [2008]: 465–475). Women, she argues, may have been supportive of cooperative behavior in order to protect their offspring. Pregnant women, in particular, stood to benefit from food sharing in times of scarcity. "Maintaining certainty in their position in the lunch line, so to speak, is of greater concern to females than males due to the fundamental trade-off between somatic effort and reproductive effort" (469). Female hunter-gatherers are believed to have cooperated among one another for gathering, hunting, and child-rearing, but Hannagan argues that their role as facilitators may have extended to the males and the group as a whole: "[I]n foraging societies women are as likely as men to curb the deviant behavior of 'upstarts'—those who attempt to disrupt the social balance by violating group norms" (469). The sexual freedom and independence of females, Campbell argues, changed with the onset of agri-

culture 10,000 years ago when women began to be confined to smaller spaces of home and land, and men, who became the suppliers of food and other resources, were able to exercise greater control over women and achieve parental certainty ("Sex Differences in Direct Aggression"). While male dominance hierarchies may have become entrenched at this time, male aggression and patriarchal practices are believed to have been one of the dominant strategies used in sexual selection during hunter-gatherer periods of human history (Smuts, "Evolutionary Origins of Patriarchy").

27. Smuts, "Evolutionary Origins of Patriarchy," 13, and Smuts, "Male Aggression Against Women," 15.

28. Napoleon A. Chagnon, "Life Histories, Blood Revenge, and Warfare in a Tribal Population," *Science* 239, no. 4843 (1988): 985–992.

29. Wrangham and Peterson, *Demonic Males*, 173.

30. Smuts, "Male Aggression Against Women," 11.

31. Ibid., 19.

32. Margo Wilson, Martin Daly, and Joanna Scheib, "Femicide: An Evolutionary Psychological Perspective," in Patricia Adair Gowaty, ed., *Feminism and Evolutionary Biology: Boundaries, Intersections, and Frontiers*, 431–465 (New York: Chapman and Hall, 1997).

33. Smuts, "Evolutionary Origins of Patriarchy," 18.

34. N. Pound, Martin Daly, and Margo Wilson, "There's No Contest: Human Sex Differences Are Sexually Selected," *Behavioral and Brain Sciences* 32, nos. 3/4 (2009): 286–287, quote from 286.

35. Mies, "Social Origins of the Sexual Division of Labor."

36. Smuts, "Evolutionary Origins of Patriarchy."

37. Smuts, "Male Aggression Against Women."

38. Ibid., 26.

39. Ibid., 6.

40. Smuts, "Evolutionary Origins of Patriarchy," 22.

41. Patricia Adair Gowaty, "Introduction: Darwinian Feminists and Feminist Evolutionist," in Patricia Adair Gowaty, ed., *Feminism and Evolutionary Biology: Boundaries, Intersections, and Frontiers*, 12 (New York: Chapman and Hall, 1997).

42. Wrangham and Peterson, *Demonic Males*, 125.

43. Ibid., 159.

44. Ibid., 146.

45. Barbara D. Miller, "The Anthropology of Sex and Gender Hierarchies," in Barbara D. Miller, ed., *Sex and Gender Hierarchies*, 22 (Cambridge: Cambridge University Press, 1993).

46. Kemper, *Social Structure and Testosterone*.

47. Malcolm Potts and Thomas Hayden, *Sex and War: How Biology Explains War and Terrorism and Offers a Path to a Safer World* (Dallas: BenBella Books, 2008), 310.

48. Ibid., 109.

49. Thayer, *Darwin and International Relations*.

50. Wrangham and Peterson, *Demonic Males*, 249.

51. Ibid., 233.

52. Thayer, *Darwin and International Relations*, 13.

53. Ibid., 76.

54. See also Potts and Hayden, *Sex and War*.

55. Ibid., 96.

56. Stephen Rosen, *War and Human Nature* (Princeton, NJ: Princeton University Press, 2005), 89–90, 95.

57. Ibid., 96.

58. Wrangham and Peterson, *Demonic Males*, 125.

59. Richard D. Alexander, "Evolution, Culture, and Human Behavior: Some General Considerations," in Richard D. Alexander and Donald W. Tinkle, eds., *Natural Selection and Social Behavior: Recent Research and New Theory*, 509–520 (New York: Chiron Press, 1981).

60. Mary Hartman, *The Household and the Making of History: A Subversive View of the Western Past* (Cambridge: Cambridge University Press, 2004), 229.

61. Ibid., 221.

62. Kemper, *Social Structure and Testosterone*.

63. Clarice Auluck-Wilson, "When All Women Lift," *Journal of Women in Culture and Society* 20, no. 4 (1995): 1029–1038.

64. John Archer and Sylvana Côté, "Sex Differences in Aggressive Behavior: A Developmental and Evolutionary Perspective," in Richard E. Tremblay, Willard W. Hartup, and John Archer, eds., *Developmental Origins of Aggression*, 425–443 (New York: Guilford Press, 2005).

65. Leonard Berkowitz, *Aggression: Its Causes, Consequences, and Control* (Philadelphia: McGraw-Hill, 1993); L. Rowell Huesmann and Nancy G. Guerra, "Children's Normative Beliefs About Aggression and Aggressive Behavior," *Journal of Personality and Social Psychology* 72 (1997): 408–419; Rolf Loeber and David P. Farrington, eds., *Serious and Violent Juvenile Offenders: Risk Factors and Successful Interventions* (Thousand Oaks, CA: Sage, 1998); Gerald R. Patterson, "A Comparison of Models for Interstate Wars and for Individual Violence," *Perspectives on Psychological Science* 3, no. 3 (2008): 203–223; Stephanie H. M. van Goozen, Graeme Fairchild, and Gordon T. Harold, "The Role of Neurobiological Deficits in Childhood Antisocial Behavior," *Current Directions in Psychological Science* 17, no. 3 (2008): 224–228.

66. Cheryl Brown Travis, "Theory and Data on Rape and Evolution," in Cheryl Brown Travis, ed., *Evolution, Gender, and Rape*, 207–220 (Cambridge, MA: MIT Press, 2003).

67. Jacquelyn W. White and Lori A. Post, "Understanding Rape: A Metatheoretical Framework," in Cheryl Brown Travis, ed., *Evolution, Gender, and Rape*, 383–411 (Cambridge, MA: MIT Press, 2003).

68. John Archer, "Sex Differences in Aggression Between Heterosexual Partners: A Meta-analytic Review," *Psychological Bulletin* 126, no. 5 (2000): 651–680, doi: 10.1037/0033–2909.126.5.651.

69. John Archer, "Sex Differences in Aggression in Real-World Settings: A Meta-analytic Review," *Review of General Psychology* 8, no. 4 (2004): 291–322, doi: 10.1037/1089–2680.8.4.291.

70. Alice H. Eagly and Wendy Wood, "The Origins of Sex Differences in Human Behavior: Evolved Dispositions Versus Social Roles," *American Psychologist* 54, no. 6 (1999): 408–423.

71. Ibid., 421.

72. Wendy Wood and Alice H. Eagly, "A Cross-Cultural Analysis of the Behavior of Women and Men: Implications for the Origins of Sex Differences," *Psychological Bulletin* 128, no. 5 (2002): 699–727.

73. Ibid., 718.

74. Ibid., 722.

75. Stephanie H. M. van Goozen, Graeme Fairchild, and Gordon T. Harold, "The Role of Neurobiological Deficits in Childhood Antisocial Behavior," *Current Directions in Psychological Science* 17, no. 3 (2008): 224–228.

76. Adrian Raine, "Biosocial Studies of Antisocial and Violent Behavior in Children and Adults: A Review," *Journal of Abnormal Child Psychology* 30, no. 4 (2002): 311–325, www-rcf.usc.edu/~raine/BioSocialStudies_Raine.pdf, accessed May 31, 2010; Angela Scarpa and Adrian Raine, "Biosocial Bases of Violence," in Daniel J. Flannery, Alexander T. Vazsonyi, and Irwin D. Waldman, eds., *The Cambridge Handbook of Violent Behavior and Aggression*, 151–169 (Cambridge: Cambridge University Press, 2007).

77. Michael Bohman, "Predisposition to Criminality: Swedish Adoption Studies in Retrospect," in Gregory R. Bock and Jamie A. Goode, eds., *Genetics of Criminal and Antisocial Behavior*, 99–114 (West Sussex, UK: John Wiley, 1996); Remi J. Cadoret, Leslie D. Leve, and Eric Devor, "Genetics of Aggressive and Violent Behavior," *Anger, Aggression, and Violence* 20, no. 2 (1997): 301–322; Remi J. Cadoret, Colleen A. Cain, and R. R. Crowe, "Evidence for Gene-Environment Interaction in the Development of Adolescent Antisocial Behavior," *Behavior Genetics* 13 (1983): 301–310; Xiaojia Ge, Rand D. Conger, Remi J. Cadoret, Jenae M. Neiderhiser, William Yates, Edward Troughton, and Mark

Stewart, "The Developmental Interface Between Nature and Nurture: A Mutual Influence Model of Child Antisocial Behavior and Parent Behaviors," *Developmental Psychology* 33, no. 2 (1996): 574–589.

78. Remi J. Cadoret, Colleen A. Cain, and Raymond R. Crowe, "Evidence for Gene-Environment Interaction in the Development of Adolescent Antisocial Behavior," *Behavior Genetics* 13, no. 3 (1983): 301–310.

79. Kenneth A. Dodge and Michelle R. Sherrill, "The Interaction of Nature and Nurture in Antisocial Behavior," in Daniel J. Flannery, Alexander T. Vazsonyi, and Irwin D. Waldman, eds., *The Cambridge Handbook of Violent Behavior and Aggression* (Cambridge: Cambridge University Press, 2007), 215–242.

80. Adrian Raine, "From Genes to Brain to Antisocial Behavior," *Current Directions in Psychological Science* 17, no. 5 (2008): 323–328.

81. Steve W. Cole, "Social Regulation of Human Gene Expression," *Current Directions in Psychological Science* 18, no. 3 (2009): 132–137.

82. Ibid., 135; Michael J. Meaney, "Epigenetics and the Biological Definition of Gene x Environment Interactions," *Child Development* 81, no. 1 (2010): 41–79.

83. Frances A. Champagne and Rahia Mashoodh, "Genes in Context: Gene-Environment Interplay and the Origins of Individual Differences in Behavior," *Current Directions in Psychological Science* 18, no. 3 (2009): 127–131. For further discussion of how social information alters gene expression in the brain to influence behavior and how genetic variation influences brain function and social behavior, see Gene E. Robinson, Russell D. Fernald, and David F. Clayton, "Genes and Social Behavior," *Science* 32, no. 5903 (2008): 896–900, doi: 10.1126/science.1159277.

84. Raymond H. Baillargeon, Mark Zoccolillo, Kate Keenan, Sylvana Cote, Daniel Perusse, and Hong-xing Wu, "Gender Differences in Physical Aggression: A Prospective Population-Based Survey of Children Before and After Two Years of Age," *Developmental Psychology* 43, no. 1 (2007): 13–26; Jamie M. Ostrov and Caroline F. Keating, "Gender Differences in Preschool Aggression During Free Play and Structured Interaction: An Observational Study," *Social Development* 13, no. 2 (2004): 255–277.

85. Janet S. Hyde, "New Direction in the Study of Gender Similarities and Differences," *Current Directions in Psychological Science* 16, no. 5 (2007): 259–263.

86. Bonnie Ballif-Spanvill, Claudia Clayton, Rebecca Nichols, and Rachel Kramer, "Good Ole Boys: Gender, Aggression, and Prosocial Behavior in Same- and Mixed-Sex Pairs" (manuscript submitted for publication, 2010).

87. Patterson, "Comparison of Models."

88. M. Katherine Weinberg, Edward Z. Tronick, Jeffrey F. Cohn, and Karen L. Olson, "Gender Differences in Emotional Expressivity and Self-Regulation During Early Infancy," *Developmental Psychology* 35, no. 1 (1999): 175–188.

89. Patterson, "Comparison of Models."

90. Carol Lyon Martin, "A Ratio Measure of Gender Stereotyping," *Journal of Personality and Social Psychology* 52, no. 3 (1987): 489–499; Gerald R. Patterson, "Siblings: Fellow Travelers in Coercive Family Processes," *Advances in the Study of Aggression* 1 (1984): 173–214; Daniel S. Shaw and Emily Winslow, "Precursors and Correlates of Antisocial Behavior from Infancy to Preschool," in David M. Stoff, James Breiling, and Jack D. Maser, eds., *Handbook of Antisocial Behavior*, 148–158 (New York: John Wiley, 1997).

91. John D. Coie and Janis B. Kupersmidt, "A Behavioral Analysis of Emerging Social Status in Boy's Groups," *Child Development* 54 (1983): 1400–1416; Patterson, "Comparison of Models."

92. Brad J. Bushman and Russell G. Geen, "Role of Cognitive-Emotional Mediators and Individual Differences in the Effects of Media Violence on Aggression," *Journal of Personality and Social Psychology* 58, no. 1 (1990): 156–163; Nicholas L. Carnagey and Craig A. Anderson, "The Effects of Reward and Punishment in Violent Video Games on Aggressive Affect, Cognition, and Behavior," *Psychological Science* 16, no. 11 (2005): 882–889; Kenneth A. Dodge and Gregory S. Pettit, "A Biopsychosocial Model of the Development of Chronic Conduct Problems in Adolescence," *Developmental Psychology* 39, no. 2 (2003): 349–371; David P. Farrington, "Origins of Violent Behavior Over the Life Span," in Daniel J. Flannery, Alexander T. Vazsonyi, and Irwin D. Waldman, eds., *The Cambridge Handbook of Violent Behavior and Aggression*, 664–687 (Cambridge: Cambridge University Press, 2007); Holly Foster, Jeanne Brooks-Gunn, and Anne Martin, "Poverty/Socioeconomic Status and Exposure to Violence in the Lives of Children and Adolescents," in Daniel J. Flannery, Alexander T. Vazsonyi, and Irwin D. Waldman, eds., *The Cambridge Handbook of Violent Behavior and Aggression*, 664–687 (Cambridge: Cambridge University Press, 2007); Uberto Gatti, Richard E. Tremblay, and Frank Vitaro, "Iatrogenic Effect of Juvenile Justice," *Journal of Child Psychology and Psychiatry* 50, no. 8 (2009): 991–998, doi: 10.1111/j.1469–7610.2008 .02057.x; L. Rowell Huesmann and Lucyna Kirwil, "Why Observing Violence Increases the Risk of Violent Behavior by the Observer," in Daniel J. Flannery, Alexander T. Vazsonyi, and Irwin D. Waldman, eds., *The Cambridge Handbook of Violent Behavior and Aggression*, 545–570 (Cambridge: Cambridge University Press, 2007).

93. Elizabeth Reed, Jay G. Silverman, Anita Raj, Emily F. Rothman, Michele R. Decker, Barbara Gottlieb, Brett E. Mollar, and Elizabeth Miller, "Social and

Environmental Contexts of Adolescent and Young Adult Male Perpetrators of Intimate Partner Violence: A Qualitative Study," *American Journal of Men's Health* 2, no. 3 (2008):. 260–271, doi: 10.1177/1557988308318863.

94. James Snyder, Lynn Schrepferman, and Carolyn St. Peter, "Origins of Antisocial Behavior: Negative Reinforcement and Affect Dysregulation of Behavior as Socialization Mechanisms in Family Interaction," *Behavior Modification* 21, no. 2 (1997): 187–215.

95. Thayer, *Darwin and International Relations*, 151–152.

96. Patterson, "Comparison of Models."

97. Santiago Yubero and Raul Navarro, "Students' and Teachers' Views of Gender-Related Aspects of Aggression," *School Psychology International* 27, no. 4 (2006): 488–512, doi: 10.1177 /0143034306070436.

98. Timothy Brezina, "Teenage Violence Toward Parents as an Adaptation to Family Strain: Evidence from a National Survey of Male Adolescents," *Youth and Society* 30, no. 4 (1999): 416–444, doi: 10.1177/0044118X99030004002.

99. Kristin L. Anderson and Debra Umberson, "Gendering Violence: Masculinity and Power in Men's Accounts of Domestic Violence," *Gender and Society* 15, no. 3 (2001): 359–380; Dianne Herman, "The Rape Culture," in Jo Freeman, ed., *Women: A Feminist Perspective*, 20–38, 3rd ed. (Palo Alto, CA: Mayfield Publishing, 1984); Ronda Redden Reitz, "Batterers' Experiences of Being Violent," *Psychology of Women Quarterly* 23 (1999): 143–165.

100. Ruth E. Mann and Clive R. Hollin, "Sexual Offenders' Explanations for Their Offending," *Journal of Sexual Aggression* 13, no. 1 (2007): 3–9; Wade C. Myers, David S. Husted, Mark E. Safarik, and Mary Ellen O'Toole, "The Motivation Behind Serial Sexual Homicide: Is It Sex, Power, and Control, or Anger?" *Journal of Forensic Sciences* 51, no. 4 (2006): 900–907.

101. Diana Scully and Joseph Marolla, "Riding the Bull at Gilley's: Convicted Rapists Describe the Rewards of Rape," *Social Problems* 32, no. 3 (1985): 251–263.

102. Patterson, "Comparison of Models."

103. Robert F. Bornstein, "The Complex Relationship Between Dependency and Domestic Violence: Converging Psychological Factors and Social Forces," *American Psychologist* 31, no. 6 (2006): 595–606.

104. Bonnie Ballif-Spanvill, Claudia J. Clayton, and Suzanne Hendrix, "Gender Types of Conflict and Individual Differences in the Use of Violent and Peaceful Strategies Among Children Who Have and Have Not Witnessed Interparental Violence," *American Journal of Orthopsychiatry* 73, no. 2 (2003): 141–153.

105. Patterson, "Comparison of Models."

106. Mark Nielsen and Keyan Tomaselli, "Overimitation in Kalahari Bushman Children and the Origins of Human Cultural Cognition," *Psychological Science* 21 (2010): 729–736, doi: 10.1177 /0956797610368808.

107. E. Mark Cummings, Marcie C. Goeke-Morey, and Lauren M. Papp, "Every-day Marital Conflict and Child Aggression," *Journal of Abnormal Child Psychology* 32, no. 2 (2004): 191–202; Jeffrey L. Edleson, "Children's Witnessing of Adult Domestic Violence," *Journal of Interpersonal Violence* 14, no. 8 (1999): 839–870; Sandra A. Graham-Bermann, "The Impact of Woman Abuse on Children's Social Development: Research and Theoretical Perspectives," in George W. Holden and Robert Geffner, eds., *Children Exposed to Marital Violence: Theory, Research, and Applied Issues*, 21–54 (Washington, DC: American Psychological Association, 1998); Gayla Margolin and Elana B. Gordis, "The Effects of Family and Community Violence on Children," *Annual Review of Psychology* 51 (2000): 445–479.

108. Joetta L. Carr and Karen M. VanDeusen, "The Relationship Between Family of Origin Violence and Dating Violence in College Men," *Journal of Interpersonal Violence* 17, no. 6 (2002): 630–646, doi: 10.1177/0886260502017006003; Daniel J. Flannery, Mark I. Singer, Manfred van Dulmen, Jeff M. Kretschmar, and Lara M. Belliston, "Exposure to Violence, Mental Health, and Violent Behavior," in Daniel J. Flannery, Alexander T. Vazsonyi, and Irwin D. Waldman, eds., *The Cambridge Handbook of Violent Behavior and Aggression*, 306–321 (Cambridge: Cambridge University Press, 2007); Todd Herrenkohl, W. Alex Mason, Rick Kosterman, Liliana J. Lengua, J. David Hawkins, and Roberta D. Abbott, "Pathways from Physical Childhood Abuse to Partner Violence in Young Adulthood," *Violence and Victims* 19, no. 2 (2004): 123–136; M. Kay Jankowski, Harold Leitenberg, Kris Henning, and Patricia Coffey, "Intergenerational Transmission of Dating Aggression as a Function of Witnessing Only Same Sex Parents vs. Opposite Sex Parents vs. Both Parents as Perpetrators of Domestic Violence," *Journal of Family Violence* 14, no. 3 (1999): 267–279.

109. Bonnie Ballif-Spanvill, Claudia J. Clayton, and Suzanne B. Hendrix, "Witness and Nonwitness Children's Violent and Peaceful Behavior in Different Types of Simulated Conflict with Peers," *American Journal of Orthopsychiatry* 77, no. 2 (2007): 206–215.

110. Richard A. Fabes, Carol L. Martin, and Laura D. Hanish, "Young Children's Play Qualities in the Same-Other and Mixed-Sex Peer Groups," *Child Development* 74, no. 3 (2003): 921–932; Robert L. Munroe and A. Kimball Romney, "Gender and Age Differences in the Same-Sex Aggregation and Social Behaviors: A Four-Culture Study," *Journal of Cross-Cultural Psychology* 37, no. 1 (2006): 3–19.

111. Ballif-Spanvill et al., "Good Ole Boys."

112. Joyce F. Benenson and Kiran Alavi, "Sex Differences in Children's Investment in Same-Sex Peers," *Evolution and Human Behavior* 25, no. 4 (2004): 258–266.

113. Joyce F. Benenson, Henry Markovits, Caitlin Fitzgerald, Diana Geoffroy, Juli-anne Flemming, Sonya M. Kahlenberg, and Richard W. Wrangham, "Males' Greater Tolerance of Same-Sex Peers," *Psychological Science* 20, no. 2 (2009): 184–190.

114. Joshua S. Goldstein, "Gender in the IR Textbook and Beyond," *International Studies Perspectives* 8, no. 3 (2007): 320–322.

115. Ibid.

116. Nicole Tausch, Katharina Schmid, and Miles Hewstone, "The Social Psychol-ogy of Intergroup Relations," in G. Salomon and E. Cairns, eds., *Handbook on Peace Education*, 75–86 (New York: Psychology Press, 2010).

117. Donelson R. Forsyth, *Group Dynamics*, 4th ed. (Belmont, CA: Thomson Wads-worth, 2006).

118. Thomas W. Farmer, Hongling Xie, Beverly D. Cairns, and Bryan C. Hutchins, "Social Synchrony, Peer Networks, and Aggression in School," in Patricia H. Hawley, Todd D. Little, and Philip C. Rodkin, eds., *Aggression and Adapta-tion: The Bright Side to Bad Behavior* (Mahwah, NJ: Lawrence Erlbaum, 2007): 209–233; Marion K. Underwood, "Introduction to the Special Issue: Gender and Children's Friendships: Do Girls' and Boys' Friendships Consti-tute Different Peer Cultures, and What Are the Trade-offs for Development?" *Merrill-Palmer Quarterly* 53, no. 3 (2007): 319–324.

119. Carol Lynn Martin and Richard A. Fabes, "The Stability and Consequences of Young Children's Same-Sex Peer Interactions," *Developmental Psychology* 37, no. 3 (2001): 431–446; Amanda J. Rose, "Structure, Content, and Socioemo-tional Correlates of Girls' and Boys' Friendships: Recent Advances and Future Directions," *Merrill-Palmer Quarterly* 53, no. 3 (2007): 489–506.

120. Mary E. Kite, "Gender Stereotypes," in Judith Worell, ed., *Encyclopedia of Women and Gender*, 1:561–570 (San Diego: Academic Press, 2001).

121. Carol Lynn Martin and Lisa M. Dinella, "Gender Development: Gender Schema Theory," in Judith Worell, ed., *Encyclopedia of Women and Gender*, 1:507–521 (San Diego: Academic Press, 2001).

122. Eleanor E. Maccoby, "Gender and Group Process: A Developmental Perspec-tive," *Current Directions in Psychological Research* 11, no. 2 (2002): 54–58.

123. Nicole Tausch, Katharina Schmid, and Miles Hewstone, "The Social Psychol-ogy of Intergroup Relations," in Gavriel Salomon and Edward Cairns, eds., *Handbook on Peace Education*, 75–86 (New York: Psychology Press, 2010).

124. Sarah K. Murnen, Carrie Wright, and Gretchen Kaluzny, "If 'Boys Will Be Boys,' Then Girls Will Be Victims? A Meta-analytic Review of the Research That Relates Masculine Ideology to Sexual Aggression," *Sex Roles* 46, nos. 11/12 (2002): 359–375.

125. Mark Bennett, Martyn Barrett, Rauf Karakozov, Giorgi Kipiani, Evanthia Lyons, Valentina Pavlenko, and Tatiana Riazanova, "Young Children's Evaluations of the Ingroup and of Outgroups: A Multi-national study," *Social Development* 13, no. 1 (2004): 124–141.

126. Mark Van Vugt, David De Cremer, and Dirk P. Janssen, "Gender Differences in Cooperation and Competition: The Male-Warrior Hypothesis," *Psychological Science* 18, no. 1 (2007): 19–23.

127. Ervin Staub, *The Roots of Evil: The Origins of Genocide and Other Group Violence* (New York: Cambridge University Press, 1989).

128. Goldstein, "Gender in the IR Textbook and Beyond."

129. Donelson R. Forsyth, *Group Dynamics*, 4th ed. (Belmont, CA: Thomson Wadsworth, 2006).

130. Gerben A. van Kleef, Christopher Oveis, Ilmo van der Löwe, Aleksandr Luo-Kogan, Jennifer Goetz, and Dacher Keltner, "Power, Distress, and Compassion: Turning a Blind Eye to the Suffering of Others," *Psychological Science* 19, no. 12 (2008): 1315–1322.

131. Nathanael J. Fast and Serena Chen, "When the Boss Feels Inadequate: Power, Incompetence, and Aggression," *Psychological Science* 20, no. 11 (2009): 1406–1413, doi: 10.1111/j.1467–9280.2009.02452.x.

132. Julia C. Babcock, Jennifer Waltz, Neil S. Jacobson, and John M. Gottman, "Power and Violence: The Relation Between Communication Patterns, Power Discrepancies, and Domestic Violence," *Journal of Consulting and Clinical Psychology* 61, no. 1 (1993): 40–50.

133. Ronald L. Akers, Marvin D. Krohn, Lonn Lanza-Kaduce, and Maria Radosevich, "Social Learning and Deviant Behavior: A Specific Test of a General Theory," *American Sociological Review* 44, no. 4 (1979): 636–655; Dana L. Haynie, "Delinquent Peers Revisited: Does Network Structure Matter?" *American Journal of Sociology* 106, no. 4 (2001): 1013–1057; Cesar J. Rebellon, "Do Adolescents Engage in Delinquency to Attract the Social Attention of Peers? An Extension of a Longitudinal Test of the Social Reinforcement Hypothesis," *Journal of Research in Crime and Delinquency* 43, no. 4 (2006): 387–411; Christine S. Sellers, John K. Cochran, and Katherine A. Branch, "Social Learning Theory and Partner Violence: A Research Note," *Deviant Behavior* 26, no. 4 (2005): 379–395.

134. Deborah M. Capaldi, Thomas J. Dishion, Mike Stoolmiller, and Karen Yoerger, "Aggression Toward Female Partners by At-Risk Young Men: The Contribution of Male Adolescent Friendships," *Developmental Psychology* 37, no. 1 (2001): 61–73; Stephen E. Humphrey and Arnold S. Kahn, "Fraternities, Athletic Teams, and Rape: Importance of Identification with a Risky Group,"

Journal of Interpersonal Violence 15, no. 12 (2000): 1313–1322, doi: 10.1177/088 626000015012005; Sarah K. Murnen and Maria H. Kohlman, "Athletic Participation, Fraternity Membership, and Sexual Aggression Among College Men: A Meta-analytic Review," *Sex Roles* 57 (2007): 145–157, doi: 10.1007/ s11199-007-9225-1; Leora N. Rosen, Robert J. Kaminski, Angela Moore Parmley, Kathryn H. Knudson, and Peggy Fancher, "The Effects of Peer Group Climate on Intimate Partner Violence Among Married Male U.S. Army Soldiers," *Violence Against Women* 9, no. 9 (2003): 1045–1071, doi: 10.1177 / 1077801203255504.

135. Claudia J. Clayton, Sally H. Barlow, and Bonnie Ballif-Spanvill, "Principles of Group Violence with a Focus on Terrorism," in Harold V. Hall and Leighton C. Whitaker, eds., *Collective Violence: Effective Strategies for Assessing and Interviewing in Fatal Group and Institutional Aggression*, 277–311 (Boca Raton, FL: CRC Press, 1999).

136. Men may also seek to harm male enemies by harming the female "possessions" of these enemies.

137. Joshua S. Goldstein, *War and Gender: How Gender Shapes the War System and Vice Versa* (Cambridge: Cambridge University Press, 2001).

138. Dorothy L. Espelage, Stanley Wasserman, and Mark Fleisher, "Social Networks and Violent Behavior," in Daniel J. Flannery, Alexander T. Vazsonyi, and Irwin D. Waldman, eds., *The Cambridge Handbook of Violent Behavior and Aggression*, 450–464 (Cambridge: Cambridge University Press, 2007).

139. Jeffry Fagan, Deanna L. Wilkinson, Garth Davies, "Social Contagion of Violence," In Daniel J. Flannery, Alexander T. Vazsonyi, and Irwin D. Waldman, eds., *The Cambridge Handbook of Violent Behavior and Aggression*, 688–723 (Cambridge: Cambridge University Press, 2007).

140. Ibid., 716.

141. Louisa J. Shirley and Anne Campbell, "Same-Sex Preference in Infancy: Visual Preference for Sex-Congruent Stimuli at Three Months," *Psychology, Evolution, and Gender* 2, no. 1 (2000): 3–18.

142. Zeev Maoz and Bruce Russett, "Normative and Structural Causes of Democratic Peace, 1946–1986," *American Political Science Review* 87 (September 1993): 624–638; Bruce Russett, *Controlling the Sword: The Democratic Governance of National Security* (Cambridge, MA: Harvard University Press, 1990).

143. Richard D. Alexander, "Evolution, Culture, and Human Behavior: Some General Considerations," in Richard D. Alexander and Donald W. Tinkle, eds., *Natural Selection and Social Behavior*, 509–520 (New York: Chiron Press, 1981); Jack P. Greene and J. R. Pole, eds., *Colonial British America: Essays in the New History of the Early Modern Era* (Baltimore: Johns Hopkins University Press, 1983).

144. Gregory A. Raymond, "International Norms: Normative Orders and Peace," in J. A. Vasquez, ed., *What Do We Know About War*, 290 (New York: Rowman and Littlefield, 2000).

145. Gerald M. Erchak, "Family Violence," in Carol R. Ember and Melvin Ember, eds., *Research Frontiers in Anthropology* (Englewood Cliffs, NJ: Prentice-Hall, 1994); Gerald M. Erchak and Richard Rosenfeld, "Societal Isolations, Violent Norms, and Gender Relations: A Re-examination and Extension of Levinson's Model of Wife Beating," *Cross-Cultural Research* 28, no. 2 (1994): 111–133; David Levinson, *Family Violence in Cross-Cultural Perspective* (Newbury Park, CA: Sage, 1989); Cynthia Cockburn, "The Gendered Dynamics of Armed Conflict and Political Violence," in Caroline Moser and Fiona C. Clark, eds., *Victims, Perpetrators or Actors?: Gender, Armed Conflict, and Political Violence*, 13–29 (New York: Zed Books, 2001).

146. Jean Bethke Elshtain, *Women and War* (New York: Basic Books, 1987); Susan Brownmiller, *Against Our Will: Men, Women, and Rape* (New York: Simon and Schuster, 1975); Betty Reardon, *Sexism and the War System* (New York: Teachers College Press, 1985); Sara Ruddick, "Pacifying the Forces: Drafting Women in the Interests of Peace," *Signs* 8, no. 3 (1983): 470–489.

147. Mary Caprioli, "Primed for Violence: The Role of Gender Inequality in Predicting Internal Conflict," *International Studies Quarterly* 49, no. 2 (2005): 161–178.

148. Johan Galtung, *Peace: Research, Education, Action: Essays in Peace Research*, vol. 1 (Bucharest: CIPEXIM, 1990); Johan Galtung, "Cultural Violence," *Journal of Peace Research* 27, no. 3 (1990): 291–305.

149. Galtung, *Peace*, 80.

150. Ibid., 264–265.

151. Galtung, "Cultural Violence," 291.

152. Caprioli et al., "The WomanStats Database."

153. V. Spike Peterson, "Gendered National: Reproducing 'Us' Versus 'Them,'" in L.A. Lorentzen and J. Turpin, eds., *The Women and War Reader*, 42–43 (New York: New York University Press, 1998).

154. J. Ann Tickner, *Gender in International Relations: Feminist Perspectives on Achieving Global Security* (New York: Columbia University Press, 1992); Hanna Papanek, "To Each Less Than She Needs, From Each More Than She Can Do: Allocations, Entitlements, and Value," in Irene Tinker, ed., *Persistent Inequalities: Women and World Development*, 162–181 (New York and Oxford: Oxford University Press, 1994); Mark Tessler and Ina Warriner, "Gender, Feminism, and Attitudes Toward International Conflict," *World Politics* 49 (January 1997): 250–281; Caprioli, "Primed for Violence"; J. Ann Tickner, *Gendering World Politics* (New York: Columbia University Press, 2001).

155. Swanee Hunt and Cristina Posa, "Women Waging Peace," *Foreign Policy* (May/June 2001): 38–47; Tickner, *Gender in International Relations.*

4. THE HEART OF THE MATTER: THE SECURITY OF WOMEN AND THE SECURITY OF STATES

Large portions of this chapter are reproduced by permission of *International Security* from Valerie M. Hudson, Mary Caprioli, Bonnie Ballif-Spanvill, Rose McDermott, and Chad F. Emmett, "The Heart of the Matter: The Security of Women and the Security of States," *International Security* 33, no. 3 (2008/2009): 7–45.

1. Samuel P. Huntington, *The Clash of Civilizations and the Remaking of World Order* (New York: Simon and Schuster, 1996).
2. Michael W. Doyle, "Kant, Liberal Legacies, and Foreign Affairs," *Philosophy and Public Affairs* 12, no. 3 (Summer 1983): 205–235; Zeev Maoz and Bruce Russett, "Normative and Structural Causes of Democratic Peace, 1946–1986," *American Political Science Review* 87 (September 1993): 624–638; James Lee Ray, *Democracy and International Conflict: An Evaluation of the Democratic Peace Proposition* (Columbia: University of South Carolina Press, 1995); Paul Huth and Todd Allee, *The Democratic Peace and Territorial Conflict in the Twentieth Century* (Cambridge: Cambridge University Press, 2003); Zeev Maoz, "The Controversy Over the Democratic Peace: Rearguard Action or Cracks in the Wall?" *International Security* 22, no. 1 (Spring 2003): 162–198.
3. Thomas Homer-Dixon, *Environment, Scarcity, and Violence* (Princeton, NJ: Princeton University Press, 2001); Lael Brainard and Derel Chollet, eds., *Too Poor for Peace? Global Poverty, Conflict, and Security in the 21st Century* (Washington, DC: Brookings Institution, 2007).
4. United Nations press conference, March 8, 2006, www.un.org/News/Press/docs/2006/sgsm10370.doc.htm, accessed November 26, 2007.
5. While it is obvious that states are composed of people, and about half of those people are women, this "human security" perspective is actually relatively new to security studies, which traditionally have treated the state as an abstraction instead of a group of human beings. That is why the gentleman who asked this question could regard it as entirely coherent.
6. Marilyn Brewer and L. Lui, "Primacy of Age and Sex in the Structure of Person Categories," *Social Cognition* 7, no. 3 (1989): 262–274; Susan Fiske and Steven Neuberg, "A Continuum of Impression Formation, from Category-Based to Individuating Processes: Influence of Information and Motivation on Attention and Interpretation," *Advances in Experimental Social Psychology* 23 (1990): 1–74; Steven Messick and Diane Mackie, "Intergroup Relations," *Annual Review of Psychology* 40 (1989): 45–81.

7. Robert Kurzban, John Tooby, and Leda Cosmides, "Can Race Be 'Erased'? Co-alitional Computation and Social Categorization," *Proceedings of the National Academy of Sciences* 98, no. 22 (2001): 15387–15392.

8. Quoted in Andrew Stephen, "Hating Hillary," *New Statesman*, May 22, 2008, www.newstatesman.com/north-america/2008/05/obama-clinton-vote-usa-media, accessed June 10, 2008.

9. Jacques Derrida, *Of Grammatology* (Baltimore: Johns Hopkins University Press, 1976); Jacques Derrida, *Writing and Difference* (London: Routledge, 1978).

10. We recognize that people in nearly every society, modern and historical, have found ways to modify their assigned gender. However, this involves a very small minority of people, with gender assignment being otherwise immutable for the overwhelming majority of society (Ramaswami Mahalingam, Jana Haritatos, and Benita Jackson, "Essentialism and the Cultural Psychology of Gender in Extreme Son Preference Communities in India," *American Journal of Orthopsychiatry* 77, no. 4 [October 2007]: 598–609).

11. Joseph Lopreato, *Human Nature and Biocultural Evolution* (Boston: Allen and Unwin, 1984); Richard Wrangham and Dale Peterson, *Demonic Males: Apes and the Origins of Human Violence* (New York: Houghton Mifflin, 1996).

12. Sylviane Agacinski, *The Parity of the Sexes* (New York: Columbia University Press, 2001), 14.

13. Eva M. Rathgeber, "WID, WAD, GAD: Trends in Research and Practice," *Journal of Developing Areas* 24, no. 4 (1990): 489–502; Martha Chen, "A Matter of Survival: Women's Right to Work in India and Bangladesh," in Martha Nussbaum and Jonathon Glover, eds., *Women and Culture and Development: A Study of Human Capabilities* (Oxford: Clarendon Press, 1992), 37–60; Jodi L. Jacobson, *Gender Bias: Roadblock to Sustainable Development* (Washington, DC: Worldwatch Institute, 1992); Amartya Sen, "Women's Survival as a Development Problem," *Bulletin of the American Academy of Arts and Sciences* 43 (1989): 14–29; Geeta Chowdery and Sheila Nair, *Power, Postcolonialism, and International Relations: Reading Race, Gender, and Class* (New York: Routledge, 2002).

14. World Economic Forum, "The Global Gender Gap Report," www.weforum.org/pdf/gendergap/report2007.pdf, accessed December 2007; World Bank, "Engendering Development: Through Gender Equality in Rights, Resources, and Voice," *World Bank Policy Research Report* (Washington, DC: Oxford University Press, 2001); John Hoddinott and Lawrence Haddad, "Does Female Income Share Influence Household Expenditure Patterns?" *Oxford Bulletin of Economics and Statistics* 57, no. 1 (2001): 77–97.

15. Duncan Thomas, "Intrahousehold Resource Allocation: An Inferential Approach," *Journal of Human Resources* 25 (1990): 635–664; Duncan Thomas, Dante Contreras, and Elizabeth Frankenberg, *Child Health and the Distribu-*

tion of Household Resources at Marriage (Los Angeles: RAND and UCLA, 1997); Elizabeth M. King and Andrew D. Mason, *Engendering Development* (Washington, DC: World Bank, 2001); Berta Esteve-Volart, "Sex Discrimination and Growth" (IMF Working Paper WP/oo/84, Washington, DC, International Monetary Fund, African Department, 2000); Shireen J. Jejeebhoy, *Women's Education, Autonomy, and Reproductive Behavior: Experience from Developing Countries* (Oxford: Clarendon Press, 1995); T. Paul Schultz, "Investments in the Schooling and Health of Women and Men: Quantities and Returns," *Journal of Human Resources* 28, no. 4 (1993): 694–725; Albino Barrera, "The Role of Maternal Schooling and Its Interaction with Public Health Programs in Child Health Production," *Journal of Development Economics* 32 (1990): 69–91; Lisa Smith and Lawrence Haddad, "Overcoming Child Malnutrition in Developing Countries," 2020 *Vision Briefs* no. 64, (Washington, DC: Food Policy Research Institute, 2000), http://ideas.repec.org/p/fpr/2020dp/30 .html, accessed December 26, 2007.

16. Daniel Kaufmann, "Challenges in the Next Stage of Corruption," in Daniel Kaufmann and Miguel Schloss, eds., *New Perspectives in Combating Corruption*, 139–164 (Washington, DC: Transparency International and the World Bank, 1998); http://siteresources.worldbank.org/INTWBIGOVANTCOR/ Resources/challenges.pdf, accessed May 23, 2011.

17. King and Mason, "Engendering Development."

18. Inter-Parliamentary Union, "Politics: Women's Insight," www.ipu.org/iss-e/ women.htm (2000), accessed December 26, 2007.

19. Swanee Hunt, "Let Women Rule," *Foreign Affairs* 86, no. 3 (2007): 109–120.

20. Cynthia Enloe, *Bananas, Beaches, and Bases: Making Feminist Sense of International Politics* (Berkeley: University of California Press, 1989, updated 2001); Jean Bethke Elshtain, *Women and War* (New York: Basic Books, 1987); Carol Cohn, "Sex and Death in the Rational World of Defense Intellectuals," *Signs* 12, no. 4 (Summer 1987): 687–718; V. Spike Peterson, *Gendered States: Feminist (Re)Visions of International Relations Theory* (Boulder, CO: Lynne Rienner Publishers, 1992); V. Spike Peterson, "Gendered National: Reproducing 'Us' Versus 'Them,'" in L. A. Lorentzen and J. Turpin, eds., *The Women and War Reader*, 41–49 (New York: New York University Press, 1998); Christine Sylvester, *Feminist Theory and International Relations in a Postmodern Era* (New York: Cambridge University Press, 1994); Christine Sylvester, *Feminist International Relations: An Unfinished Journey* (Cambridge: Cambridge University Press, 2001); Christine Sylvester, "'Progress' as Feminist International Relations," in Frank P. Harvey and Michael Brecher, eds., *Critical Perspectives in International Studies*, 150–167 (Ann Arbor: University of Michigan Press,

2002); J. Ann Tickner, *Gender in International Relations: Feminist Perspectives on Achieving Global Security* (New York: Columbia University Press, 1992); J. Ann Tickner, *Gendering World Politics* (New York: Columbia University Press, 2001); J. Ann Tickner, "Hans Morgenthau's Principles of Political Realism: A Feminist Reformulation," *Millennium: Journal of International Studies* 17, no. 3 (1998): 429–440; Rebecca Grant and Kathleen Newland, *Gender and International Relations* (Bloomington: Indiana University Press, 1991); Jan Jindy Pettman, *Worlding Women: A Feminist International Politics* (New York: Routledge, 1996); Marysia Zalewski and Jane Papart, eds., *The "Man" Question in International Relations* (Boulder, CO: Lynne Rienner Publishers, 1998); see also Francis Fukuyama, "Women and the Evolution of World Politics," *Foreign Affairs* 77, no. 5 (September/October 1998): 24–40. A new generation continues this important tradition; see, for example, Laura Sjoberg, ed., *Gender and International Relations: Feminist Perspectives* (New York: Routledge, 2009); Laura Shepherd, ed., *Gender Matters in Global Politics: A Feminist Introduction to International Relations* (New York: Routledge, 2010); Natalie Florea Hudson, *Gender, Human Security, and the United Nations: Security Language as a Political Framework for Women* (New York: Routledge, 2009), to cite but a few such works.

21. Swanee Hunt and Cristina Posa, "Women Waging Peace," *Foreign Policy* (May/June 2001): 38–47; Natalie Florea Hudson, "Securitizing Women and Gender Equality: Who and What Is It Good For?" (paper presented at the International Studies Association, Chicago, March 2007); see also www.peacewomen.org.

22. J. Ann Tickner, "What Is Your Research Program? Some Feminist Answers to IR's Methodological Questions," *International Studies Quarterly* 49, no. 1 (2005): 1–21; V. Spike Peterson, "(On) The Cutting Edge: Feminist Research in International Relations" (presentation at the University of Arizona Association for Women Faculty Meeting, Tucson, February 1991); Sylvester, "'Progress' as Feminist International Relations"; Jill Steans, "Engaging from the Margins: Feminist Encounters with the 'Mainstream' of International Relations," *British Journal of Politics and International Relations* 5, no. 3 (2003): 428–454.

23. See, for example, Lene Hansen, *Security as Practice: Discourse Analysis and the Bosnian War* (New York: Routledge, 2006); Sandra Whitworth, *Men, Militarism, and UN Peacekeeping* (Boulder, CO: Lynne Rienner Publishers, 2004); Dubravka Zarkov, *The Body of War: Media, Ethnicity, and Gender in the Break-up of Yugoslavia* (Durham, NC: Duke University Press, 2007); Dyan Mazurana, Angela Raven-Roberts, and Jane Parpart, eds., *Gender, Conflict, and Peacekeeping* (New York: Rowman and Littlefield, 2005).

24. Sylvester, *Feminist International Relations*.

25. Mary Caprioli, "Feminist IR Theory and Quantitative Methodology: A Critical Analysis," *International Studies Review* 6, no. 2 (2004): 253–269; see also Mary Caprioli, "Making Choices," *Politics and Gender* 5, no. 3 (2009): 426–431.

26. M. Steven Fish, "Islam and Authoritarianism," *World Politics* 55, no. 1 (October 2002): 4–37.

27. Mary Caprioli, "Gendered Conflict," *Journal of Peace Research* 37, no.1 (2000): 51–68.

28. Mary Caprioli and Mark A. Boyer, "Gender, Violence, and International Crisis," *Journal of Conflict Resolution* 45, no. 4 (2001): 503–518.

29. Mary Caprioli, "Gender Equality and State Aggression: The Impact of Domestic Gender Equality on State First Use of Force," *International Interactions* 29, no. 3 (2003): 195–214. These results were replicated by Erik Melander, "Gender Equality and Interstate Armed Conflict," *International Studies Quarterly* 49, no. 4 (2005): 695–714; see also Monty G. Marshall and Donna Ramsey, "Gender Empowerment and the Willingness of States to Use Force" (unpublished research paper, Center for Systemic Peace, 1999, available at www. members .aol.com/CSPmgm/).

30. Mary Caprioli, "Primed for Violence: The Role of Gender Inequality in Predicting Internal Conflict," *International Studies Quarterly* 49, no. 2 (June 2005): 161–178.

31. Fish, "Islam and Authoritarianism," 30.

32. Mary Caprioli and Peter F. Trumbore, "Human Rights Rogues in Interstate Disputes, 1980–2001," *Journal of Peace Research* 43, no. 2 (2006): 131–148; Mary Caprioli and Peter F. Trumbore, "Hierarchies of Dominance: Identifying Rogue States and Testing Their Interstate Conflict Behavior," *European Journal of International Relations* 9, no. 3 (2003): 377–406; Mary Caprioli and Peter Trumbore, "Ethnic Discrimination and Interstate Violence: Testing the International Impact of Domestic Behavior," *Journal of Peace Research* 40, no. 1 (2003): 5–23.

33. David Sobek, M. Rodwan Abouharb, and Christopher G. Ingram, "The Human Rights Peace: How the Respect for Human Rights at Home Leads to Peace Abroad," *Journal of Politics* 68, no. 3 (2006): 519–529.

34. Rose McDermott and Jonathan Cowden, "The Effects of Uncertainty and Sex in a Crisis Simulation Game," *International Interactions* 27, no. 4 (2002): 353–380.

35. Dominic Johnson, Rose McDermott, Emily Barrett, Jonathan Cowden, Richard Wrangham, Matthew McIntyre, and Stephen Rosen, "Overconfidence in Wargames: Experimental Evidence on Expectations, Aggression, Gender, and Testosterone," *Proceedings of the Royal Society (Biology)* 273 (2006): 2513–2520.

36. Natalie B. Florea, Mark A. Boyer, Scott W. Brown, Michael J. Butler, Magnolia Hernandez, Kimberly Weir, Lin Meng, Paula R. Johnson, Clarisse Lima, and Hayley J. Mayall, "Negotiating from Mars to Venus: Gender in Simulated International Negotiations," *Simulation and Gaming* 34, no. 2 (2003): 226–248.

37. Huntington, *The Clash of Civilizations and the Remaking of World Order.*

38. Ronald Ingelhart and Pippa Norris, "The True Clash of Civilizations," *Foreign Policy* 135 (March/April 2003): 63–70; Ronald Ingelhart and Pippa Norris, *Rising Tide: Gender Equality and Cultural Change Around the World* (New York: Cambridge University Press, 2003).

39. Martha Nussbaum, *Women and Human Development: The Capabilities Approach* (Cambridge: Cambridge University Press, 2000); Martha Nussbaum, "Human Capabilities, Female Human Beings," in Martha Nussbaum and Jonathon Glover, eds., *Women, Culture, and Development*, 61–104 (New York: Oxford University Press, 1995).

40. David L. Cingranelli and David L. Richards, "The Cingranelli-Richards (CIRI) Human Rights Dataset," version 2006.10.02, www.humanrightsdata.org.

41. UNECA, "The African Gender and Development Index," available at www.uneca.org/eca_programmes/acgd/publications/agdi_book_final.pdf, 2005, accessed July 24, 2007.

42. Mary Caprioli, Valerie M. Hudson, Rose McDermott, Bonnie Ballif-Spanvill, Chad F. Emmett, and S. Matthew Stearmer, "The WomanStats Project Database: Advancing an Empirical Research Agenda," *Journal of Peace Research* 46, no. 6 (November 2009): 1–13.

43. The data are freely accessible to anyone with an Internet connection (www.womanstats.org), thus facilitating worldwide scholarship on these issues. Contribution of data via remote upload is also possible for approved credentialed sources.

44. Good primers on polytomous logistic regression, sometimes called ordinal regression, are available here: Marija Norusis, "Ordinal Regression," in her book *SPSS Advanced Statistical Procedures Companion* (New York: Prentice Hall, 2010), 69–89, www.norusis.com/pdf/ASPC_v13.pdf; and also Richard Williams, "Statistics II: Ordered Logit Models—Overview" (Department of Sociology, University of Notre Dame, n.d.), www.nd.edu/~rwilliam/stats2/l91.pdf.

45. To test the civilizational explanation for state peacefulness, a particular identity associated with greater levels of conflict or a lack of state peacefulness must first be identified. In the early years of the twenty-first century, Islamic civilization—rightly or wrongly—has been singled out for this dubious distinction (see, for example, Lee Harris, *Civilization and Its Enemies: The Next Stage of History* (New York: Free Press, 2004); Norman Podhoretz, *World War IV: The*

Long Struggle Against Islamofascism (New York: Doubleday, 2007); Oriana Fallaci, *The Force of Reason* (London: Rizzoli, 2006). Huntington himself makes particular reference to Islam's "bloody borders" (*The Clash of Civilizations*).

46. Hansen, *Security as Practice*.

47. Valerie M. Hudson and Donna Lee Bowen, "Family Law, Violence Against Women, and State Security: The Hajnal-Hartman Thesis and the Issue of Legal Enclaves" (paper presented at the annual conference of the International Studies Association, New Orleans, February 17–20, 2010).

48. Robert Wright, *The Moral Animal* (New York: Vintage, 1995), 98.

49. Laura Betzig, *Despotism and Differential Reproduction: A Darwinian View of History* (New York: Aldine de Gruyter, 1986).

50. Marvin Harris, "The Evolution of Human Gender Hierarchies," in Barbara D. Miller, ed., *Sex and Gender Hierarchies*, 57–79 (Cambridge: Cambridge University Press, 1993).

51. James L. Boone, "Noble Family Structure and Expansionist Warfare in the Late Middle Ages: A Socioecological Approach," in Rada Dyson-Hudson and Michael A. Little, eds., *Rethinking Human Adaptation: Biological and Cultural Models*, 79–96 (Boulder, CO: Westview, 1983).

52. Hillary Clinton, "Remarks at the TEDWomen Conference," Washington, DC, December 8, 2010, www.state.gov/secretary/rm/2010/12/152670.htm.

53. Johnson et al., "Overconfidence in Wargames"; Caprioli, "Gendered Conflict"; Caprioli, "Primed for Violence"; Caprioli, "Gender Equality and State Aggression"; Melander, "Gender Equality and Interstate Armed Conflict"; Sobek, Abouharb, and Ingram, "The Human Rights Peace."

54. Bradley A. Thayer and Valerie M. Hudson, "Sex and the Shaheed: Insights from the Life Sciences of Islamic Suicide Terrorism," *International Security* 34, no. 4 (Spring 2010): 37–62.

55. Valerie Hudson and Andrea Den Boer, *Bare Branches: The Security Implications of Asia's Surplus Male Population* (Cambridge, MA: MIT Press, 2004).

56. Ronald Inglehart, Roberto Foa, Christopher Peterson, and Christian Welzel, "Development, Freedom, and Rising Happiness: A Global Perspective (1981–2007)," *Perspectives on Psychological Science* 3, no. 4 (2008): 264–285.

57. Malcolm Potts and Thomas Hayden, *Sex and War* (Dallas: BenBella Books, 2008), 25–26, 197, 301.

58. Ibid., 329.

59. Ibid., 14–15.

60. Ibid., 369.

5. WINGS OF NATIONAL AND INTERNATIONAL RELATIONS, PART ONE

1. V. Spike Peterson, "Security and Sovereign States: What Is at Stake in Taking Feminism Seriously?" in V. Spike Peterson, ed., *Gendered States: Feminist (Re)Visions of International Relations Theory* (Boulder, CO: Lynne Rienner Publishers, 1992), 31–64.
2. We thank *Foreign Policy* magazine for permission to use material from our article Valerie M. Hudson and Patricia Leidl, "Betrayed," *Foreign Policy*, May 10, 2010, www.foreignpolicy.com/articles/2010/05/07/the_us_is_abandoning_afghanistan_s_women?page=0,0, accessed May 22, 2010.
3. Hudson and Leidl, "Betrayed."
4. Wheatley Institution, Brigham Young University, Provo, Utah, March 26, 2010.
5. "Subjugation of Women Is Threat to US Security: Clinton," *Agence France-Presse*, March 12, 2010, www.google.com/hostednews/afp/article/ALeqM5ib71t2 EuWmwDahxNKDaHxcEbfcYA, accessed May 18, 2010.
6. V. Spike Peterson, ed., *Gendered States: Feminist (Re)Visions of International Relations Theory* (Boulder, CO: Lynne Rienner Publishers, 1992); V. Spike Peterson, "Gendered National: Reproducing 'Us' Versus 'Them,'" in Lois A. Lorentzen and Jennifer Turpin, eds., *The Women and War Reader* (New York: New York University Press, 1998), 41–49
7. Arthur N. Gilbert and James F. Cole, "Revolutionary Theory and Gender Theory: The Iranian Case" (paper prepared for the International Studies Association annual conference, Chicago, February 21–25, 1995), 12.
8. CNN, "New Protest Statement Builds in Iran—Men in Head Scarves," December 14, 2009, http://edition.cnn.com/2009/WORLD/meast/12/14/iran.head scarf.protest/, accessed May 18, 2010.
9. UN Treaties, http://treaties.un.org/Pages/ViewDetails.aspx?src=IND&mtdsg_no=IV-8&chapter=4&lang=en, accessed May 18, 2010.
10. UN Treaties, http://treaties.un.org/Pages/ViewDetails.aspx?src=TREATY&mtdsg_no=IV-8&chapter=4&lang=en, accessed May 18, 2010.
11. "Grassroots Politics and Women's Activism Forum in D.C.," Muslimahmediawatch, November 17, 2009, http://muslimahmediawatch.org/2009/11/grass roots-politics-and-womens-activism-forum-in-d-c/, accessed May 18, 2010.
12. "Understanding Islamic Feminism: An Interview with Ziba Mir-Hosseini, February 7, 2010, http://madrasareforms.blogspot.com/2010/02/understanding-islamic-feminism.html, accessed May 18, 2010.
13. "Middle East: Regional Coalition 'Equality Without Reservation,'" Women Living Under Muslim Laws, n.d., www.wluml.org/node/4563, accessed May 18, 2010.

14. Democratic People's Republic of Korea, CEDAW Report, September 11, 2002, www.bayefsky.com/reports/dprkorea_cedaw_c_prk_1_2002.pdf, 10–11, accessed May 18, 2010.

15. International Women's Rights Action Watch (IWRAW), "What Is Shadow Reporting?" n.d., www1.umn.edu/humanrts/iwraw/faqs.html#shadowreport, accessed May 18, 2010.

16. Hudson and Leidl, "Betrayed."

17. Amnesty International, "Make the United Nations More Effective in Realizing Women's Rights," February 25, 2010, www.amnesty.org/en/appeals-for-action/gear, accessed May 18, 2010.

18. Ronald D. Bachman, ed., *Romania: A Country Study* (Washington, DC: GPO for the Library of Congress, 1989), http://countrystudies.us/romania/37.htm, accessed May 18, 2010.

19. Karen Dente and Jamie Heiss, "Pediatric AIDS in Romania," *Medscape General Medicine* 8, no. 2 (2006):11, www.medscape.com/viewarticle/528693, accessed May 18, 2010.

20. Touchingly Naïve, "Forced Abortion, Forced Sterilisation," January 8, 2008, http://touchinglynaive.wordpress.com/2008/01/08/forced-abortion-forced-sterilisation-warning-not-nice/, accessed May 18, 2010.

21. Chicago Committee to End Sterilization Abuse (CESA), "Sterilization Abuse: A Task for the Women's Movement," January 1977, https://www.uic.edu/orgs/cwluherstory/CWLUArchive/cesa.html; also "Mississippi Appendectomy," November 20, 2009, http://mississippiappendectomy.wordpress.com/, accessed May 18, 2010.

22. Matthew Connelly, *Fatal Misconceptions* (Cambridge, MA: Harvard University Press, 2008), 322.

23. Reggie Littlejohn, "China—The Consequences of Coercion: China's One Child Policy and Violence Against Women and Girls," November 10, 2009, www.womensrightswithoutfrontiers.org/index.php?nav=congressional (accessed May 18, 2010); Richard Jones, "Parental Responsibility: Challenging the Injustices of the One-Child Policy." *South China Morning Post*, electronic ed., October 5, 2008.

24. European Commission, "Harmful Practices," September 8, 2009, www.harmfulpractices.org/site/, accessed May 18, 2010.

25. Defending Women Defending Rights, n.d., www.defendingwomen-defendingrights.org/, accessed May 18, 2010.

26. WUNRN, "Jordan: Limited Access to Justice for Women," February 26, 2003, www.wunrn.com/news/2006/02_19_06/022506_jordan_womens.htm, accessed May 18, 2010.

27. Kristine Pearson of Lifeline Energy (http://lifelineenergy.org) (remarks presented at the Radcliffe Institute conference "Driving Change, Shaping Lives: Gender in the Developing World," Cambridge, MA, March 3–4, 2011).

28. Marilyn Waring, *Counting for Nothing: What Men Value and What Women Are Worth*, (2nd ed., Toronto: University of Toronto Press, 2004).

29. Office of the High Commissioner for Human Rights, "Project on a Mechanism to Address Laws That Discriminate Against Women.," March 6, 2008, www .ohchr.org/Documents/Publications/laws_that_discriminate_against_women .pdf, accessed May 18, 2010.

30. BBC, "New Poster to Attack Prostitution," May 5, 2008, http://news.bbc .co.uk/2/hi/uk_news/7384006.stm, accessed May 18, 2010.

31. Julie Bindel, "Iceland: The World's Most Feminist Country," *Guardian*, March 25, 2010, www.guardian.co.uk/lifeandstyle/2010/mar/25/iceland-most-feminist-country, accessed May 18, 2010.

32. Jeanne Sarson and Linda MacDonald, "Defining Torture by Non-State Actors in the Canadian Private Sphere," *First Light*, Winter 2009, 29–33, www.ccvt .org/pdfs/firstlighwinter2009.pdf, accessed May 18, 2010.

33. Julia Preston, "New Policy Permits Asylum for Battered Women," *New York Times*, July 15, 2009, www.nytimes.com/2009/07/16/us/16asylum.html?_r=1&scp =1&sq=asylum%20domestic%20violence&st=cse, accessed May 18, 2010.

34. Bruce Crumley, "French Bid to Ban Marital Abuse That's Psychological," *Time*, January 9, 2010, www.time.com/time/world/article/0,8599,1952552,00 .html, accessed May 18, 2010.

35. WUNRN, "Sierra Leone Judgment on Forced Marriage," March 23, 2009, www .wunrn.com/news/2009/03_09/03_23_09/032309_sierra.html, accessed May 18, 2010.

36. Una Hombrecher, "Overcoming Domestic Violence" (Stuttgart: Social Service Agency of the Protestant Church in Germany, 2007), 68, www2.wcc-coe.org/dov .nsf/41c6b7355083931ec1256c14002d2a77/6714af73bd48efe9c12574aa003d0616/ $FILE/BfdW-BUCHHuslGewENGL_final2.pdf, accessed May 18, 2010.

37. Robert Jensen (remarks at the Radcliffe Institute conference "Driving Change, Shaping Lives: Gender in the Developing World," Cambridge, MA, March 3–4, 2011). In another experiment, in which Jensen provided information, recruitment, and follow-up on job opportunities in the big cities for girls who were located in rural Indian communities, he found a significant increase in vaccination rates, school attendance, and even the weight of girls in the villages over three years. Again, envisioning a different life for girls is one of the first steps to greater family investment in girls.

38. Americans are noticeably less vigilant in this area than their European counterparts, which is lamentable. For example, there has been no movement at all on the proposed House Bill 1822, the Susan B. Anthony and Frederick Douglass Prenatal Nondiscrimination Act. No matter what one's position on abortion, this is a bill well worth supporting. Already, birth sex ratios among certain ethnic groups in America are significantly increasing, and the United States has an obligation to act to make sex-selective abortion illegal now before its prevalence spreads. See Nadwa Mosaad, "Sex Ratio at Birth Deteriorating Among Asian Immigrants in the United States" (Population Reference Bureau, November 2008), www.prb.org/Articles/2008/sexratioatbirth.aspx, accessed May 18, 2010.

39. Human Rights Watch, "Syria: No Exceptions for Honor Killings," July 28, 2009, www.hrw.org:80/en/news/2009/07/28/syria-no-exceptions-honor-killings, accessed May 18, 2010.

40. Gulf News, "Syria Stiffens Punishment for Honour Killings," January 11, 2011, http://gulfnews.com/news/region/syria/syria-stiffens-punishment-for-honour-killing-1.744322, accessed February 9, 2011.

41. Matt Bradley, "Egypt's Rate of Female Mutilation Drops to 66%," National, March 16, 2010, www.thenational.ae/apps/pbcs.dll/article?AID=/20100316/FOREIGN/703159842/1002, accessed May 18, 2010.

42. Katie Zoglin, "Morocco's Family Code: Improving Equality for Women," Human Rights Quarterly 31, no. 4 (November 2009), http://muse.jhu.edu/journals/human_rights_quarterly/v031/31.4.zoglin.html, accessed May 18, 2010.

43. Doron Shultziner and Mary Ann Tetreault, "Paradoxes of Democratic Progress in Kuwait: The Case of the Kuwaiti Women's Rights Movement," Muslim World Journal of Human Rights 7, no. 2 (2011), article 1.

44. "First Ladies in the Gulf Make Mark in Public Roles," Gulf News, September 22, 2008, http://gulfnews.com/news/gulf/uae/general/first-ladies-in-the-gulf-make-mark-in-public-roles-1.132527, accessed May 18, 2010.

45. David Knowles, "12 Year Old Saudi Girl Wins Divorce from Husband, 80," AOLNews, April 22, 2010, www.aolnews.com/world/article/12-year-old-saudi-girl-wins-divorce-from-80-year-old-husband/19450389, accessed May 18, 2010.

46. Interview with Mirai Chatterjee of the Self-Employed Women's Association of India (SEWA), Radcliffe Institute, Harvard University, March 4, 2011. Chatterjee also indicated that traditional birth attendant training was a very effective tool to promote literacy. The midwives were highly motivated to be able to take notes on what they were learning, rather than having to take notes by pictograms or by repeating the day's information to a literate child at home who would then transcribe what the midwife remembered. Often, the midwives

would simply determine that they absolutely must be literate,ʹ and then have their children teach them basic literacy at home in a very short time.

47. Encyclopedia.com, "Court Bans Fatwas," February 2, 2001, www.encyclopedia .com/doc/1G1–71202881.html, accessed May 18, 2010.

48. Chris Kiwawulo, "Bride Price Petition, Uganda MIFUMI Court Case," *Mifumi*, April 7, 2010, http://mifumi.org/blog/?tag=bride-price-petition-uganda-mifumi-court-case, accessed May 18, 2010.

49. Paola Bergalla and Augustina Ramon Michel, "Argentina: Two Judicial Decisions Regarding Abortion in the Case of Rape" (Universidad de San Andres, April 19, 2010), www.wunrn.com/news/2010/04_10/04_19_10/041910_argentina .htm, accessed May 18, 2010.

50. Asia-Pacific Forum on Women, Law, and Development, "Negotiating Culture: Intersections of Culture and Violence Against Women in the Asia-Pacific," 2006, http://pacific.ohchr.org/docs/Culture_and_VAW-Final_Report_Oct_30_ (2).doc, accessed May 18, 2010.

51. Sara Israelson-Hartley and Wendy Leonard, "Talking About Religion May Solve the World's Big Problems," *Deseret News*, November 22, 2009, www .deseretnews.com/article/705346068/Talking-about-religion-may-solve-worlds-big-problems.html?pg=2, accessed May 18, 2010.

52. Ann Jones, "The Terrifying Normalcy of Assaulting Women," *Alternet*, May 14, 2008, www.alternet.org/reproductivejustice/85282?page=entire, accessed May 18, 2010.

53. Elaine Ganley, "France: Polygamy Banned, but Complex Issues," Human Rights Without Frontiers, May 3, 2010, www.wunrn.com/news/2010/05_10/05_ 03_10/050310_france.htm, accessed May 18, 2010.

54. Women Living Under Muslim Laws, "UK: Muslim Institute Launches New Model Muslim Marriage Contract," August 11, 2008, www.wluml.org/node/ 4749, accessed May 18, 2010.

55. Harry Eckstein, *A Theory of Stable Democracy* (Princeton, NJ: Center of International Studies, Woodrow Wilson School of Public and International Affairs, Princeton University, 1961), iii, http://hdl.handle.net/2027/mdp .39015008254560.

56. Frances Harrison, "Egypt Bans 92-Year Old's Marriage," *BBC News*, June 13, 2008, http://news.bbc.co.uk/2/hi/7452456.stm, accessed May 18, 2010.

57. PhilGAD Portal, "PGMA Signs Magna Carta of Women," Philippine Commission on Women, August 14, 2009, www.ncrfw.gov.ph/index.php/ncrfw-press-releases/349-news-ncrfw-pgma-signs-mcw, accessed May 18, 2010.

58. Guatemalan Human Rights Commission, "Guatemala's Femicide Law: Progress Against Impunity?" 2009, www.ghrc-usa.org/Publications/Femicide_Law_ ProgressAgainstImpunity.pdf, accessed May 18, 2010.

59. Eugene Kwibuka, "Rwanda: Gender Violence Law to Be Passed in Two Weeks," *AllAfrica*, February 11, 2009, http://allafrica.com/stories/200902110118.html, accessed May 18, 2010.

60. Hombrecher, "Overcoming Domestic Violence."

61. Association for Women's Rights in Development, "Call for Pakistan Divorce Law Change Causes Stir," October 12, 2008, www.awid.org/eng/Women-s-Rights-in-the-News/Women-s-Rights-in-the-News/Call-for-Pakistan-divorce-law-change-causes-stir, accessed May 18, 2010.

62. Ahmed Al-Haj, "Yemen Cleric: Fight Law Banning Child Brides," *Arab News*, April 21, 2010, http://arabnews.com/middleeast/article46941.ece, accessed May 18, 2010.

63. Esther Duflo (remarks at Radcliffe Institute conference "Driving Change, Shaping Lives: Gender in the Developing World," Cambridge, MA, March 3–4, 2011).

64. Dan Bilefsky, "Women's Influence Grows in Bulgarian Public Life," *New York Times*, February 7, 2010, www.nytimes.com/2010/02/08/world/europe/08iht-bulgwomen.html?emc=eta1, accessed May 18, 2010.

65. "Gender and Power in the Nordic Countries: A Study of Politics and Business" (Nordic Gender Institute, 2009), http://flipflashpages.uniflip.com/2/13467/51823/pub/document.pdf, accessed May 18, 2010.

66. The Hunger Project, "Two Million Women Leaders and Counting" (International Museum of Women, 2008), www.imow.org/wpp/stories/viewStory?storyId=100, accessed May 18, 2010.

67. Alexandra Zavis, " Women Take on a Security Role," *Los Angeles Times*, June 4, 2008, http://articles.latimes.com/2008/jun/04/world/fg-daughters4, accessed May 18, 2010.

68. Jack Healy and Yasir Gahzi, "Iraqi Women Work to Halt Bombers, but Paycheck Is Elusive," *New York Times*, February 28, 2011, www.nytimes.com/2011/02/28/world/middleeast/28iraq.html, accessed March 1, 2011.

69. Debbie Taylor, ed., *Women: A World Report* (Oxford: Oxford University Press, 1985), 87.

70. UN Office for the Coordination of Humanitarian Affairs, "Women UN Peacekeepers – More Needed," IRIN, May 20, 2010, www.irinnews.org/Report.aspx?ReportId=89194, accessed May 24, 2010.

71. Africa for Women's Rights, "Commit to the Protection of Women's Rights!" July 10, 2009, www.africa4womensrights.org/post/2009/07/10/COMMIT-TO-THE-PROTECTION-OF-WOMEN-S-RIGHTS, accessed May 18, 2010.

72. Morice Mendoza, "Davos 2009: Where Are the Women?" *Der Spiegel*, January 28, 2009, www.spiegel.de/international/business/0,1518,604003,00.html, accessed May 18, 2010.

73. Steven Erlanger, "For Women Who Lead, a Forum of Their Own," *New York Times*, October 19, 2008, www.nytimes.com/2008/10/20/world/europe/20france .html, accessed May 18, 2010.

74. Donald Steinberg, "Combating Sexual Violence in Conflict: Using Facts from the Ground" (address to the United Nations, December 17, 2008), www.wunrn .com/news/2009/01_09/01_12_09/011209_combating.htm, accessed May 18, 2010.

75. Measure Evaluation, "Violence Against Women and Girls: A Compendium of Monitoring and Evaluation Indicators," n.d., www.cpc.unc.edu/measure/tools/ gender/violence-against-women-and-girls-compendium-of-indicators; see also Report of the Secretary-General, United Nations, "Women and Peace and Security," April 6, 2010, www.un.org/ga/search/view_doc.asp?symbol=S/2010/173, accessed May 18, 2010.

76. Lizette Alvarez, "Sweden Faces Facts on Violence Against Women," *New York Times*, March 30, 2005, www.nytimes.com/2005/03/29/world/europe/29iht- letter-4909045.html?pagewanted=1&emc=eta1, accessed May 18, 2010.

77. "Peace and Security for All" (Feminist Institute of the Heinrich Boll Foundation, May 2006), www.boell.de/publications/feminism-gender-democracy- 8878.html, accessed June 1, 2010.

78. Nobel Women's Initiative Conference, "Women Redefining Democracy" (Antigua, Guatemala, May 10–12, 2009), www.nobelwomensinitiative.org/search/ results/post/redefining-democracy-declaration, accessed May 18, 2010.

6. WINGS OF NATIONAL AND INTERNATIONAL RELATIONS, PART TWO

1. Barry Schwartz, "In 'Sticky' Ideas, More Is Less," *Washington Post*, January 17, 2007, www.washingtonpost.com/wp-dyn/content/article/2007/01/16/ AR2007011601625.html, accessed May 27, 2010.

2. Some of our favorite such groups include GirlEffect, Women for Women International, and Equality Now, but there are many fine groups worldwide. Peace-women.org provides a very detailed list of both indigenous and transnational groups working for a better situation for women and girls. Another excellent source of information on local groups and their efforts is the Women News Network video collection, at http://womennewsnetwork.vodpod.com/. Our own project website, Womanstats.org , is a critical piece of infrastructure for chronicling the situation of women; our home page at www.womanstats.org provides information on how to support our research, through donating either time or funds.

3. Donna Abu-Nasr, "Saudi Girls Should Be Allowed to Play Sports, Says Prince," *Huffington Post*, June 23, 2009, www.huffingtonpost.com/2009/06/23/saudi- girls-should-be-all_n_219692.html, accessed May 27, 2010.

4. James Brooke, "Dowry Too High. Lose Bride and Go to Jail," *New York Times*, May 7, 2003, www.nytimes.com/2003/05/17/world/dowry-too-high-lose-bride-and-go-to-jail.html?scp=1&sq=dowry%20too%20high&st=cse, accessed May 27,2010; Nisha Sharma, *Encyclopedia of World Biography*, www.notable biographies.com/news/Sh-Z/Sharma-Nisha.html, accessed May 27, 2010.

5. Barbara Crossette, "Amid the Isolation, Finally, a Friend: A Movement to Confront Hidden Abuse in Immigrant Families," *New York Times*, October 16, 2000, www.nytimes.com/2000/10/16/nyregion/amid-isolation-finally-friend-move ment-confront-hidden-abuse-immigrant-families.html?scp=1&sq=crossette %20abuse%20immigrant%20families&st=cse, accessed May 27, 2010.

6. Nicholas D. Kristof, "Mother of a Nation," *New York Times*, April 2, 2006, http://query.nytimes.com/gst/fullpage.html?res=9C00EED71230F931A35757 C0A9609C8B63&scp=9&sq=kristof%20mother%20of%20nation&st=cse, accessed May 27, 2010; Nicholas D. Kristof, "Mukhtar Mai," *New York Times*, November 26, 2008, http://kristof.blogs.nytimes.com/2008/11/26/mukhtar-mai/ ?scp=3&sq=kristof%20mukhtar&st=cse, accessed May 27, 2010.

7. Denise Grady, "In War and Isolation, a Fighter for Afghan Women," *New York Times*, July 28, 2009, www.nytimes.com/2009/07/28/health/28midw.html, accessed May 27, 2010.

8. Ilene R. Prusher, "The Birth of Hope," *Christian Science Monitor*, March 17, 2004, www.csmonitor.com/2004/0317/p14s01-lifp.html, accessed May 27, 2010.

9. Ruth Eglash, "Sisters Doing It for Themselves," *Jerusalem Post*, September 15, 2009, retrieved from www.jpost.com, accessed November 13, 2009; now available only through *Jerusalem Post* archives.

10. Nujood Ali and Delphine Minoui, *I Am Nujood, Age 10 and Divorced* (New York: Three Rivers Press, 2010), 42.

11. Ibid.

12. "CNN Heroes: Child Rape Survivor Saves 'Virgin Myth' Victims," *CNN.com*, October 1, 2009, www.cnn.com/2009/LIVING/06/04/cnnheroes.betty.makoni/ index.html?iref=allserch, accessed May 27, 2010.

13. Elizabeth Vargas, "Person of the Week: Dr. Massouma al-Mubarak," *ABC News*, June 17, 2005, http://abcnews.go.com/WNT/PersonOfWeek/story?id= 859044&page=2, accessed May 27, 2010.

14. Robert F Worth, "First Women Win Seats in Kuwait Parliament," *New York Times International*, May 18, 2009, www.nytimes.com/2009/05/18/world/ middleeast/18kuwait.html?_r=1&scp=1&sq=first%20women%20win%20seats% 20Kuwait&st=cse, accessed May 27, 2010.

15. Mona Mehta and Chitra Gopalakrishnan, "'We Can': Transforming Power in Relationships in South Asia," *Gender and Development* 15, no. 1 (2007): 41–49.

16. Ed Vulliamy, "Breaking the Silence," *Guardian*, October 5, 2005, www.guard ian.co.uk/media/2005/oct/05/broadcasting.saudiarabia, accessed May 27, 2010.

17. "My Mother Held Me Down," *BBC News*, July 10, 2007, http://news.bbc.co .uk/2/hi/health/6287926.stm, accessed May 27, 2010.

18. Waris Dirie Foundation, "About Waris Dirie," 2010, www.waris-dirie-foundation .com/en/about-waris-dirie/, accessed May 27, 2010.

19. HBDGWerbeagentur. "Waris Dirie: Stop FGM Now" (video file), February 5, 2010, Retrieved from http://adsoftheworld.com/media/tv/waris_dirie_ stop_fgm_now, accessed May 27, 2010.

20. Middle East Media Research Institute (MEMRI), "Saudi Cleric, Women's Rights Activist in TV Debate on Types of Marriage in Arab World (special dispatch no. 2144), December 8, 2008, www.memri.org/report/en/0/0/0/0/0/0/2979 .htm, accessed May 27, 2010.

21. Katherine Zoepf, "Saudi Women Find an Unlikely Role Model: Oprah," *New York Times*, September 19, 2008, www.nytimes.com/2008/09/19/world/ middleeast/19oprah.html?scp=1&sq=zoepf%20saudi%20oprah&st=cse.

22. Jamel Arfaoui, "New Tunisian Film Calls Attention to Inheritance Law," *Magharebia*, August 10, 2008, www.magharebia.com/cocoon/awi/xhtml1/en_ GB/features/awi/features/2008/10/08/feature-01, accessed May 27, 2010.

23. Nazila Fathi. "Starting at Home: Iran's Women Fight for Rights," *New York Times*, February 12, 2009, www.nytimes.com/2009/02/13/world/middleeast/ 13iran.html?scp=1&sq=nazila%20fathi%202009%20starting%20at%20home&st =cse, accessed May 27, 2010.

24. journeymanpictures, "Iran's Fearless Film Maker" (video file), February 4, 2008, www.youtube.com/watch?v=QFIjKBsuZTQ&feature=fvw, accessed May 27, 2010.

25. Tahmineh Milani, Internet Movie Database, www.imdb.com/name/nm 0586841/, accessed May 27, 2010.

26. "New Films to Debut at Iranian Theaters in Noruz," *Tehran Times*, March 9, 2010, www.tehrantimes.com/index.asp?newspaper_no=10826&B1=View+the+ newspapr, accessed May 27, 2010.

27. "The Seventh Biennial Conference on Iranian studies: Toronto, Canada, July 31– August 3, 2008," *Payvand*, http://payvand.com/news/08/jun/1066.html, accessed May 27, 2010.

28. Fathi, "Starting at Home."

29. "Saudi Women Make Video Protest," *BBC News*, March 11, 2008,http://news .bbc.co.uk/2/hi/middle_east/7159077.stm, accessed May 27, 2010.

30. "Saudi Women Challenge Driving Ban," *BBC News*, September 18, 2007,http:// news.bbc.co.uk/2/hi/middle_east/7000499.stm, accessed May 27, 2010.

31. Faiza Saleh Ambah, "An Olympic Door Opens for Saudi Woman,"*Washington Post Foreign Service*, August 18, 2008,. www.washingtonpost.com/wp-dyn/ content/article/2008/08/17/AR2008081702539.html, accessed May 27, 2010.

32. Stephanie Hancock, "Saudi Lingerie Trade in a Twist," *BBC News*, February 25, 2009, http://news.bbc.co.uk/2/hi/middle_east/7908866.stm, accessed May 27, 2010.

33. Women's Undergarments for Women Only [ca. 2008], on *Facebook* [group page], www.facebook.com/group.php?gid=20469931029, accessed May 27, 2010.

34. Robert F. Worth, "As Taboos Ease, Saudi Girl Group Dares to Rock," *New York Times International*, November 24, 2008, www.nytimes.com/2008/11/24/world/ middleeast/24saudi.html?scp=3&sq=worth%20Saudi%20rock%20gorup%20girl &st=cse, accessed May 27, 2010.

35. Fathi, "Starting at Home."

36. Eman Al Nafjian, http://saudiwoman.wordpress.com, accessed May 27, 2010.

37. Firuzeh Shokooh Valle, "Silence Speaks: Multimedia Storytelling in Republic of Congo," *Global Voices*, February 26, 2010, http://globalvoicesonline .org/2010/02/26/silence-speaks-multi-media-storytelling-in-republic-of-congo/, accessed May 27, 2010; Amy L. Hill, "Silence Speaks—Digital Stories for Healing and Empowerment," 2009, www.wunrn.com/news/2009/02_09/02_ 09_09/020909_silence.htm, accessed May 27, 2010.

38. Neil MacFarquhar, "Iranian Women's Dress Code Is Modest but Golf Friendly," *New York Times*, July 5, 2005, www.nytimes.com/2005/07/05/inter national/middleeast/05golf.html?scp=1&sq=iranian%20women's%20dress%20 golf%20friendly&st=cse, accessed May 27, 2010.

39. Carol Strickland, "Mosque Modern," *Christian Science Monitor*, August 3, 2009, www.csmonitor.com/The-Culture/Arts/2009/0803/p17s01-algn.html, accessed May 27, 2010.

40. Doron Shultziner and Mary Ann Tetreault, "Paradoxes of Democratic Progress in Kuwait: The Case of the Kuwaiti Women's Rights Movement," *Muslim World Journal of Human Rights* 7, no. 2 (2011): 1–25.

41. Ian Fisher, "Sometimes a Girl's Best Friend Is Not Her Father," *New York Times*, March 2, 1999, www.nytimes.com/1999/03/02/world/kajiado-journal-sometimes-a-girl-s-best-friend-is-not-her-father.html?scp=1&sq=girl's%20best% 20friend%20not%20her%20father&st=cse, accessed May 27, 2010.

42. Dexter Filkins, "Afghan Girls, Scarred by Acid, Defy Terror, Embracing School," *New York Times International*, January 14, 2009, www.nytimes.com/ 2009/01/14/world/asia/14kandahar.html?scp=1&sq=afghan%20girls%20scarred %20by%20acid%20filkins&st=cse, accessed May 27, 2010.

43. Mark Lacey, "Genital Cutting Shows Signs of Losing Favor in Africa," *New York Times*, June 8, 2004, www.nytimes.com/2004/06/08/international/africa/08 cutt.html?scp=2&sq=lacey%20genital%20cutting%20favor%20africa&st=cse, accessed May 27, 2010.

44. "Experts: Black Church Can Better Address Domestic Violence," Weblog entry, *ReligionNewsBlog*, September 10, 2007, www.religionnewsblog.com/19324/domestic-violence-3, accessed May 27, 2010.

45. Yigal Schliefer, "In Turkey, Muslim Women Gain Expanded Religious Authority," *Christian Science Monitor*, April 27, 2005, www.csmonitor.com/2005/0427/p04s01-woeu.html, accessed May 27, 2010.

46. Kwame Anthony Appiah, "The Art of Social Change," *New York Times*, October 22, 2010, www.nytimes.com/2010/10/24/magazine/24FOB-Footbinding-t.html, accessed 1 March 2011.

47. Quoted in Doron Shultziner and Mary Ann Tetreault, "Paradoxes of Democratic Progress in Kuwait: The Case of the Kuwaiti Women's Rights Movement," *Muslim World Journal of Human Rights* 7, no. 2 (2011): 17.

48. Stephanie Hancock, "Creating a Woman's World in Arabia," *BBC News*, March 4, 2009, http://news.bbc.co.uk/2/hi/middle_east/7922279.stm, accessed May 27, 2010.

49. Michael Slackman, "Sidewalks, and an Identity, Sprout in Jordan's Capital, *New York Times*, February 23, 2010, www.nytimes.com/2010/02/24/world/middleeast/24amman.html?scp=1&sq=slackman%20sidewalks%20jordan&st=cse, accessed May 27, 2010.

50. Huma Yusuf, "People Making a Difference: Sheema Kermani," *Christian Science Monitor*, June 8, 2009, www.csmonitor.com/The-Culture/Home/2009/0608/p47s01-lihc.html, accessed May 27, 2010.

51. Tom Engelhardt, "Tomgram: Ann Jones, Changing the World One Shot at a Time," *TomDispatch.com*, May 13, 2008, www.tomdispatch.com/post/174931, accessed May 27, 2010.

52. Abdullah Nasser al-Fouzan, "Moudhi Riding on a Donkey," *Saudi Gazette*, May 29, 2010, www.saudigazette.com.sa/index.cfm?method=home.regcon&contentID=2010040168079, accessed May 29, 2010. Some have suggested this story is apocryphal, while others insist it is true. The fact that such a story is still circulating shows its deep resonance within the culture.

53. Isabel Kershner, "On One Field, Two Goals: Equality and Statehood," *New York Times*, October 28, 2009, www.nytimes.com/2009/10/29/world/middleeast/29westbank.html?scp=1&sq=kershner%20one%20field%20two%20goals&st=cse, accessed May 27, 2010.

54. Women for Women International, "Ending Violence Against Women in Eastern Congo: Preparing Men to Advocate for Women's Rights," 2007, www

.womenforwomen.org/news-women-for-women/files/MensLeadershipFull
Report_002.pdf, accessed May 27, 2010.

55. Nadia Muhanna, "Q & A: Bassam al-Kadi, Director of the Syrian Women
Observatory," *Syria Today*, November 2009, www.syria-today.com/index
.php/november-2009/452-society/4282-qaa-bassam-al-kadi-director-of-the-syrian-
women-observatory, accessed May 27, 2010.

56. WUNRN, "Pan-Arab Training Guide on Practical Ways to Engage Men and
Boys in the Fight to End Violence Against Women," 2010, www.wunrn.com/
news/2010/05_10 /05_10_10/051010_arab.htm, accessed May 27, 2010.

57. Bonnie Ballif-Spanvill and Heather Farrell, "The Personalization of Peace
Education" (paper presented at the Comparative and International Education
Society, Baltimore, February 2007); Bonnie Ballif-Spanvill, C. Campbell, and
Hwanhi Chung, "Worldwide Efforts to Teach Children How to Be Peaceful"
(unpublished paper, 2010).

58. Sarah Touahri, "Child Marriage in Morocco Criticized," *Magharebiaý*, May 5,
2009, www.magharebia.com/cocoon/awi/xhtml1/en_GB/features/awi/features/
2009/05/05/feature-01, accessed May 27, 2010.

59. Margaret [pseud.], "Foreign Firsts: Egypt Jails a Man for Sexual Harassment
of a Woman," *Jezebel*, October 23, 2008, http://jezebel.com/5067775/foreign-
firsts-egypt-jails-a-man-for-sexual-harassment-of-a-woman, accessed May 27,
2010.

60. Jeffrey Fleishman and Noha El-Hennawy, "In Egypt, Harassed to Their Limit,"
Los Angeles Times, December 17, 2008, http://articles.latimes.com/2008/dec/17/
world/fg-harassment17, accessed May 27, 2010.

61. Ruth Gledhill, "Victory for Saudi Girl, 8, Sold by Her Father to a 50-Year-Old
Man," *Times*, May 1, 2009, www.timesonline.co.uk/tol/news/world/middle_
east/article6201769.ece, accessed May 27, 2010.

62. "Girl, 12, Fighting to Divorce 80-Year-Old Husband in Saudi Arabia," Tele-
graph.co.uk, February 9, 2010, www.telegraph.co.uk/news/worldnews/middle
east/saudiarabia/7192960/Girl-12-fighting-to-divorce-80-year-old-husband-in-
Saudi-Arabia.html, accessed May 27, 2010.

63. Salman Masood, "Pakistani Woman Who Shattered Stigma of Rape Is Married,"
New York Times International, March 18, 2009, www.nytimes.com/2009/03/18/
world/asia/18mukhtar.html?scp=1&sq=masood%20pakistani%20married&st=
cse, accessed May 27, 2010.

64. Mark Lacey, "From Broken Lives, Kenyan Women Build Place of Unity," *New
York Times*, December 7, 2004, http://query.nytimes.com/gst/fullpage.html?re
s=9C03E4D71431F934A35751C1A9629C8B63&scp=1&sq=lacey%20kenyan%2
0women%20build%20place&st=cse, accessed May 27, 2010.

65. Emily Wax, "In India, New Seat of Power for Women," *Washington Post*, October 12, 2009, www.washingtonpost.com/wp-dyn/content/article/2009/10/11/AR2009101101934.html, accessed May 27, 2010.

66. Fathi, "Starting at Home."

67. Robert F. Worth, "Arab TV Tests Societies' Limits with Depictions of Sex and Equality," *New York Times*, September 2008, 26, www.nytimes.com/2008/09/27/world/middleeast/27beirut.html?scp=1&sq=arab%20tv%20tests%20depictions%20sex%20equality&st=cse, accessed May 27, 2010.

68. Karin Laub and Dalia Nammari, "Soap Opera Shakes Customs of Arab Married Life," *USA Today*, July 27, 2008, www.usatoday.com/life/television/2008–07–27–733717293_x.htm , accessed May 27, 2010.

69. Hunt Alternatives Fund, "Asha Hagi Elmi: Expert Spotlight," April 2007, www.huntalternatives.org/download/498_4_26_07_somali_woman_leader_peace_cal.pdf, accessed May 27, 2010.

70. Susan McKay, "How Do You Mend Broken Hearts? Gender, War, and Impacts on Girls in Fighting Forces," in G. Reyes and G. A. Jacobs, eds., *Handbook of International Disaster Psychology*, 4:45–60 (Westport, CT: Praeger, 2006).

71. Iris Bohnet, "Gender Equality: A Nudge in the Right Direction," *Financial Times*, October 13, 2010, FT.com.

72. Bonnie Ballif-Spanvill, "The Most Critical Education for the 21st Century, Particularly for Girls and Women, Is Teaching People to Get Along with Each Other" (paper presented at the UN Commission on the Status of Women, New York, March 2010).

73. Interview with S. Matthew Stearmer, May 27, 2010.

74. Blaine Harden, "Learn to Be Nice to Your Wife, or Pay the Price," *Washington Post*, November 26, 2007, www.washingtonpost.com/wp-dyn/content/article/2007/11/25/AR2007112501720.html, accessed May 27, 2010.

75. Thomas L. Friedman, "Postcard from Yemen," *New York Times*, February 8, 2010, http://topics.nytimes.com/top/news/international/countriesandterritories/yemen/index.html?scp=1&sq=postcard%20from%20yemen&st=cse, accessed May 27, 2010.

76. Greg Mortenson and David Oliver Relin, *Three Cups of Tea: One Man's Mission to Promote Peace . . . One School at a Time* (New York: Penguin, 2006), 153.

77. Colleen Johnson, "The Social Problems That Deter Xhosa Women from Marriage and How Education and Westernization Allow Them to Refuse Marriage" (honors thesis, Brigham Young University, Provo, Utah, 2006), 9–10.

78. Michael Hall, "The Mechanics of Relations Submission," WomanStats Blog, September 17, 2009, womanstats.org/blog2nd09.htm#submission, accessed May 27, 2010, abridged with the permission of the author.

79. Dexter Filkins, "A School Bus for Shamsia," *New York Times*, August 23, 2009, www.nytimes.com/2009/08/23/magazine/23school-t.html?scp=1&sq=school%2obus%20for%20shamsia&st=cse, accessed May 27, 2010.

80. Agence France-Presse, "Subjugation of Women Is Threat to US Security: Clinton," March 12, 2010, www.google.com/hostednews/afp/article/ALeqM5ib71t2EuWmwDahxNKDaHxcEbfcYA, accessed May 27, 2010.

7. TAKING WING

1. Bahá'í Faith, "Two Wings of a Bird: The Equality of Women and Men," http://info.bahai.org/article-1-9-1-9.html, accessed May 27, 2010.

2. Hillary Clinton, "Remarks at the TEDWomen Conference," U.S. Department of State, 8 December 2010, www.state.gov/secretary/rm/2010/12/152670.htm., accessed February 10, 2011.

3. Gayle Tzemach Lemmon, "The Hillary Doctrine," *Newsweek*, March 6, 2011, www.newsweek.com/2011/03/06/the-hillary-doctrine.html, accessed March 10, 2011.

4. Rajiv Chandrasekaran, "In Afghanistan, U.S. Shifts Priorities on Women's Rights as It Eyes Wider Priorities," *Washington Post*, March 6, 2011, www.washingtonpost.com/wp-dyn/content/article/2011/03/05/AR2011030504233.html, accessed March 10, 2011.

5. CNN, "Egypt's Million Women March Fizzles Into Shouting Matches," March 8, 2001, www.cnn.com/2011/WORLD/meast/03/08/egypt.women/index.html?hpt=T2, accessed March 10, 2011.

6. Kristen Chick, "In Egypt's Tahrir Square, Women Attacked at Rally on International Woman's Day," *Christian Science Monitor*, March 8, 2011, www.csmonitor.com/World/Middle-East/2011/0308/In-Egypt-s-Tahrir-Square-women-attacked-at-rally-on-International-Women-s-Day, accessed March 10, 2011.

7. Michelle Bachelet, "Remarks at UN Women Launch," United Nations Entity for Gender Equality and the Empowerment of Women, February 24, 2011, www.unwomen.org/2011/02/un-women-launch-remarks-by-usg-michelle-bachelet/, accessed March 10, 2011.

8. Human Rights Watch, "Your Dress According to Their Rules: Enforcement of an Islamic Dress Code for Women in Chechnya," March 10, 2011, www.hrw.org/en/reports/2011/03/10/you-dress-according-their-rules-0, accessed March 10, 2011.

9. Michele Keleman, "Women Should 'Play a Part' in the 'New Egypt,'" March 9, 2011, www.npr.org/2011/03/09/134384804/Clinton-Urges-New-Egypt-Government-To-Include-Women, accessed March 10, 2011.

CONTRIBUTORS

VALERIE M. HUDSON is Professor and George H. W. Bush Chair in The Bush School of Government and Public Service at Texas A&M University, having previously taught at Brigham Young, Northwestern, and Rutgers universities. Her research foci include foreign policy analysis, security studies, gender and international relations, and methodology. Hudson's articles have appeared in such journals as *International Security, Journal of Peace Research, Political Psychology,* and *Foreign Policy Analysis.* She is the author or editor of several books, including (with Andrea Den Boer) *Bare Branches: The Security Implications of Asia's Surplus Male Population* (MIT Press, 2004), which won the American Association of Publishers Award for the Best Book in Political Science, and the Otis Dudley Duncan Award for Best Book in Social Demography, resulting in feature stories in the *New York Times,* the *Economist, 60 Minutes,* and other news publications. Hudson was named to *Foreign Policy* magazine's list of Top 100 Global Thinkers for 2009.

BONNIE BALLIF-SPANVILL is an emeritus professor of psychology and was the last director of the Women's Research Institute at Brigham Young University. After twenty-five years as a professor and department chair in the graduate school of Fordham University at Lincoln Center in New York City, she returned to her alma mater in 1994. Her research publications and papers in human motivation and emotion earned her the Fellow status in both the American Psychological Association, in 1984, and the Association for Psychological Science, in 1987. Currently, she is studying the ramifications of violence and development of peace in women and men across ages and in different circumstances and cultures worldwide. Her recent publications address intergenerational domestic violence, the impact of witnessing violence, and the design of techniques to increase peacefulness. She has also published a global anthology of poetry by women, revealing their experiences with violence and their resilient visions of peace.

MARY CAPRIOLI is an associate professor and Head of political science and Director of International Studies at the University of Minnesota Duluth. She has researched the role of gendered structural inequality on political conflict and violence. Caprioli pioneered a new line of scholarly inquiry between the security of women and the national and international behavior of states and confirmed the link using quantitative methodology. Her expertise has been sought by scholars worldwide. She is an associate editor for *Foreign Policy Analysis,* is a member of the WomanStats board of directors, and is an advisory board member of the Minorities at Risk Project. She received her PhD from the University of Connecticut.

CHAD F. EMMETT is an associate professor of geography at Brigham Young University. He is interested in finding ways for competing peoples to peacefully share space. Previous research and publications have focused on Christian-Muslim relations throughout the Islamic world, with a special emphasis on Indonesia and on Nazareth, as found in his book *Beyond the Basilica: Christians and Muslims in Nazareth,* In other publications he has explored ways for Israelis and Palestinians to peacefully share the sacred space of the Holy Land and Jerusalem. He has been associated with the WomanStats project from its inception and hopes that greater parity between men and women will lead to greater peace and security for all. At BYU he has served as the director of the international studies program and the Middle East studies/Arabic program. Before his PhD studies at the University of Chicago, he worked as an Indonesian linguist for the U.S. Department of Defense.

INDEX

Abdullah of Saudi Arabia, 140, 166
abortion: forced, 129–31; laws, 60. *See also* sex-selective abortion
acid attacks, 21
activists: demonstrations by, 122–23, 181, 203; organizations, 161–63
adaptive choices, female, 75–76
adultery, 9, 28, 34–35, 56
Afghanistan, 152, 208; acid attacks, 21; Afghan Midwives Association, 160; cultural practices, 128–29; domestic violence, 22; education, 171; government policies affecting women, 120; marriage laws, 181; Polygyny Scale, 59; protection of women, 203; quotas for women in government, 42, 149; Required Codes of Dress for Women in the Islamic World, 66; sale of daughters into marriage, 31–32; United States policy on, 202, 206–208; women's participation in government, 150
Africa: African Gender and Development Index, 105; agriculture, 14; AIDS widows and orphans, 37; Discrepancy in Education Scale (sub-Sahara), 61; education (North Africa and sub-Sahara), 44; Governmental Participation by Women Scale, 62; Inequity in Family Law/Practice Scale, 60; malnourishment of girls, 27; Maternal Mortality Scale, 61; Physical Security of Women Scale, 56; polygamy, 33, 34; Polygyny Scale, 59;

radio programs, women's, 135; Required Codes of Dress for Women in the Islamic World, 66; West Africa, 186
Agacinski, Sylviane, 98
agency of women, 157
age of consent, 28–29; Inequity in Family Law/Practice Scale, 59–60
aggression: group contexts, 88–90; imitation by children, 86–87; male use of, 71–72, 73–75; masculinity and, 88–89; out-groups, 76–78; sex differences in, 81; state, 78; testosterone and, 45–46; training children in use of, 83–84
agriculture: origins of patriarchy and, 70, 71, 74, 237n15; women's role in, 14
Ahmed, Nazir, 9
AIDS epidemic: myths about cures, 13, 162; promiscuity, 11; sexual exploitation of women, relationship to, 2, 25–26; transmission, 34, 37, 130; widows and orphans, 37
Albania, gender change, 227n11
Alexander, Richard, 70
Alexandra, Czarina, 39
Algeria, Discrepancy in Education Scale, 61
Ali, Nujood, 161
al-Jazeera, 165
American Political Science Association, 41
AmericasWatch, 36
Ammodi, Fawziya, 30
Anani, Ghida, 179

of laws against, 36–37; global rates of, 21–22; Ivory Coast, 143; laws against, 146, 152; legal aspects, 28; Physical Security of Women Scale, 55–56; rewards for batterers, 85; root of gendered micro-aggression, 91; societal conflict, correlation with, 92; terms used to describe, 136–137; United States, 172

domination, male, 197. *See also* male dominance hierarchies

double standards, criminal punishment, 35–36

dowry, 12–13, 147, 173, 178

dress codes: failure to follow, 65–68; gender based, 29; Required Codes of Dress for Women in the Islamic World, 65–68; Western societies, 137

driving, ban on women, 166–167, 176–177

droit de seigneur, 29

Dubai, 140; Dubai TV, 165

Duflo, Esther, 52–53, 148

Eagly, Alice, 81, 98

East Asia, forced abortion and sterilization, 130

East Timor, domestic violence, laws against, 146

Eckstein, Harry, 145

economic factors in violence, 73

economics: caregivers, 14–15, 150–151; development, role of women in, 98–99; economic system, exclusion of women from, 47–50; national economic performance, 44; national system of accounts, 47; resources, distribution of, 73–74; study of, 49–50. *See also* labor

Ecuador, 8

education of women and girls, 44, 141, 166, 170–171, 175, 192–193; Discrepancy in Education Scale, 61–62; fertility, correlation with, 51; rights under state law, 134–135; Taliban, opposition to, 21

Egypt: child brides, 29; Discrepancy in Education Scale, 62; divorce laws, 146; female genital cutting, 18, 138; Intermingling in Public in the Islamic World Scale, 64; marriage laws, 145; Required

Codes of Dress for Women in the Islamic World, 67; sexual harassment laws, 182; Supreme Judicial Council, 149; women's participation in government, 170, 203, 206–208, 236n2

Elizabeth I, 233n52

Elmi, Asha Hagi, 188–189

enforcement of laws, 64–65, 68, 106, 117, 146–147, 181–182

environmental conditions: antisocial behavior, influence on, 82–83; behavior, influence on, 81–82

epigenetics, 83

equality, defined, 6–7

Equality Now, 263n2

Equality Without Reservation (CEDAW), 128

Estonia, CEDAW, 124

Ethiopia, maternal mortality, 13–14

ethnopolitical differences, 3

Europe: forced abortion and sterilization, 130; marriage, egalitarian, 79–80, 188

European Union: domestic violence, 152; Harmful Traditional Practices Survey, 134

evolutionary theory, 45–46, 108; biology and psychology, 69–70; family law, influence of reproductive interests on, 28–29; misconceptions about, 69–70; violence, 74–75

exogamy, 39, 76

exploitation: context of, 15; structural violence, 93

Facebook, 167

Fagan, Jeffry, 90

family, patrilocal. *See* patrilocality

family law, 112–113; enclaves, 143–144; equity in, 16, 144–145; inequity in, 28–38, 108, 112–113, 206; Inequity in Family Law/Practice Scale, 59–60; Islamic societies, 127–128

Fazal, Mohammed, 31–32

FBI, homicides, statistics, 21–22

female alliances, 80, 91, 238n26

female circumcision, 26, 138, 172, 189. *See also* female genital cutting (FGC); infibulation

scripts for gender relations, 16, 184–190
security demographics, 115
security of states: defined, 115–116; gender
    equality, role in, 3; link to security
    of women, 91–92, 95–118, 199–200,
    203–205, 208–209
security studies, 5, 95–98, 115–118; research
    questions for, 154; status of women,
    99–103
Seker, Zuleyha, 173
self-sufficiency, women's, 184
Serbian forces, rape of captives, 10, 19–20
sex: defined, 6; differences in animal spe-
    cies, 70; segregation, 63–65; sex tourism,
    13; sexual dimorphism, 71, 75; world
    peace, linkage between, 15–16
sex ratios, 4, 117; incentive structures for
    families, 147; Son Preference and Sex
    Ratio Scale, 56–57; world wide, 4
sex-selective abortion, 4, 96–97, 110, 115;
    Asia, 28; China, 128; enforcement of
    laws against, 117; India, 13; Son Prefer-
    ence and Sex Ratio Scale, 57; United
    States, 260n38; Western societies, bans
    on, 137
sexual assault, 19–23. *See also* physical
    security of women; rape
sexual harassment, 51, 182
sexuality, female. *See also* chastity, female:
    harm related to, 23–27; honor, associa-
    tion with, 8–11; male control of, 70–72
shadow CEDAW reports, 124, 128, 182
shari'a law, 113, 120–121, 146–147
Sharkar, Tanika, 40
Sharma, Nisha, 158
Sheikholeslam, Mahvash, 166
Sherrill, Michelle, 83
Shi'a, 181
Shi'ites, 66, 120
Shtar Mahaba (Half the Love), 165
Shuaka, Christine, 171
Shuichi Amano, 192
Shultziner, Doron, 139, 174
Shuriye, Isnino, 171–172
Sierra Leone: community responses to girl
    soldiers, 189; forced marriages, 136–137;

maternal mortality, 23; Special Court,
    141–142
Silence Speaks (storytelling initiative),
    167–168
Singapore: Governmental Participation by
    Women Scale, 63; Son Preference and
    Sex Ratio Scale, 57
Sixth Clan (Somalia), 188–189
slogans, 186–187, 203
Slovakia, CEDAW, 124
Slovenia, Governmental Participation by
    Women Scale, 63
Smith, Adam, 49
Smuts, Barbara, 70–74
Snowe, Olympia, 44
soap operas, 187–188
Sobek, David, 102
social behavior, 80–91. *See also* behavior
social contagion, 90
social diffusion theories, 91–94
social networking sites, 166–167
social role theory, 81–82
social sanctions on violence, 180–181
Social Security system, 48
social structures, male-dominated, 69–94
SOCIC (States of Concern to the Interna-
    tional Community) scale, 107, 109–113
Somalia: female genital cutting (FGC),
    164; sixth clan, 188–189
son preference, 12, 115; dowry, influence
    on, 13; Son Preference and Sex Ratio
    Scale, 56–57
South Africa, 68; Governmental Participa-
    tion by Women Scale, 62, 63; marriage,
    193; rape, 140, 153; survivors of abuse,
    168
South America: defense ministers, female,
    116; leaders, women, 42
South Asia: campaigns against violence
    against women, 162–163; Discrepancy in
    Education Scale, 61; Governmental Par-
    ticipation by Women Scale, 62; Physical
    Security of Women Scale, 56; women's
    education, 44
South Korea: Governmental Participation
    by Women Scale, 63; Son Preference

MECHANICS' INSTITUTE
MECHANICS'
MERCANTILE LIBRARY